UNBOXING
GOD

AN UNEVANGELICAL GUIDE TO CHRISTIANITY

UNBOXING GOD

ALDEN SWAN

ONBrand Books

an imprint of W. Brand Publishing

NASHVILLE, TENNESSEE

j.brand@wbrandpub.com
ONBrand Books
www.wbrandpub.com

Cover design by JuLee Brand / designchik

Unboxing God / Alden Swan —1st ed.

Available in Paperback, eBook and Kindle formats.

Paperback ISBN: 978-1-956906-94-3
eBook ISBN: 978-1-956906-95-0

Library of Congress Control Number: 2024915501

CONTENTS

To My Family

BECOMING UNLOST IN THE EVANGELICAL WOODS

"Which woods?" you ask.

"Good question," I respond. *"Just look around: hundreds of denominations. Buildings. TV and radio preachers. A music and film industry. Hundreds of millions of dollars in donations. Preachers. Crackpots. Programs. Rules and expectations. Meetings. And theologies—hundreds of them. A dark, dank, and often frightening forest full of wolves and gingerbread houses and utter nonsense."*

"Is all of it nonsense?"

"No, of course not. But some of it is."

"Which parts?"

"That's what we need to find out."

Christianity is a relationship with God that began several millennia ago, as was revealed to our ancestors and handed down through the years. During that time, the people of God were embattled, enslaved, exiled, persecuted, and dispersed around the world. Prophets and kings came and went. God himself showed up at times. Stories were written down and structures were put in place to hold the stories. Ideas were added, removed, or changed. Groups split. Teachings were lost and others were invented. Along the way, religion became big business, and a lot of "fluff" (to put it very nicely) was added.

People are leaving Christianity in droves. Church leaders and laypeople alike spend too much time talking about *postmodernism*, *deconstruction*, and other big words that no one seems to understand (and that I try not to use). I am not interested in deconstruction (which has to do with language, not theology or faith). And I don't claim to be postmodern. I am not a progressive and neither am I a conservative (which, to me, is simply yesterday's progressive that stopped progressing). I'm just a wanderer and a wonderer seeking truth while remaining rooted in the ancient creeds and beliefs.

Many years ago, a friend called me "the eternal seeker" because I refused to be satisfied with his or anyone else's pat answers. I think it's a good phrase. I believe that once God is freed from our mental, philosophical, and theological boxes, there's always something new to discover. Seek and you shall find. Go where no man has gone before. Wonder. Wander. Grow.

A few years ago, having wandered through my fill of "progressive" Christian thinking, and having studied a bit of history and theology, I hypothesized that it all started to go south with Augustine. So, I sought to find out what Christianity was like before Mr. Augustine started creating new doctrines. Lo and behold, I discovered that some of the so-called "progressive" thinking was nothing but ancient Christianity! Some—not all of it. I also discovered that Western Christians had some good ideas not based on Augustinian heresy. Surprisingly, there are a lot of contemporary scholars who embrace the ancient, pre-Augustinian mentalities. This causes great offense to people (e.g. American conservative evangelicals) who tend to like their Christianity packaged in nice little controllable boxes. I hope this book opens a few boxes.

Unboxing God seeks to bring a semblance of order to my wandering studies of old and new sources and sets them down for others to follow. This book is essentially an ordered series of research papers. Hopefully, it is not as boring as that sounds! I have written this book for my family and friends, to explain why I am the way I am. It's also a bit of a spiritual travelogue, detailing my journey through and out of the woods. I'd rather be right than wrong. So, as you could perhaps guess, my thoughts have changed and grown as I've read, studied, and written. I've included quotes and sources along the way, and I strongly encourage you to go deeper into any subject if you so desire.

Mostly, I just want to set people free from the incredible burden of trying to be "right" about Christianity, from the fear of questioning what you're told, or from simply having to believe what anyone else believes. You are unique, and your faith is unique. You can be a Christian (a follower of Jesus) without being a flake, a mind-controlled zombie, or an evangelical.

Once you're out of the woods (or out of the box), you can see the light. Because, as I said in my earlier book (okay, Paul said it first), it is for freedom that Jesus has set us free (Galatians 5:1).

THE GOD BOX–A SHORT STORY

Andy and Caroline stood briefly outside the study as Andy gave the slightly open door a short rap.

"Come in," a booming voice responded. Andy opened the door and allowed his wife to enter first. A tall, balding man in his mid-fifties was hunched in front of a computer screen as he deliberately stabbed a keyboard with his index fingers.

"Sorry to keep you waiting," he spoke into the air as he made one final poke and rose to greet them. "Sending off the weekly prayer email," he explained. "I'm not much of a typist." He paused for a split second, "Let me see if I can get this right . . . Carol, isn't it?"

"Caroline."

"Of course; my apologies. Andy, nice to see you again." He shook their hands in turn and led them to two imitation leather chairs, of which there were three arranged in a conversation grouping in the corner of the study.

"Thank you for seeing us on such short notice, Reverend," Andy began.

"Oh, call me John. I don't like titles." He took the third chair, which was arranged in such a way that his long legs had a chance to extend without danger of kicking his guests. "I continue to get a handful of people calling me 'Pastor' around here, but I am trying to break that habit. Religious formality just gets in the way. That's why I like to come out from behind the desk and avoid as many religious clichés as I can. The world has too much religion, not enough Jesus, I always say."

Andy was silent, not really having a clue what the distinction between "religion" and "Jesus" was, or how you could have one without the other. He glanced over at Caroline, who nodded knowingly. Right, he thought. She doesn't get it, either.

"Can I get you some coffee?" Pastor John broke eye contact momentarily as he reached behind him for his well-used, seldom-washed mug on his desk. The couple both replied in the negative as Pastor John readjusted himself in the chair.

"This is certainly a pleasure," he affirmed. "We are all so excited to adopt you into our family. It's rare to have a couple come forward together, but it's definitely a plus." Seeing their somewhat confused looks, he continued, "You see, when a husband or wife alone accepts Christ, it can create great stress in a marriage. However, as you begin your new lives together, it's a most wonderful opportunity—both for you and for us—as we get to participate in your journey. Yes, a very wonderful thing indeed. As I mentioned Sunday, the Bible tells us that the angels rejoice when one is saved. I'd say they had quite a celebration last Sunday!"

Andy and Caroline smiled politely, still not quite sure what kind of a journey they were on. This was all very new to them, as neither had come from a family for which religion played a part. Caroline responded first, "This is all very new to us . . ."

"Of course, of course," John jumped in. They could see that he was obviously used to doing most of the talking. "I understand completely. Don't try to figure everything out all at once—you've got plenty of time to learn the ins and outs of Christianity and church life. We're just glad you're here." He took a sip from his cup. "Tell me," he said, looking at Andy, "a little about your backgrounds."

"Well, neither of us have ever been what you'd call religious . . ."

Andy was interrupted by a knock on the study door. "Excuse me," said John, rising to get the door. The church secretary, Joan, according to the nameplate on her desk, handed the pastor what looked like two business cards. He thanked Joan and re-closed the door.

"Carry on," he nodded to Andy as he returned to his chair, setting the cards on the coffee table in front of them.

Andy's eyes fell to the cards, which he noticed had "Andy" and "Caroline" lettered on them. "As I was saying, we've never been what you could call religious. Neither of our families ever attended church, and at least in my family, the subject of God never came up."

"Unless somebody was swearing," Caroline added, smiling. She continued, determined to carry her side of the conversation. "My family went to church for weddings, funerals, and sometimes Christmas, if there was a special program. My mom believed in God and even claimed to have seen Him once."

Pastor John nodded silently, either not catching or not acknowledging the humor.

"Religion never made any sense to us—to me," Andy continued. "In fact, it still doesn't."

Caroline nodded in agreement, "I'm not even sure why we came on Sunday, other than the Nelsons had been after us forever to come. I told Andy, 'We've got to go once, then we can tell them that it's just not for us.' But," she paused, looking over at Andy to make sure she had his agreement, "we both felt something

Sunday that we'd never felt before. I guess you call it the presence of God, or at least that's what I think it was. I thought it was just me, but then before I knew it, I was down front kneeling next to Andy. I don't even know how I got there!"

"I'm still not even sure what it all means," said Andy earnestly. "I mean, I feel different—lighter, I guess you could say—but I have absolutely no language to really explain it. I started reading that Bible you gave us on Sunday, but it honestly hasn't helped explain anything at all to us yet. So far, it's very subjective."

Caroline was shaking her head, "It's all so foreign. Christianity is like a different language, a different culture. I feel inside that it's true, but I guess my head hasn't arrived there yet."

The pastor smiled. "I am very excited for you two. I really am. You are in the best possible place to learn about God and what it means to be a Christian."

"What do you mean?" Caroline asked.

Pastor John leaned forward, "What I mean is, many people have preconceived notions about God and Christianity, many of them wrong. It's sometimes very hard to shake those wrong notions loose and get them on the right track."

"My mom always said," Caroline interrupted, "that there are many tracks. That's why there are so many churches."

Andy grinned, "Caroline's mom is sometimes on several tracks at once."

Caroline gave him one of her looks and continued, "I mean, Judy Nelson warned me about that church down on the corner of 5th, to make sure we didn't go there instead. She said they had some strange ideas. How do we know which church has it right?"

Pastor John sat for a moment, his hands pressed together with the index fingers pressed against his lips. "I can tell you're both real thinkers," he said slowly. "That's good . . . that's very good. I think our church is a good place for you. We have classes that will help you to sort out all of these questions."

With that he reached down and picked up the two cards, handing one to each, glancing at the names to make sure they had the right ones. "These are for you," he said.

John took the card, which had a scanner code on the back, and after a moment he looked up. "What is this?"

John smiled warmly, "These are the links to your God Boxes. I am told you can just scan the code with your phone, and it will log you in. Our church tech department can help you if you have any problems."

Whatever expectations Andy may have had, this did not fit in with any of them. "God Boxes? I don't think I've ever heard the term before." Caroline nodded in agreement, her face the picture of pure bewilderment.

"The God Box is an invention of mine, a space on our church's Internet cloud where we can all put everything we know about God. It helps keep our faith orderly, and, regarding Caroline's comment, it helps us keep on the right track."

"I don't think I understand," said Andy slowly.

"It's really very simple," Pastor John continued, unfazed by their lack of understanding. "Religion can be a very messy thing." To this, both Andy and Caroline nodded in agreement.

"We have had many people come into this church over the years, and most of them arrive with all kinds of strange ideas and doctrines that simply don't belong."

"Belong where?" interjected Caroline.

"In the church," replied John quickly. "It just doesn't belong here. I'm talking strange ideas about the past, strange ideas about the future—all kinds of mumbo jumbo that we simply don't need. Christianity can be a very simple, neat thing. That's what the God Box is all about."

"So, ideas go in the box?" ventured Andy.

"Ideas, guidelines, disciplines—it all goes in the God Box. Everything you need to live a nice, normal Christian life will fit in this little online box. Amazing, isn't it?"

"Yes," they replied together, although not at all sure. "I am truly amazed," answered Andy.

"Reincarnation," said the Pastor, "will not fit into the God Box. There is simply no place for it. Therefore, we know we don't need it. The same goes for polygamy. No room at the inn, so to speak. The same goes for drinking, extramarital sex and homosexuality, as well as for wild-eyed healers and visions of Mary. See? The God Box gives us a nice, orderly way to live our lives. We have the freedom of boundaries!"

Pastor John stretched and draped his left arm over the back of his chair. "So, what do you think?"

"Well . . ." hesitated Caroline.

"Does everyone in this church have a God Box?" asked Andy.

"Certainly. It's how we keep on the same page around here. The pastoral staff can always check to see that no one is slipping into dangerous thinking. We've never had a big mess like some of the other churches. No heresies, no scandals, no surprises. Just peace and contentment."

"We did notice the church was very calm and orderly," offered Caroline.

"Absolutely. No swinging from the chandeliers here," John affirmed.

Andy leaned forward. "Do other churches have God Boxes?"

Pastor John smiled, "Ah, I knew you were a thinker, Andy. And I like that about you." He stood and walked over to a picture window looking out down Main Street. Andy could see at least two other church steeples.

"Yes, they all have God Boxes. Only," he gestured with his right index finger in the air for emphasis, "we're the only ones who admit it."

He turned and once again sat down opposite them. "Let's take a quick look at your boxes." He pulled up Caroline's box on his computer screen. "You will notice several labeled compartments inside. Don't be fooled by the relative size of the compartments—that has nothing to do with a thing's importance."

They stared into the screen, as if they might suddenly see something that could make them comprehend what Pastor John was telling them.

"For example, there's a small compartment for Salvation. You've prayed the prayer, you're born again, you're bound for heaven, and that's all we need to say about it. See, we've written the date right in there. In case you ever start doubting, all you need to do is glance in the box."

John let this sink in for his guests and then continued, "You will now notice that the 'Don't' section is somewhat larger than the 'Do' section. That's not because they are more important than the Dos, it's just that the Don'ts take more room—there are more of them. The Dos are mainly prayer and Bible reading. Not much room for negotiation there!

"In the Do compartment is a large place for tithing. That's important, but you don't really need to understand why for now. There's plenty of time for that."

Sensing he was perhaps losing their focus, John raised his voice slightly, "The entire bottom half of the boxes is called 'Eschatology,' which is a big word meaning the last days." Andy looked over at Caroline, both thinking that "last days" meant nothing to them, either.

"The other compartment is the Belief section, with compartments of the Infallibility of the Bible, the Trinity, and so on. Don't worry; you have plenty of time to figure all of this out. That's exactly what the box is for!"

Andy shifted in his chair, wondering when exactly a good time to leave would be.

"The God Box takes all of the thinking and worrying away from living the overcoming Christian life. Now, if you are thinking that perhaps the box is too limited, let me assure you that I am fully satisfied that these boxes are perfect to hold everything you need. If it won't fit in here, it's not worth thinking about! And," he paused to get their full attention, "the fifteen hundred members of this church will agree."

"Well," said Caroline, her mind racing. "Thank you. You've sure given us some things to think about."

"Yes," added Andy, getting to his feet. "Thank you so much for your time. I can't wait to start using this." Andy waved the card slightly.

"You're very welcome," replied Pastor John, beaming. "Again, it's such a pleasure to have you with us. Before long, you'll be just like one of the family— happy, content, and never having to think about your spiritual lives again."

"Thank you again," they both chimed and escorted themselves out.

Andy and Caroline were silent as they walked to their car, parked just out of sight of the Pastor's study window. Andy pushed the black control on his key fob and beeped the doors open. "Whaddya think?"

"I don't know . . ." Caroline's voice trailed off. She thought for a moment but remained silent. "How about you?"

Andy shrugged. "It's certainly not what I was expecting."

"Me either. Judy never mentioned a God Box."

"Can't say I blame her." Andy leaned back against the car. "It sounds nuts. I mean, I don't claim to know anything about religion, but even to me..."

Caroline looked Andy in the eyes, "You know that feeling we had in church last Sunday, like we could feel God?" Andy nodded as Caroline continued, "And that feeling, like lightness, that you've talked about?" Andy nodded again.

"Well," Caroline said thoughtfully, "I was just thinking, I don't think there's any room in this box for those."

Andy paused a moment, then he quietly breathed, "Yeah." He opened Caroline's door, then he considered what to do with his card. They looked at each other with a newfound wisdom and smiled. Without speaking, Caroline handed Andy hers.

Andy looked at the cards. "Recycling?"

"Recycling."

He stuck the cards in an empty coffee cup in the cup holder and drove away.

BORN TO WONDER

If there were a God, I think it very unlikely that he would have such an uneasy vanity as to be offended by those who doubt his existence. –Bertrand Russell

"Why would you start this book with a quote from a famous atheist?" you ask.

"Another good question," I answer. "This means that you are already questioning what you are reading. I like that. The reason I would quote Russell is that he had discarded all religious boxes and could ask questions about things that those trapped in theological boxes might not."

"So does that mean that he could have been right about not believing in God?"

"He could have been, but he's not. Just because he asks good questions doesn't mean he has the right answers. But, I think he's probably correct in the above statement. I don't believe God minds that we ask questions. In fact, He might be frustrated that so many of us don't ask them."

I have a confession to make, and it makes me somewhat nervous. I know a lot of people won't understand, but here it is: I am, by many standards, a terrible Christian. I don't do a lot of "Christian" things. A lot of what presents itself as Christianity makes me cringe, and I would rather not be associated with it. I can't listen to Christian radio, I *never* watch Christian TV, and I avoid Christian "music"—aside from outsiders like Bruce Cockburn, Jennifer Knapp, and some classic U2. It's all I can do not to scream at the "Jesus memes" on Facebook. Furthermore, I've developed an allergic reaction to many churches—they make me break out in anger (just ask my wife). As a result, I think I'm a much better Christian by staying out of many churches.

That said, I remain firmly and confidently Christian. My faith in Jesus is as strong as ever—perhaps even stronger, as I have gotten so much stuff out of the way. I believe the Apostles' and Nicene Creeds, I believe Jesus is God and literally, physically rose from the dead, and I believe the Bible is inspired. I believe Jesus has saved me/us, and that he will return, somehow, sometime (only without all that Tribulation and Rapture stuff). I believe I will spend eternity in God's presence. I am, by these standards, quite orthodox. I have, however, discarded many "add-on" beliefs, which unfortunately have become quite mainstream. In some cases, they dominate western Christianity.

The problem with many so-called "Christian" things is not Jesus or the Bible, it's all of the stuff that people *do* to Christianity to make it into something else as if the gospel—the good news—isn't enough. Instead of just seeing Jesus, we see rules, judgment, guilt, expectations, hatred, division, exclusion, racism, sexism, manipulation, and abuse. We also see intentional ignorance and denial of reality, baseless claims and conspiracies, and theologies that defy common sense and sound Bible study. Somewhere in this milieu there is truth. But how can you find it? How can you tell the truth from nonsense? How do we even know what God is really like?

I think it's time that we give God a little credit, and by "we" I am including atheists who don't believe in God. Seriously. Don't just imagine God is as shallow as evangelicals and fundamentalists paint him to be. If you are going to go to the trouble of deciding whether to believe or not that someone exists, at least try to know who you do or don't believe in (a little attempt at humor), and don't go with the dime-store version. Is God a mysterious unknown figure like Keyser Söze in *The Usual Suspects*? Or is he like the legendary Wizard of Oz, pushing buttons and hiding behind a curtain? Is he the old, bearded man surrounded by clouds and angels? Or is he perhaps really what you'd imagine God to be?

As a mental experiment, imagine God as you would expect the Creator of all that exists to be. Who is he? Toss out all the boxes and use your imagination. Is God the angry god who "abhors" us, as Jonathan Edwards wrote in the following passage from his famous sermon "Sinners in the Hands of an Angry God?"

> *The God that holds you over the pit of hell, much as one holds a spider, or some loathsome insect over the fire, abhors you, and is dreadfully provoked: his wrath towards you burns like fire; he looks upon you as worthy of nothing else, but to be cast into the fire; he is of purer eyes than to bear to have you in his sight; you are ten thousand times more abominable*

*in his eyes, than the most hateful venomous serpent
is in ours.*

Or is God the one represented by Jesus, who said,

> *"Blessed are the poor in spirit, for theirs is the
> kingdom of heaven. Blessed are those who mourn, for
> they will be comforted. Blessed are the meek, for they
> will inherit the earth. Blessed are those who hunger
> and thirst for righteousness, for they will be filled."
> (Matthew 5:3-6)*

And,

> *"Come to me, all you who are weary and are carrying
> heavy burdens, and I will give you rest." (Matthew
> 11:28)*

"I know," as Paul wrote to Timothy, *"whom I have believed"* (2 Timothy 1:12 KJV). And it is not the god of
condemnation who resembles the pagan gods of old—
so if that's the God you want to find, don't look here.

I happen to *not* believe in the god that many other
people believe in, which happens to be the same god
that many atheists don't believe in. I also *do* believe in a
God that many people don't believe in (because they're
too busy believing in something else). People are free
to make up their own minds about what they do and
don't believe, but it seems to me that if they choose not
to believe in God, they should at least know what god
they don't believe in, and why. Even more so, people
who choose to believe in God should know who they
believe in, and why. Unfortunately, America and the
broader Western world have been handed a caricature

of Christianity based on bad logic and theology, so that the god that many people believe in—or don't believe in—is probably different than the God that's presented in Jesus.

In America, the fundamentalist evangelical packaging of God has been promoted over and above all other beliefs. This is not because they have the best beliefs, by any means, but because they have been the loudest and pushiest. Their quick grasp of electronic media (radio, TV, and the Internet) likely has a lot to do with it. A thoughtful theological discussion can't compete in a ratings contest with empty promises, showmen, faith healers, and, unfortunately, purveyors of guilt. As a result, this TV religion is what many people, both Christian and non, understand Christianity to be. Those Christians who have doubts find themselves either having to act the part to fit in or drift away. I have heard it said that fundamentalism is one of the main causes of atheism, and I don't doubt it for a minute.

I have spent a lot of my life as an "amateur theologian," trying to work through the grab bag of theologies and traditions that all identify as Christian. At times, I feel like this unattributed quote I found on the Interweb: *"My analysis is severely limited by my lack of understanding of what I am doing."* As I've said, I am a wanderer, a wonderer, and a seeker, but I don't think I'm lost. I can agree with the great G. K. Chesterton, who wrote, *"The more I considered Christianity, the more I found that while it had established a rule and order, the chief aim of that order was to give room for good things to run wild."*[1] I excel at running wild.

However, I happen to still believe in the same God I believed in as a child. I don't know how I came to this belief, but I have always believed that God loves me unconditionally and that I need have no fear of God or his judgments. That doesn't mean my theology hasn't changed about peripheral things—as Madeleine L' Engle said, *"I do not think that I will ever reach a stage when I will say, 'This is what I believe. Finished.' What I believe is alive . . . and open to growth."* If your beliefs are static, you are not growing or learning. It means that you need to go on a little journey and experience a bit of danger, as I have done.

Along the way, some of my church experiences have caused trauma and others have brought hope and understanding. I can't think of any that haven't had any impact whatsoever, even if to cause me to blow smoke out my ears. There are many, many false teachers, some who are sincere but dangerously wrong, and others who are wolves in sheep's clothing (Matthew 7:15). In my experience, most false teachers are simply ignorant rather than evil, but you often can't be sure. It's easy for even someone of above-average intelligence to get swayed by a smooth-talking teacher with a slick or attractive theology, even if it is abusive. In my book with Ken Blue, *The Gospel Uncensored: How Only Grace Leads to Freedom*, we discuss this phenomenon in more depth.[2] I strongly suggest you buy a copy because I could use the royalties.

Christianity—the *Gospel* or "good news" of Jesus—is quite simple, and it is free. It's meant to be given away. In its true form, you can't make money from it, you can't get power or position from it, and you can't get authority over other people with it. It is not a commodity that can be packaged and marketed, it is not based on any special knowledge that you can only find at some special seminar. It's just here, and it's free for the taking. And get this: it doesn't make you special!

It doesn't give you a whiter smile or fresher breath or improve your love life and doesn't even make you a better person! How great is that? It won't make you rich and may not even make you "happy." It will, however, give you a different context for your life and challenge you to be a more loving person.

That didn't fly in a consumerist culture. So, one thing led to another. Simple organizational structures created to benefit people became power centers, and within only a few years branding was taking place (1 Corinthians. 3:4), and then there were competing gospels being preached (Galatians 1:6-9). Now, 2,000 years later, we have countless denominations, competing theologies, and marketing out the wazoo (that's theological language).

A BIT OF COMMON SENSE

Despite all of the publicity and attention around the more outrageous representations of Christianity, I do believe that there is a commonsense approach to understanding God and Christianity that normal people will identify with, which is what this book is about. We don't need rules and programs and seminars to achieve some certain level of spirituality, because we all have what we need. As Peter wrote,

> His divine power has granted to us **all things that pertain to life and godliness,** through the knowledge of him who called us to his own glory and excellence . . . For this very reason, **make every effort to supplement your faith with virtue, and virtue with knowledge . . .** (2 Peter 1:3, 5 ESV, emphasis mine)

I believe that there is a commonsense approach to Christianity that bypasses the wackos and flakes and guilt and work that you may have run across in your journey. As Jesus said, *"Take my yoke upon you, and learn from me, for I am gentle and humble in heart, and you will find rest for your souls"* (Matthew 11:29). The phrase "common sense" does not mean common or average thinking, contrary to popular belief. "Average" thinking is usually not something to aspire to at all. As we all know, public opinion is powerful, but rarely is it a good test of truth. As Gore Vidal wrote, *"At any given moment, public opinion is a chaos of superstition, misinformation, and prejudice."*[3] Likewise, as Bertrand Russell wrote in *Marriage and Morals*, *"The fact that an opinion has been widely held is no evidence whatever that it is not utterly absurd."*

Entire segments of the Church have at times had some rather strange ideas, and we shouldn't simply strive to go with the flow. Rather, a "commonsense approach" means using the faculties available to most humans—that is, the ability to think and reason or the good sense God gave us. Humans are created in the image of God, though not physically. But we of all his creation have the abilities to think and create and reason. (I've often thought that if it were up to me, I wouldn't have been so trusting.) As Galileo wrote: *"I do not feel obliged to believe that the same God who has endowed us with senses, reason, and intellect has intended us to forego their use."*

In the more than thirty years of experience I have investigating liability scenarios for insurance companies, I often referred to the "reasonably prudent person" standard, which is precisely what it sounds like. I'd ask, "What would a reasonably prudent person have done in this situation?" Again, "reasonably prudent" doesn't necessarily mean average, which can be a low bar. When we don't have a specific statute or rule to follow, we must evaluate based on what we think makes the most sense to someone who is "reasonably prudent." This principle, by the way, is used in many fields. And just to go a bit deeper, we must also use common sense to choose the standards by which we measure things. For example, someone with special knowledge—like a doctor or an engineer—has "professional" standards that are higher than those of the average person. Fortunately, God does not require us to have a PhD in theology, because he's already given us *"all things that pertain to life and godliness"* (2 Peter 1:3 ESV). Just use the good sense God gave you, and that can include a bit of learning from the experts. (I, again, am not an expert, I just quote them.)

In applying common sense standards, as well as professional standards, we must keep in mind that standards change over time, along with an increase in knowledge. Medical standards 1,000 years ago differ significantly from those today and the common understanding of illness differed. The same is true of science and even literature. We must be cautious to apply the proper standard to whatever we are looking at. At one time, bloodletting was the highest medical standard—today, not so much. At the time of Christ, the world believed that the Sun revolved around the Earth. Scientific knowledge has evolved; had Jesus, for example, taught that the Earth revolved around the Sun, he may have been killed for a completely different reason. It is important to understand "common sense" as it existed in the first century.

We will find this is necessary when looking at Christian thinking, especially as it concerns our understanding of the Bible. It is undeniable that we (humans) have grown in general knowledge over the years, especially over the last 100 years, and our understanding of natural phenomena will likely be thought of as archaic to those 500 years from now, and with it, our understanding of things in the Bible. That's right, we haven't "arrived." We are still adapting to new understandings of, well, everything. So where do we start with our commonsense approach to Christianity? How do we start utilizing the good sense God gave us? There are so many versions of Christianity available, let's start by unpeeling the onion of Christendom just a bit to expose the complexity of the subject, which I hope to simplify as we push through.

STORIES

We all have stories about who we are and what led us to be where and who we are today. These stories provide important contexts for how we view the world and evaluate information. For example, this is a tidbit of my story: I was raised in such a small, rural community where we belonged to the Lutheran church with about half of the other folks in and around the area. There were other churches in town, including Catholic, Presbyterian, Episcopal, and Evangelical Covenant. In later years, a new "franchise" appeared: the Baptists. Later yet, the Assemblies of God. Aside from a Catholic wedding and a couple of Episcopal funerals (my mom's family was Episcopalian), I never went to the other churches. Until I was older, while

I was immersed in Lutheran Christianity, my experience of the Church at large was quite limited.

We were taught some church history and a little comparative theology in our confirmation classes (basic theological education we went through in our junior high years), but otherwise, I had no clue about dispensationalism, the end times, Pentecostalism, or double predestination. We believed in salvation by grace, and I was raised knowing—not just believing, but with a deep knowledge—that God loved me unconditionally. I would sometimes worry that my parents may stop loving me, but for whatever reason I was absolutely certain that God always would. That was enough for me. (For the most part, it still is, despite my continued thinking and questioning of all things theological.)

There are countless other stories and experiences, ranging from "I've never been inside a church" to "I've belonged to more churches than you can count" to "I've spent my whole life in a cult." Some are happy and thriving in their church, and some are confused, hurt, or incredibly damaged. Growing up in a Christian environment is not necessarily a good thing.

Whatever our background, things can get confusing when we start to develop relationships with people from different backgrounds and traditions. I can recall being asked, "Are you Calvinist or Arminian?" My response was something like, "What??" Or perhaps, "I'm Lutheran and we don't care." It can be kind of confusing when you realize that being a Christian is not enough for everyone, and being a Christian does not mean you agree with what other Christians believe.

There are up to 3,000 different Christian denominations (the number depends on how you distinguish one from another) around the world. I read somewhere that there may be 200 different kinds of Baptists—I really don't know. I've been involved in enough non-denominational (or multi-denominational) groups to know that we share some core beliefs, especially when you're dealing with people who never really paid attention to the fine points of their church's teachings.

More often than we would think, many people not only don't understand the doctrines of the church they attend, but they also can't define their own beliefs. You may be surprised by this, but I think that's probably okay if they're part of a normal, functioning community. There's nothing wrong with having simple faith. It's when the problems start (abuse, manipulation, or weird restrictive teachings) that we need some understanding of what's going on. Knowing people outside of your group can be of great value when determining the normalcy of your church experience.

Today, there are a growing number of people being called the "nones." On March 21, 2019, Jack Jenkins wrote in the Religion News Service,[4]

> According to newly released General Social Survey data, Americans claiming "no religion"—sometimes referred to as "nones" because of how they answer the question "What is your religious tradition?"— now represent about 23.1 percent of the population, up from 21.6 percent in 2016. People claiming evangelicalism, by contrast, now represent 22.5 percent of Americans, a slight dip from 23.9 percent in 2016.[5]

The nones are also made up of people with many diverse backgrounds and experiences. Some of the nones are wandering believers (somewhere on the spectrum of belief), and others would consider themselves non-believers, completely off the faith spectrum. However, anyone who has been raised in America has probably formed some opinion about Christianity, or at least about Christians. Virtually everywhere are those claiming the label of Christianity, from rappers to the occupant of the White House. However, one version seldom looks like another.

NO JUDGMENT HERE

These examples, of course, are broad generalizations and are not meant to pigeonhole anyone or judge anyone's past or present. I'm just trying to show the breadth of church and non-church experiences and backgrounds. We are each a product of our past and we can't change that, and we shouldn't be ashamed of where we come from. The important thing is that we're here, and so is God.

Regardless of our background and where we might be today, Christianity—especially in America—tends to be a confusing mess in which even the label "Christian" is difficult to define. This project is an attempt to help myself and others navigate the paths through the treacherous Christian labyrinth, with more than a little of my own opinions showing through. (After all, it's my book.)

UNBOXING THE CHURCH—A VERY BRIEF AND LIKELY INACCURATE HISTORY

This short history will hopefully be helpful to those who haven't spent time trying to figure out how the Church got from the New Testament (NT) era to where it is today. It will be brief and fairly general, which means it won't be completely accurate. Think of it as a world map sketched by hand on a chalkboard. It only has value in a very general sense, but it may have some worth as we delve into Christianity.

THE EARLY CHURCH

A long, long time ago in a place half a world away, there was one church that didn't even have a name. Over time, it grew up into Europe and down into Africa, and became very organized, especially after the emperor Constantine converted to Christianity. The Church had leaders in various parts of the world, including one in Rome. Most of the Church used Greek as their official language, but the Church in Rome leaned toward Latin. As the years passed, the Roman portion of the Church grew away from the rest, even adopting some different theological viewpoints (which will be discussed down the road). In 1054, they officially split, and the Roman Catholic Church was born. The Eastern (now collectively known as "Orthodox") Church continued, eventually separating into various groups as countries became more politically divided. There now is the Greek Orthodox, the Russian Orthodox, the Armenian Orthodox, the Egyptian Coptic Church, and so on.

The Orthodox Churches are still fairly aligned with each other theologically, and the Roman Church is what it is—a very Western religion quite different from that of the East. Because of the apparent similarities, it is often assumed that the Roman and Eastern Churches are alike, but in reality the Roman Church has more in common with the Protestant Churches than with the Orthodox because of the teaching of a guy named Augustine and the later Enlightenment, out of which came a whole new worldview. The Eastern Church-es, as we will see, bypassed these philosophical and theological changes. The original Christian Church is closest to the current Orthodox Churches, and the Roman Catholic Church is, in my opinion, a Western distortion of Christianity out of which the Western Church has evolved.

THE REFORMATION AND BEYOND

In the fifteenth century, and moving into the sixteenth century, there were a few people who tried to bring some reform to the Roman Catholic Church (RCC). The official date for the start of what is called the Reforma-tion is October 31, 1517, when a young German monk named Martin Luther posted a topic for discussion on the door of Wittenberg Chapel, much like we do today on Facebook. This led to him questioning more and more of the RCC's teachings, and eventually, he had to leave the RCC. Thus, the church known as "Lutheran" came to be. The central teaching that set the Lutherans apart is that we are saved by God's grace alone, not by doing penance or buying indulgences (a Middle Ages RCC fundraising scheme). It is important to note here that the Reformation only happened in the Western Church—the Orthodox Church required no such refor-mation and have changed very little over the years.

This reformation, of course, inspired others to break away. Reformers like John Calvin went a differ-ent direction, with Calvin inspiring what is known as the Reformed tradition, or Calvinism. While Calvin-ists like to talk about their similarities with Lutherans, there are quite few. Calvinists also believe in salvation by grace, but with a twist: God only saves the people he chooses or predestines, regardless of what people do or want. For Calvin, the sovereignty of God was the keystone. Some Calvinists are brave enough to say that God even chooses which people he will send to hell. There are some other fun things about Calvinism that we'll get into down the road. The Puritans were Calvinists, and the modern Presbyterians descended from that tradition. Calvinism has impacted the entire Western Church, even those parts which claim to reject Calvinism.

One thing these early groups have in common is that they are *credal*, holding to the ancient creeds of the Church, particularly the Apostle's Creed (although Calvin had his own twist on that) and the Nicene Creed, with some language disagreements between Eastern and Western traditions. Most of the historic churches through the Reformation (and some later) hold to the Apostle's Creed and the Nicene (or, more accurately, the Nicene-Constantinopolitan) Creed as stating the essential beliefs of Christianity. Some churches reject these, as they don't believe in confessing "the words of men" over that of the Bible. This sounds very holy but can open the door to many heretical interpretations. Essentially, they are just replacing the historic creeds with newer "words of men."

As more and more splinter groups developed, each with their own theological peculiarities, this resulted in a variety of "statements of faith" that for the most part have replaced the creeds. Also, along with these new statements of faith, an emphasis developed on "personal" experiences of salvation, which has led to what we know as the current evangelical movement.

IN CLOSING

Now that I have provided something of a background to the Christian landscape, we will start to look at more of the nuts and bolts and do more in-depth exploration of the reasoning (or lack thereof) for Christianity. But first, let's look at issues of faith, reason, and doubt, which all come into play as we inspect Christianity and our own thinking.

CHAPTER 2

WONDER | DOUBT | FEAR | FAITH

"So, is this book going to be complicated?" you ask.

"Not at all," I respond. *"While at times I present various amounts of information, the goal is always to free us from the theological boxes that serve to keep us in line with someone else's ideas. These boxes also create a sense of fear of what could happen should we break out of the box. My theory is that if we can overcome our fear of having questions and doubt, we can find a bigger faith, still grounded in the basics of Christianity but will all the wonder that comes from discovery."*

"That sounds quite ambitious."

"It is," I agree. *"Let's see how successful I am."*

THE ONLY THING TO FEAR . . .

As we look at various aspects of Christianity, I first should explain a bit more about my own approach to Christianity, which has morphed throughout the years and continues to do so almost daily. As I have said elsewhere, and will say again, I have long stopped being afraid of asking questions, and I am more than fine with not having answers. The practice of asking questions, doubting pat answers, and discovery is a truly wonderful thing. Every time I discover something new or understand something in a new way—when I have one of those "lightbulb" moments—I am overcome with wonder and amazement. That has happened several times in writing this book. Perhaps I'm just weird. But, when one of those truths lets me see God in a new, bigger way, it's a worship moment. You can keep your worship bands and all that—just give me a bit of truth.

I suspect it was that kind of wonder-worship that inspired Walter C. Smith to write this hymn:

Immortal, invisible, God only wise,
In light inaccessible, hid from our eyes,
Most blessed, most glorious, the Ancient of Days,
Almighty, victorious, Thy great name we praise.

Unresting, unhasting, and silent as light,
Nor wanting, nor wasting, Thou rulest in might;
Thy justice, like mountains, high soaring above
Thy clouds, which are fountains of goodness and love.

To all, life Thou givest, to both great and small;
In all life Thou livest, the true life of all;
We blossom and flourish as leaves on the tree,
And wither and perish—but naught changeth Thee.

Great Father of glory, pure Father of light,
Thine angels adore Thee, all veiling their sight;
All praise we would render; O, help us to see
'Tis only the splendor of light hideth Thee.[6]

Wonder is one of the great things in life. I think that we all have a sense of wonder as children, but we somehow lose that as we grow older and are taught structures that curb that sense, or to have our knowledge of something challenged by new information. That sense of wonder and hunger for understanding is something that we may have to fight to regain and hold on to—there is much in the world that would steal it. But first, we must get rid of the fear of questioning and doubt of our beliefs about God, which hinder us from learning and experiencing anything new.

This may not seem to be much of an issue for some of you, as you may be agnostic or even an atheist and have little invested in a particular mindset in religion (or so you think). For others who have been taught a more structured or fundamentalist mindset, as is common in many evangelical or conservative communities, you may feel concerned about a loss of faith—even a partial loss of faith—and what that could mean for you. As Peter Enns writes,

> It is upsetting to redraw our maps and change what we see as the anchor of our security—and if left to ourselves, we would never go there. So we build walls to prevent that from happening, walls within which we preserve what makes us feel secure, where we are in control and our God makes perfect sense to us.

> Watching certainty slide into uncertainty is frightening. Our beliefs provide a familiar structure to our messy lives. They give answers to our big questions of existence: Does God exist? Is there a right religion? Why are we here? How do I handle suffering and tragedy? What happens to us when we

die? What am I here for? Answering these questions provides our lives with meaning and coherence by reining in the chaos.[7]

Redrawing our maps, as Enns put it, is unsettling for us regardless of our beliefs, or even our unbelief. Even those not inclined to believe in a God have beliefs—in science, in nature, in the existential abyss, or what have you—that provide a sense of security, but also restrict growth. While a fear of losing faith is not uncommon, one can also have a fear of *gaining* faith. What will it mean for me if I start believing in God? What will it mean if I start believing in a *bigger* God?

LETTING GOD OUT OF THE BOX

One book that has had a great impact on my early life is the short book *Your God Is Too Small: A Guide for Believers and Skeptics Alike* by J.B. Phillips, also known for his modern English translation of the New Testament. His point was to demonstrate that our preconceptions of who God is can be extremely limited, impacting our faith and life. It has been about forty years since I read the book, but that concept has remained with me. There are many things that can impact how we see God, from our early concept of God as an extension of our parents and other authority figures to how God is presented in many overstructured theologies. These images have the effect of placing God in a hypothetical box that limits how we see him and what we expect from him, also limiting how we see ourselves (being created in God's image) and all of life. This can cause us to be spiritually and intellectually "stingy," restricting our thinking and living within this "God Box." If you don't have such a box yourself, there are many teachers and churches that would be glad to provide you with one.

For example (and jumping ahead a bit to a topic we'll discuss more), what if you believe that God is somehow controlled or limited by his own wrath and justice, and has a primary need to protect his own glory? Obviously, God would have no alternative but to torture most of humanity for eternity. God *wants* to save everyone (the Bible says so), but he's like, "I'd really love to save you all, but I'm kind of stuck here, so you'll all just have to burn in this lake of fire because you never prayed that prayer." And, knowing you're a worthless sinner, you live in fear, even if you *did* pray the prayer . . . several times. You might even secretly resent God and feel terrible about that. But what if your God was bigger than that?

Maybe your God will judge America for allowing LGBTQ+ people to have equal rights, or because we don't pray in schools, or because (gasp) abortion is legal in your state. What if you don't support the current state of Israel, such as it is? Will your God send tornadoes and earthquakes, or cause bridges to collapse as one well-known preacher claimed? But what if your God was bigger? People, let your God out of the box. Or better yet, throw out the box and find the real God, who will not be confined to anything we can devise.

I have often run into Christians who live very superstitious lives because of their theological boxes. Not that they throw salt over their shoulders or avoid black cats, but they live in fear that something they do or don't do will cause some cosmic punishment (not unlike the concept of karma), so they're afraid to do anything without seeking God for direction first, and then they convince themselves that God has told them to do whatever they decided to do. You likely know one or two of these "God told me to . . ." people. I'm often amazed at the bad advice that "God" gives these people, including getting divorced so they can marry the person that "God" wanted them to. I think not. These people are, by the way, easy prey for unscrupulous leaders who look for people to control and manipulate. I have seen many of these wolves preying on entire churches. God is bigger than karma and prefers mercy over retribution.

The most flagrant abuse—and it is abuse—of superstitious teaching is the "tithe," which is an "offering" equal to 10 percent of your income (often gross rather than after taxes). Some churches teach that Christians need to give the tithe to their particular church, and their support of other charities has to come out of their 90 percent. This practice is often a regular sermon topic, as it needs to be reinforced so that the Church's income won't drop. The teaching is often that if you are faithful to give the Church your 10 percent, God will repay you several times over. And, of course, if you don't, you'll likely be poor for the rest of your life. "It's a test of faith," they say to encourage you to give to the Church rather than pay your bills or feed your family. But in reality it is a type of Ponzi scheme. I have always wondered why, if these pastors have so much faith, they need *your* money? Where is their faith? I get so mad at these people I could scream.

To me, this is an issue of commonsense Christianity. If people would bother to think and read their Bibles for themselves, they'd realize that this is not a teaching found anywhere in the Bible. Certainly, Jesus taught generosity, but not as a mechanism to receive a blessing . . . and surely not to fund some church's building plans. This superstition is a theological box that people have been taught in order to control them (and raise money). Again, God is much bigger than the tithing investment plan.

There are also theological boxes that are based on us believing in certain interpretations of select verses. If you have ever really paid attention, you will know that no one—that is, absolutely no one—reads the entire Bible literally. I mean, they've got problems in the first two chapters of Genesis. Their literalness seems to apply to key passages, and then only to their own interpretation of what the Bible "literally" says. Which, as is often the case, reminds me of a joke: What is the difference between a literalist and a kleptomaniac? A literalist takes things literally, and a kleptomaniac takes things, literally. (My apologies for that.)

Again, I will explore this later, but for now just remember that God is bigger than any single interpretation of the Bible. And, I should point out that there is no such thing as a purely correct interpretation of the Bible. Every one of us projects our own biases into what we are reading. We're just human.

To shift to a new analogy, many of these God constructs that we hold are essentially a house of cards, where any wrong move can cause our cards to collapse, leaving us with nothing to cling to. That is a frightening proposition indeed. What, for example, do we cling to if we cannot rely on the inerrancy of the Bible? How can we believe anything? What if the Rapture doesn't happen and we really have to deal with the impacts of climate change? Or what of our belief that God will make all our decisions for us? What if God wants us to decide what kind of macaroni to buy, or even more scary, what if we need to choose our own spouses?

What if God doesn't plan everything? What if God being in control doesn't mean that God controls all of the details? I have heard many, many people voice the opinion that everything happens for a reason. One of my favorite quotes from some unknown genius is, *"Everything happens for a reason. And sometimes the reason is that you're stupid and make bad decisions."* I've proven that one myself, many times.

These constructs provide a great deal of perceived protection from personal responsibility (as all superstitions are meant to do), and they sometimes keep us prisoners to imaginary rules. It doesn't matter whether the construct is of our own design or if it was placed upon us by others. Once we have accepted that our God Box is reality, we are imprisoned by the box, and often by fear as well.

YOUR GOD IS TOO SMALL

I was raised on a farm, where we did pretty much everything ourselves. My dad was multi-talented and could do nearly anything, from constructing buildings to rebuilding diesel engines. As soon as I was old enough, I was his assistant, learning carpentry, wiring, plumbing, etc. I remember being given tasks and my fear of making a mistake. What if, for example, I ruined this piece of wood? If my dad was as small in understanding as I was at eight or nine, he would have berated me for the error and the lost wood. However, my "big" dad saw beyond the wood and knew that it wasn't the end of the world. There were fixes, as well as more wood. My error allowed me to understand that there were possibilities beyond my own under-standing that my big dad understood.

The good news (the reality) is that your imaginary God—whatever box they're in—is too small. There is a larger world and a larger God out there. As we will deal with in a later chapter, God is not going to throw you into the lake of fire for stepping out of the box or scattering cards all over the table. God is not that petty or frightened of the world (which, of course, he created). As 1 John 4:18 says, *"There is no fear in love. But perfect love drives out fear, because fear has to do with punishment"* (NIV). That's right—in the real world, no punishment. Stay tuned.

Unfortunately, many Christians live in fear of any-thing outside of their little box, which often includes anything new or different. I have been around long enough to have seen many waves of fear go through the Church. When I was a teenager, it was rock music with that evil syncopated 4/4 beat that was somehow "sa-tanic," causing physical, emotional, and spiritual harm. Led Zeppelin's "Stairway to Heaven" contained satanic messages if you played it backward, and there were all kinds of evil things in the Eagles' "Hotel California." Now, of course, it's hard to find a church that doesn't have a full drum kit on the stage and a band that tries to sound its best like early U2.

I knew people who were afraid of demons living in owl figures (I never understood that one), evil con-spiracies in kids' cartoon shows, and of course, *Harry Potter*, which our family loved. (I do, however, believe that Barney was terrifying, but not necessarily be-cause of Satan.) Come up with something new outside of the Church that people like, and the Church will react in fear. Fears change like the weather, and boxes are remade to adapt. It all comes down to not believing in a God who is bigger than the bogeyman of the month. The important thing, it seems, is to have a box you can manage.

Stop for a minute and think about the history of Israel and of the Church. Consider Jesus being crucified, the apostles being martyred, and the early church persecuted. God had plans for all of that—do you for one minute think that God was afraid of rock music or cartoon characters or even postmodernism?

I have no problem repeating myself: My God is a big God, and there is no room for that kind of fear in my life. As a wise man once wrote, *"Little children, you are from God and have conquered them, for the one who is in you is greater than the one who is in the world"* (1 John 4:4). He is also bigger than any box you can imagine.

What we must do is to stop believing that faith in our theology is faith in God. I will say this again: Stop believing that faith in your theology is faith in God. For all you know, your theology might be total crap. Does that mean that God has in any way changed? Not at all. Do you believe in God because you also believe that the Bible is without error? Stop that! Abraham believed in God without having a Bible, and he's celebrated as one of the great men of faith (even though he proved time and again that he didn't understand God at all). Perhaps one of the reasons he's known as a man of faith is that he didn't need a Bible to trust God. As Jesus told the Jewish scholars of his day, *"You search the scriptures because you think that in them you have eternal life, and it is they that testify on my behalf"* (John 5:39). It is easy to replace faith in God with faith in the Bible, because it is something physical that we can see and touch and interact with, not unlike the golden calf created by the

Israelites. And Bibles come in boxes (we call them *versions*). An invisible God can be a challenge.

It's just as easy to replace faith in God with faith in *our idea* of God. We create a God that's comfortable for us (or sometimes uncomfortable for us), that fits our needs and helps us make sense of things. Whether we like our god or not, he fills some basic needs—or the needs of whoever created him. Just like that golden calf or that white Jesus hanging on your wall.

It's okay to let go of what we think we know because God is bigger than all of that. God is certainly not going to punish someone for challenging their ideas about God, especially when they are trying to know God more accurately. Your pastor may not be happy about being challenged, but I think God will be just fine with it. And I don't think your salvation will be in jeopardy whatsoever.

WHAT DID JESUS SAY?

Several years ago, my wife and I taught a high school Sunday School class that included my two sons and a future daughter-in-law, taking two years to go through the Gospel of John. (Yes, two years!) As we looked closely at what John was saying, my childhood belief in God's unconditional love was reinforced, and I started seeing some things that I hadn't seen in the past. One thing that stood out was that in the Gospels Jesus repeatedly talked about sin as if it were a sickness that we needed to be healed from, instead of something we needed to be punished for. What a game-changer that was! I doubted my own thoughts on this for a long time until I found that this was actually the original belief of the Church.

If we needed to be healed instead of punished, then the concept of Jesus having to be punished for our sins was not correct, and that whole theological construct came crashing down. As we will see later, this is in keeping with the belief of early Christianity, before some very strange thinking was adopted that has poisoned much of the Western Church.

Another point that is made in John Chapters 6 and 10 is that Jesus takes responsibility for our spiritual safety:

> "*My sheep hear my voice. I know them, and they follow me.* **I give them eternal life, and they will never perish. No one will snatch them out of my hand.** *My Father, in regard to what he has given me, is greater than all, and* **no one can snatch them out of the Father's hand.** *The Father and I are one*" *(John 10:27-30, emphasis mine)*

The "no one" seems pretty comprehensive. There is no exception for sin, doubt, wondering how the Bible fits in with modern science, or wondering if your church is a cult. Keeping you safe in "the Father's hand" is not your responsibility, or the responsibility of your pastor. But what, you might think, if it turns out that you are not one of those that Jesus called "my sheep?" Just a bit earlier, John records Jesus as saying:

> "*I am the good shepherd. I know my own, and my own know me, just as the Father knows me, and I know the Father. And I lay down my life for the sheep.* **I have other sheep that do not belong to this fold. I** *must bring them also, and they will listen to my voice. So there will be one flock, one shepherd*" *(John 10:14-16, emphasis mine)*

This very intriguing statement—"sheep not of this fold"—has sparked some debate over the years. It seems rather obvious to me that it refers to people who are not a part of the Jewish community. But how far out of the community? Does that include the pagan Romans and Greeks? What about those people on other continents that the Jews were not even aware of? Food for thought . . .

I do have thoughts on the subject, but I don't think the topic is that important for my purpose here. Instead, let's look at who Jesus' immediate audience was. John, for the most part, only identifies them as "the Jews," which is a bit unusual to me as they were all Jews, including John and Jesus. In Chapter 9, we have a reference to the Jewish group known as the Pharisees, which were sort of a legalistic, fundamentalist bunch. And we can assume the disciples were there, as well as ordinary people. Jesus seemed to draw quite diverse crowds, including a few Samaritans and Roman soldiers at times.

Jesus is talking about who his "sheep" are. In the immediate context, it seems that Jesus is pointing out that his sheep are those interested in what he has to say, as opposed to those Jews who only mean to discredit and oppose him. It is important to note that most of these people, including some of his disciples, had no concept that he was, in fact, God. None of them would have believed at that time that Jesus would be crucified and rise from the dead. None of them would understand the concept of the Trinity. So even his best followers were basically heretics by more modern standards. None of them had Jesus "living in their hearts," and the phrase "lord and savior" from someone not interested in overthrowing Rome may have been met with some confused looks. None of them had received the

Holy Spirit (who did not arrive until later), and none of them had been baptized after believing in Jesus. Some of them weren't even good Jews.

Furthermore, Jesus didn't seem to think that these things were important. His sermons sounded nothing like Billy Graham. He taught about God's love and about how he was the source of life, without really explaining what that meant, and according to his own statement, he meant to confuse people (Mark 4:12). He never had an altar call. He taught about the Kingdom of God/Kingdom of Heaven in stories that even his closest disciples didn't understand. Rather than converting the "rich young ruler," he frustrated him and chased him away (Mark 10:17-27). He healed people and told them not to tell anyone about it. (No TV cameras or anything!) On the face of it, this does not seem like a good example of a successful—or even Christian—ministry.

STOP!

I want to stop here and reemphasize this point because I don't think I can emphasize it enough: **None of these people that Jesus interacted with would qualify as Christians by today's standards**, and Jesus does not seem concerned about this. Basically, he tells them to "love God and love other people." Rather than making it into heaven, he tells them how to live their "best lives now."[8] Again, take some time to think about this. Perhaps read through one or two of the gospels to see for yourselves what I am saying. Why isn't Jesus more concerned with correct doctrine, especially concerning salvation? Why doesn't he even tell people who he is?

At this point, we might start to wonder if Jesus really cared about these people's eternal destiny at all. Or we might start to wonder if **maybe Jesus' mission was just a bit bigger than we think**. Maybe there is a larger and grander plan. Perhaps God is already holding all these people in his hand. Just perhaps God really does have the whole world in his hand. Just how big is God, anyway?

Now, we are starting to think the right way.

NO FEAR

It is quite easy to conclude that Jesus had no fear of losing any of these people. His attitude was, "No worries, no one can snatch you from my hand. It's under control." Jesus even gave this illustration:

> *"What do you think? If a shepherd has a hundred sheep and one of them has gone astray, does he not leave the ninety-nine on the mountains and go in search of the one that went astray?" (Matthew 18:12)*

Even as a child listening to this being read in church I thought, "Wouldn't he be afraid the ninety-nine would be in danger?" Apparently not. When people talk about God having everything in control, it doesn't mean that God controls everything (or the one wouldn't wander off). It means that he's certain he won't lose any sheep.

So, what are *we* afraid of? Do you think that God gets a bit concerned when we start to doubt or ask questions about things that do not make sense to us? Did God get worried when Darwin started publishing his books? Is he worried about scientific knowledge about human origins or historical discoveries that don't quite fit our beliefs? Does he worry when some philosopher proclaims, "God is dead?" Does he sit up in heaven with his head in his hands wondering what's going to happen when people stop believing in a literal seven-day creation? Just how small is your God, anyway? Remember to shift your thinking back to just how enormous God is.

One thing you can be sure of: He's bigger than you are. He's bigger than your pastor. He's bigger than your church. And he's bigger than any theology dreamt up by man.

BUT WHAT ABOUT THAT OLD TESTAMENT GOD?

Lest you think, as many seem to, that the God of the New Testament is different from the God of the Old Testament (OT), let's take a look at what King David wrote about God:

> The LORD is merciful and gracious,
> slow to anger and abounding in steadfast love.
> He will not always accuse,
> nor will he keep his anger forever.
> He does not deal with us according to our sins
> nor repay us according to our iniquities. (Psalm 103:8-10)

If we assume that David is speaking the truth about God, as most Christians certainly agree he is, David has just pulled the rug out from under a lot of false beliefs. *He does not treat us as our sins deserve or repay us according to our iniquities*—and this was centuries before Jesus came! Think about this for an hour or three and watch your paradigms shift. It is amazing to realize that God is not bound or limited by man's rules, which are always so much smaller than God truly is.

Why do you think God kept letting his people make mistakes, over and over? Why didn't God swoop down and stop Adam from eating the apple (or whatever fruit it was)? Time and again, God could have just made things simpler; why didn't he? As Peter Enns has written, *"God is not a helicopter parent."*[9] The reason there are helicopter parents is because they have control issues, meaning a lack of trust and fear of what could happen if they aren't in control. Because they know they're not in control. God is not one of those parents, precisely because he is in control. And as some (not all) of his people came to realize, they don't have to fear, because their God is huge.

THERE IS NO SHORTAGE OF GOOD NEWS

I may be just a bit odd here, but I get really excited about theology. As I have been preparing for each chapter, I have been reading a ton of books, rereading a ton of books, and finding new books to read. The more I find out about things, such as what we have learned from years of archeological finds in places like Iraq (where Abraham came from), and about other non-Jewish writings from the same time, I am not worried about finding out that many of the stories are similar, suggesting that some of the Bible's stories were adapted from the culture in which they lived or were stories shared with pagan cultures. And, when I find that there is good reason to believe that the earliest books of the Bible were likely written much later than thought and that later books disagree with the earlier books, and so on, I am not worried about paradigm crashes. Just the contrary, I am thrilled because I see over and over again how

God has worked through real people to reveal himself and that God is obviously fine with the questions.

Bottom line: My faith is not in the Bible (remember, Abraham didn't even have a Bible), in a church, in traditions, or in theology. My faith is not in my being right. In fact, I always make a point of saying that one of the few things I am sure of is that I am wrong (at least to some extent) about everything I think I know. That doesn't bother me in the slightest. I will believe the best truth I can find, and when I find a more correct truth, I will update my beliefs. That's growth. I'm not concerned, because I know God will not let me fall from his grasp.

I still believe and have faith in the God I came to know as a child, and I still marvel and wonder at the immensity of the universe and its Creator.

> *"Ask, and it will be given to you; search, and you will find; knock, and the door will be opened for you. For everyone who asks receives, and everyone who searches finds, and for everyone who knocks, the door will be opened. Is there anyone among you who, if your child asked for bread, would give a stone? Or if the child asked for a fish, would give a snake? If you, then, who are evil, know how to give good gifts to your children, how much more will your Father in heaven give good things to those who ask him!" (Matthew 7:7-11)*

THE TRUTH IS OUT THERE

Jesus said, *"You shall know the truth, and the truth will set you free"* (John 8:32, my paraphrase). So why should we be afraid of the truth, whatever it is? If we believe Jesus, or if we believe something else, we should want to know the truth about whatever we are wondering about. It's like the now-classic line from the movie *The Matrix*: *"Do you want the red pill or the blue pill?"* Do you want reality, or would you rather close your eyes and be someone's pawn? Because you have no freedom if your life is based on someone's virtual reality, which is what a lot of what passes for Christianity is.

But Isn't Christianity All About Faith?

Ah, yes. Faith. Let's quickly turn to the biblical definition of faith:

FAITH

Now faith is the assurance of things hoped for, the conviction of things not seen. Indeed, by faith our ancestors received approval. By faith we understand that the worlds were prepared by the word of God, so that what is seen was made from things that are not visible (Hebrews 11:1-3).

What does this mean? Chances are, not what you think. The first sentence, verse 1, is usually quoted without any context as if it's a definition out of *Webster's*, which it isn't. In fact, this passage is not meant to be taken out of context of the entire letter of Hebrews, which is directed to Jews to support belief in Jesus above all else. They didn't have a problem with faith, they needed to understand that Jesus was more than an angel or another prophet. Chapter 12:2 goes on to state that Jesus is *"the founder and perfecter of our faith . . ."* There is no longer any need for a sacrifice, as Jesus fulfilled everything.

So, what is faith? If you look at the examples in Chapter 11, you could conclude that faith is obeying God, in the midst of doubt and failure. Despite hardship. Despite persecution. The great men of faith believed God had a plan, even though they didn't know what it was, and never received that which was promised. I liken this to soldiers who fight and die in overwhelming battles because they believe in a cause. For the Jewish people, faith was a belief in the Abrahamic Covenant and the purposes of God, regardless of periods of oppression. Another analogy would be a long-term retirement plan. You know that you're in for the long haul, perhaps 20, 30 years or more. So, you expect there to be periods of loss but are counting on the long-term increase, based on sound financial analysis. That's faith.

Faith, then, is not believing impossible or unbelievable things, or believing without any understanding. There is certainly such a thing as "blind faith," but only cults (and religions that act like cults) push that kind of belief. True faith, in my opinion, requires two things: trustworthy authority and wisdom (i.e., common sense).

Hang in there, and we'll get to those in a few moments.

CHAPTER 3

FAITH AND REASON–A COMMON SENSE APPROACH

"Reason?" you ask. "I was told that Christianity was a matter of faith, and that reason was relying on man's wisdom."

"But where does man's wisdom come from?" I reply. "As I will show you, God is still the source of man's wisdom. Sometimes our reasoning is correct and sometimes it isn't, because we aren't perfect. That's why we have the Bible, the Holy Spirit, and each other. Reason can be a great asset to faith."

"I'm not sure . . ."

"See, you're already using reason. You can't help it . . . you just need to apply it consistently. This chapter is one of my favorites, as we talk a little history, a little philosophy, and some good old-fashioned reason, all leading to faith."

A REASONED FAITH

I do not feel obliged to believe that the same God who has endowed us with senses, reason, and intellect has intended us to forego their use. –Galileo Galilei

There are far too many Christians who, believing in a God that is way too small, hang on to and promote inadequate and incorrect beliefs that make themselves specifically, and Christianity in general, look foolish. Years ago, there was a little saying, *"I'm a fool for Christ—whose fool are you?"* Cute, but—yes, foolish. The Apostle Paul wrote about foolishness and wisdom in the letter we know as 1 Corinthians, and it seems that many Christians misunderstood his point and have used it to justify ignorance. The fact that the wisdom of the world is foolishness to God (1 Corinthians 3:19) does not mean that the inverse is true.

If one were to do a little Bible search on the topic of foolishness—in fact, just look through Proverbs—you should not want to be a fool:

> *The fear of the LORD is the beginning of knowledge; fools despise wisdom and instruction. (Proverbs 1:7)*

> *One who is clever conceals knowledge, but the mind of a fool broadcasts folly. (Proverbs 12:23)*

> *A fool takes no pleasure in understanding, but only in expressing personal opinion. (Proverbs 18:2)*

Jesus never said, "Blessed be the fools." Nor is foolishness listed as a fruit of the Spirit. No, foolishness gets no biblical support in either the Old or New Testaments. My advice: Don't be one.

Neither does church history applaud "foolish faith." As early as the fifth century there was a mistaken competition between a blind belief in our understanding of what the Bible says and knowledge that existed outside of the Bible, as evidenced by this comment from St. Augustine concerning the meaning of Genesis:

Usually, even a non-Christian knows something about the earth, the heavens, and the other elements of this world, about the motion and orbit of the stars and even their size and relative positions, about the predictable eclipses of the sun and moon, the cycles of the years and the seasons, about the kinds of animals, shrubs, stones, and so forth, and this knowledge he hold to as being certain from reason and experience. **Now, it is a disgraceful and dangerous thing for an infidel to hear a Christian, presumably giving the meaning of Holy Scripture, talking nonsense on these topics; and we should take all means to prevent such an embarrassing situation, in which people show up vast ignorance in a Christian and laugh it to scorn.** *The shame is not so much that an ignorant individual is derided, but that people outside the household of faith think our sacred writers held such opinions, and, to the great loss of those for whose salvation we toil, the writers of our Scripture are criticized and rejected as unlearned men (emphasis mine).*[10]

This kind of faith is still an issue today, despite everything we've learned about the physical world and about the Bible. I would venture to say that it is even worse today *because* of what we know about the physical world and the Bible. People's ability to ignore a reality that is right in front of their faces or **to hold on to beliefs that do not need to be believed** is truly amazing. Consider again *beliefs that do not need to be believed.* If you highlight things as I do, highlight that. What happens if we let go of some beliefs? What if we let go of our need for certainty? What difference does this make? For example, Augustine, the hero of the Western Church, didn't take the creation story literally. His views are consistent with others of the Church Fathers. It wasn't until the eighteenth century that this modern literal belief structure was laid on the Church.

It's okay if you want to believe in a literal six-day creation, but your entire faith shouldn't rest upon something so extrinsic to the gospel. You can still believe in the essence of Christianity while doubting certain non-essential aspects. Adherence to peripheral issues can even blind you to more important matters.

I grew up on a farm in Northwestern Minnesota that was several miles outside of town. If you've ever been to Northwestern Minnesota, you know that it is flat as a pancake with hardly any trees. There are unregulated intersections everywhere you look, even on some fairly busy roads (that is, a road with more than one car in sight), but it's not a problem because you can see cars coming from a mile or two away. It is just assumed that if you are on a smaller gravel road that intersects a major road, you'll wait until the road is clear before you cross. Back then, we knew better. Those we referred to as "old farmers" were those who learned to drive in the 1930s (or earlier) when cars traveled slower and were even fewer and farther between. And perhaps they didn't want to deal with the reality that someone could be coming down that paved road going 75 or 80 mph. More than once, I saw one of these "old farmers" come up to a paved road and just keep on going across without turning to even look left or right, as if they had blinders on. It seemed that their thinking was, If I don't see it, it isn't there.

Some Christians take the same approach to their beliefs. If I refuse to acknowledge factual reality and keep on plowing ahead, I can hold on to faith in my belief in whatever it might be, such as the Earth being the center of the solar system. This might be faith and may have been reasonable in the first century, but it's no longer a reasonable faith because we all know differently now. To continue to believe in this scientific error is a "blind" faith. As philosopher Mortimer Adler wrote:

> I suspect that most of the individuals who have religious faith are content with blind faith. They feel no obligation to understand what they believe. They may even wish not to have their beliefs disturbed by thought. **But if God in whom they believe created them with intellectual and rational powers, that imposes upon them the duty to try to understand the creed of their religion. Not to do so is to verge on superstition** (emphasis mine).[11]

There is nothing wrong (and a lot right) with having a reasonable faith.

TIMES HAVE CHANGED

One thing we should always be aware of in dealing with anything in the past is that times have changed . . . a lot. It is one thing to read letters from 2,000 years ago when they were written by hand and copied by hand and read aloud as very few people could read. It is quite another to transpose those letters to the twenty-first century, where not only access to the Bible has changed, but the languages have changed, the meanings of words have changed, the culture has changed, and our very under-standing of the world has changed—considerably more than most of us realize.

Surprisingly, the concept of reason has not changed much over the years, although our collective viewing lens has completely changed. Aristotelian logic, developed by Aristotle in the fourth century BCE, became foundational to philosophy as well as theology with the rise of scholasticism and on through the Enlightenment. It is obvious from reading the New Testament that the first century Christians would likely be somewhat familiar with both Plato and Aristotle; we only have to read "In the beginning was the *Logos*" to know this, as *logos* was a Greek philosophical concept. I would also hazard a guess that Paul was knowledgeable of Greek philosophy from comments in Acts:

> *So he argued in the synagogue with the Jews and the devout persons, and also in the marketplace every day with those who happened to be there. Also some Epicurean and Stoic philosophers debated with him . . . (17:17, 18a)*

> *Every sabbath he would argue in the synagogue and would try to convince Jews and Greeks. (18:4)*

Paul's use of logic and reasoning throughout his writings make him particularly attractive to those from a modern, Western background, which sees everything from this rationalist, reasoned mentality. However, this has not always been the case, and there are significant changes in the application of reason. In fact, until the seventeenth century, reason played a much more limited role, usually in the context of theology, and reliance upon reason is still looked at with suspicion in the Eastern Church and is seen as the origins of Augustine's heresy. In the Eastern Church, reliance on the traditions takes precedence over reason, although there is still a great deal of reasoning and discussion in

Eastern theology. It seems to be more of an attitudinal thing—it's how you view reason.

Virtually none of us who have been raised "on the grid" have any concept of the thought processes that existed before Augustine, or even before the Enlightenment. There have been a handful of thinkers in the Western world who have introduced ideas that are so revolutionary that they have significantly changed the way we view the world forever, so much so that it's hard for us to now think any other way.[12] This concept in itself is nearly impossible for us to grasp; I've been working on it for years, and it still makes me dizzy.

THE MEN WHO CHANGED THE WORLD (THE WESTERN WORLD, ANYWAY)

Augustine

Augustine of Hippo was an Algerian (not the European that many might envision) theologian, philosopher, and Roman Catholic Bishop who lived from 354 to 430 AD. He originally studied Manichaeism, the predominant Persian religion at that time, and later became a Neoplatonist. He eventually converted to Christianity in his thirties but remained influenced by his earlier beliefs. Mani (for whom Manichaeism is named and who was thought to be a successor prophet to Jesus), taught a dualistic universe with an ongoing battle between the good spiritual world and the evil, dark, material world.

Neoplatonism, which continued in the thinking of Plato, was also a dualist philosophy, presenting the material world as a shadow of the more real, spiritual world of ideas. This dualistic worldview stayed with Augustine in developing his Christian theology. It's easy to see how this concept could be applied to Jesus' teachings on the Kingdom of God, although Jesus never reduced the physical world to the dark, evil place that Augustine seemed to see.

Augustine's philosophy also included his view of mankind, which is where his real problem lies, in my opinion. He developed the concept of *original sin* (building on some ideas by Ambrose, who believed that sex was the worst sin of all, and Tertullian, who taught that sin was transmitted through sperm), which was the sin of Adam transmitted to all of humanity through sexual intercourse. Augustine had lived quite somewhat of a hedonistic life before converting to Christianity, and he seemed to have a lifelong sense of guilt over his sexual indiscretions, which I believe figured into his views of dualism and original sin. One of the takeaways here is that you should never follow someone who is plagued by his guilt.

In 426 AD Augustine published *The City of God*, in which he developed for the first time the doctrine that the non-elect (those not fortunate enough to be "chosen" by God) will spend eternity burning in hell. That's right, this was a new—or perhaps, progressive—theology for its time. Augustine cherry-picked Bible verses to create an argument for eternal damnation—which seemed to work as long as you didn't bring up all those other verses or pay attention to Gregory of Nyssa's theological work on the subject.

His teachings did not catch on immediately, but the Western portion of the Church (which eventually became the Roman Catholic Church) eventually adopted Augustine wholeheartedly (with the notable exception of his later thoughts on double predestination). When you think Medieval, think of Augustine. Augustine's ideas permeated the Catholic Church, highly influencing both Luther and Calvin among others, which then spread through the entire Western Protestant Church as well. Unless you were raised Orthodox, your thinking is likely influenced at least somewhat by Augustine, even if you are an atheist.

Augustine also believed that humans had an innate capacity for reason, although he believed that reason had to be complemented by faith to discover truth.

Anselm

Centuries later, an Italian priest named Anselm (1033-1109), came on the scene. He attempted to create a rational approach to Christianity, developing what is known as the ontological argument for the existence of God. However, he believed that faith came before understanding rather than faith being the result of reason. His thinking greatly influenced a movement in the Catholic Church known as scholasticism, which would soon catch on in Roman Catholic circles.

Scholasticism was a method of study that rose to popularity in the twelfth century and continued for a few hundred years. The scholastics combined Greek philosophy and logic with theology, using dialectical reasoning and Aristotelian logic to arrive at a truth. This approach ran counter to the Augustinian approach to Christianity, as it emphasized Aristotelian logic over Plato. Note that both schools of thought are reliant on pre-Christian Greek philosophy.

Thomas Aquinas

It was Thomas Aquinas (c. 1225-1274) who, in effect, "resurrected" Aristotle, much to the dismay of many of his time who were firm Augustinians. After his death, a couple of Augustinian Catholic bishops declared this thinking heretical. However, a few years after that the pope declared Aquinas a saint, which caused his writings to become more popular. Five hundred years later, another pope declared Thomistic theology as official Catholic doctrine, firmly placing Aristotle over Plato. One of the things Aquinas believed was that one could deduce the existence of God by human reason alone, which would be complemented by supernatural revelation. His was a faith supported by reason. As the RCC had now officially adopted the Thomistic approach to theology, this thinking spread wherever the RCC was in existence.

THE WORLD UNDER AUTHORITY

Even with the major theological changes from Augustine through to the scholastics, with the changes in how we viewed humanity and our eternal destinies, and how we even viewed God (which we will get into more in a later chapter), our basic worldview is still the same. Thinking in the Western world (the Eastern Orthodox are happy on their course, having rejected the Augustinian nonsense) is still basically the same. However, the East and West agree on one aspect, and that is that truth is based on belief in authority, although there are different opinions about what that authority is. In the "postmodern" West, personal opinion seems to have risen in esteem, from beliefs in conspiracy theories to what we believe about God. I reject such foolishness—not all authorities are equal, and you must have some basis for your choice of authorities.

But in a world where literacy was a scarce commodity and access to books was even more limited, there were three main sources of authority: the State, the Church, and Tradition.

THE STATE

Wherever and whenever one lives, there has always been a source of propaganda passing for truth, in some cases more divergent from truth than others. History is written by the victors, and current events are interpreted by those with a vested interest in the population's opinion. Whether speaking truth, lies, or opinion, the State has always been a source of authority. If the State tells you that you need to pay taxes, you pay taxes. If the state says that you're the "good guys," then that's what you are. Again, in a world with limited access to independent information, the authority of the State is more pronounced, which is why some totalitarian governments try to limit access to the Internet—information is power. And, of course, the State always has consequences built in to keep people adhering to that authority.

THE CHURCH

The Church since Constantine had been a source of authority concerning spiritual and moral matters, and sometimes drifting into issues of the State. We are all probably most familiar with the Roman Catholic papacy, which has made decisions for thousands and even millions of people around the world, concerning such things as marriage, birth control, and even salvation. And, when the Bible was only available in Latin (and even when many priests couldn't read Latin), when the Church tells you what the Bible says, that's what it says. The Church also had a system of consequences, which have been largely lost over time (although not completely). Most evangelical churches rely on social consequences as opposed to threats of damnation or whatever.

TRADITION

Tradition, the third authority, has played different roles in different places. In the West, the traditions—beliefs passed down through the years, including the liturgies used in church services—were occasionally rewritten as needs arose by the Church. Traditions in any culture are a natural source of authority, and medieval Europe was no different. In the Eastern Church, that which is known as capital "T" Tradition is highly revered and still carries the weight of the Church behind it. The Orthodox, as a rule, have been more reverent to church Tradition and have also taken the time to educate their parishioners, so that the Church, rather than its leadership, possesses the Tradition, and therefore, the authority of the Church. It is a very different mindset, and difficult for a Westerner to fully grasp. One thing to note when attempting to dismiss Tradition is that the existence of the New Testament relies on Tradition. The same folks who wrote the creeds and argued about the Trinity also decided which NT books were inspired and should be added to the collection that we have today.

MARTIN LUTHER

As I've said, not everyone was happy with the direction the scholastics were going, notably Martin Luther, who, after all, was an Augustinian monk who had high regard for both Augustine and Plato and was rather dismissive of Aristotle, whom he considered a weak philosopher. Upon first glance, some of his comments seem to suggest that Luther was dead set against reason:

> *"Reason is a whore, the greatest enemy that faith has; it never comes to the aid of spiritual things, but more frequently than not struggles against the divine Word, treating with contempt all that emanates from God."*[13]

And:

> *"Reason must be deluded, blinded, and destroyed. Faith must trample underfoot all reason, sense, and understanding, and whatever it sees must be put out of sight and . . . know nothing but the word of God."*[14]

However, Luther was himself educated in philosophy and even taught university courses on Greek philosophy, including Aristotle. And anyone who has read Luther knows that he is not shy in using reason and logic in presenting his arguments. However, as I have said, Luther had high respect for Plato and thought very little of Aristotle. Among other things, he felt that Aristotle's teaching on morality was dangerous as it suggested that people become good or moral by doing virtuous things, which contradicted Luther's belief that we only do good through God's grace.

But Martin Luther is perhaps known for one thing that changed the authority structure of the world at that time: **He declared the Bible as the sole authority for the Church**, which challenged not only the Church as an authority but also tradition. *Sola Scriptura* ("the Bible alone") became the cry of the Reformation, as Luther translated the Bible into German and, thanks to Gutenberg's invention of the printing press, started making the Bible available to the German people in their own language. Now, for the first time, people could read for themselves what the Bible said.

Martin Luther and others walked away from the Roman Catholic Church and monks and priests started to marry (Martin himself married a nun, Katie). While the RCC maintained considerable power, the Reformation floodgates had been opened, and the absolute authority of the Church was broken.

So, if you were someone living in Europe in the 1400s, your source of authority and truth (for the most part) was now the State, the Church, Tradition, and the Bible, for those who grabbed at freedom and grace. These were still authorities that existed outside of everyday human experience, and for the most part they were not questioned. The cycle of the seasons continued, there were births and deaths, and life went on. Then came Descartes.

DESCARTES

Now we are coming to the most drastic shift in thinking in the last 2,000 years, with Rene Descartes, born in France in 1596. Descartes introduced a way of thinking that brought a fundamental change to the Western world. As Russell Shorto writes:

The change was in a way more profound than the American and French revolutions, the Industrial Revolution, or the information age because it affected the very structure of people's thought—the way they perceived the world, the universe, and themselves in it.[15]

Another philosopher put it this way: "The modern world is Cartesian to the core."[16]

It was as if a second Garden of Eden experience had occurred. Descartes ate from the Tree of Reason and Doubt and the innocence of the faith in the old authorities was lost. He was banned from the Garden never to return, along with all those who came after him. The revolution in thinking is "so fundamental to modern consciousness that it is hard to regard them as part of the natural property of the human mind."[17] In years of trying to access the mentality of pre-Cartesian theologians, I have found that I am too thoroughly modern to do so; I can only process through modern, Cartesian eyes.

What Descartes did was to conduct a thought experience in which he implemented doubt to question everything in the hopes of arriving at something finally, that could not be questioned. In the end, he arrived at, "I am thinking/doubting, therefore there must be something that thinks/doubts." Logically, he could not doubt that he was doubting without acknowledging that he was doing the doubting. While his famous *"cogito ergo sum"* ("I think, therefore I am") has had various applications through the years, his most important contribution to thinking was the process of doubting everything.

This doesn't mean that Descartes didn't believe in anything; in fact, he remained a lifelong dedicated

Christian. Rather, he realized that everything *could* be doubted and examined and questioned, and by doing so he ceased to rely solely on the established authorities for knowledge. The most obvious outcome of this process is modern science, which could not exist without Descartes' philosophical foundation. This, of course, was not an instant change, but by the early 1700s reason began to be "applied outside the boundaries of theology—'free thinking'—caught fire and swept across the Continent with a speed and force that bewildered churchmen."[18]

THE BATTLE LINES ARE DRAWN

So, after many centuries of Western Christianity, thinking about things has become distinct—freed—from the authorities of the Church and the State. That does not mean that Church and State were necessarily at odds with one another, but you can see where the tension existed for those who wanted to maintain the control of the Church, and for those who wanted their freedom from that brand of authoritarianism. What began as a philosophical exercise quickly developed into that nemesis of fundamentalist Christianity—science.

Science, in all its forms, started establishing something new: Truth (more accurately, facts and theories) which existed outside of religious belief. Of course, as we've seen with Augustine's comments on Genesis, there already existed some knowledge of the world that challenged the literal reading of the Bible. As science went on, Galileo was shown to be partially right, new lands were discovered, and then, we had the evil theory of evolution. The Church no longer could claim exclusivity on the narrative—there was a new narrative in town that threatened the status quo. Besides scientific discoveries, archeology began to discover not only the bones of dinosaurs but also early manuscripts that brought new readings and understandings of the Bible texts. It seems that not everyone is happy about the new truth.

While more established churches like the Roman Catholic and Reformation Churches have been in recent times more open to embracing new knowledge, the more fundamentalist groups have become more and more entrenched in tradition and denialism. To these folks "science" is abjectly anti-God, and is not to be trusted (except when it comes to things like flying on airplanes and microwave ovens). I agree with Augustine here, that this kind of thinking holds the whole church up to ridicule, even though many of our scientists are committed Christians who do not see any conflict between faith in God and science. Francis Collins, the current head of the National Institutes of Health (NIH), is one such Christian. Before his current role, he was the head of the Human Genome Project (HGP) that mapped human DNA. In a 2004 interview given in connection with the PBS show *The Question of God*, Collins says:

> *Actually, I don't see that any of the issues that people raise as points of contention between science and faith are all that difficult to resolve. Many people get hung up on the whole evolution versus creation argument — one of the great tragedies of the last 100 years is the way in which this has been polarized. On the one hand, we have scientists who basically adopt evolution as their faith, and think there's no need for God to explain why life exists. On the other hand, we have people who are believers who are so completely sold on the literal interpretation of the*

first book of the Bible that they are rejecting very compelling scientific data about the age of the earth and the relatedness of living beings. It's unnecessary. I think God gave us an opportunity through the use of science to understand the natural world. The idea that some are asking people to disbelieve our scientific data in order to prove that they believe in God is so unnecessary.[19]

The fact remains that many, many of our conservative evangelicals have chosen to revert to a pre-enlightenment type of thinking, relying on the authority of their churches and leaders rather than on their own five senses and their ability to think and reason, even when it comes to understanding the Bible. This also results in many of these same people embracing several strange doctrines and conspiracy theories.

The Enlightenment and the rise of reason brought many good things, but some jumped to the conclusion that reason was all you need so we could dispense with God altogether. As the philosopher Immanuel Kant said, *"All our knowledge begins with the senses, proceeds then to the understanding, and ends with reason. There is nothing higher than reason."*[20] The reaction of the Church was, of course, to jump to the opposite corner and argue that faith was all you need, so we could dispense with reason. This is where a lot of contemporary conflicts arise.

THE NEW ATHEISTS

New Atheism is a quasi-movement that took hold around the start of the twenty-first century, led mainly by four anti-religion atheist authors, Richard Dawkins, Sam Harris, Daniel Dennett, and Christopher Hitchens, who are more or less the antithesis of the anti-science fundamentalists. Besides championing science and reason over religion and faith, they believe that more than just unnecessary, religion and faith are destructive forces in society. As Dawkins put it,

> *Faith is the great cop-out, the great excuse to evade the need to think and evaluate evidence. Faith is the belief in spite of, even perhaps because of, the lack of evidence.*[21]

Dawkins, however, had his own self-serving definition of "faith" that limited it to what we think of as blind faith—that is, belief without evidence, thinking, or reason. This strawman definition made it easy for people to agree with, therefore concluding that science was the clear winner. Furthermore, it makes discussions about faith nearly impossible, as he fails to acknowledge any other perspective. So, when someone accuses someone from the new atheist perspective of having faith in science (which is a valid claim), it is immediately handwaved away as being an impossibility, as faith by their definition is faith without evidence.

Faith, however, is not belief devoid of reason, it is belief that is based on something. When we sit down in a chair, we have faith that the chair will support us, even if we haven't seen that particular chair before. Our knowledge and experience with chairs provide a basis for us to trust in a chair. By this definition, scientists have *faith* in the scientific method. They use it and rely on it because they believe that empirical study is effective and provides reliable results. If they didn't have faith in their methods of study and observation, they wouldn't spend so much time doing it. However, calling it "faith" will often drive them crazy because science, to them, is the antithesis of faith (aka belief without reason).

PHILOSOPHICAL ISSUES OF FAITH AND REASON AND THE UNCERTAINTY OF SCIENCE

If I had my life to live over, I might have finished my philosophy degree, rather than transferring to business school, and spent my time studying epistemology, or the study of how we know what we know. I just love thinking about this stuff. Now that I'm retired, I am free to study whatever I want, and that makes me happy. Apologies for the personal detour.

To get just a little background on the question of faith and reason from a philosophical perspective, let's go back to Enlightenment philosopher **David Hume**, born in Scotland in 1711. While many atheists refer to Hume's arguments against miracles, what I find most interesting is his proposition that you can never logically deduct the effect from the cause, which goes to the foundation of scientific study. Just showing that something happened ninety-nine times does not guarantee that it will happen a one hundredth time. Along comes another philosopher of the same period, **Immanuel Kant**, quoted earlier, who was bothered by Hume's thinking, and made an end run around Hume by coming up with different categories of knowledge, saying that we simply can't know everything by reason alone.

Zipping along to the twentieth century, we have philosopher **Bertrand Russell**, also mentioned earlier, a renowned atheist:

Our nature is as much a fact of the existing world as anything, and there can be no certainty that it will remain constant. It might happen, if Kant is right, that tomorrow our nature would so change as to make two and two become five. This possibility seems never to have occurred to him, yet it is one which utterly destroys the certainty and universality which he is anxious to vindicate for arithmetical propositions . . .[22]

To my knowledge, no one has come up with a good argument to refute Hume's initial proposition that a cause does not guarantee a specific effect. There is no guarantee that the universe will not someday change, so that 2 + 2 = 5. It seems quite unlikely, but we cannot prove it. And the fact that the Sun comes up (in a manner of speaking) in the east every morning does not mean it will be there tomorrow. No amount of experience in the past will guarantee the same experience at any point in the future. To return to our chair example, we can never be truly sure that a chair will not break under our weight. While unlikely, it may have been sabotaged by spies. We simply cannot be 100 percent certain. What scientists do when they send men to the moon is to have faith (here, a belief in probability) that what has happened in the past will happen in the future. We have no reason to expect that what we have seen will not happen in the future, but we have no absolute proof that it will. The best we have is a high probability that what has happened 10,000 times or more will continue to happen and that 2+2 will still equal 4.

Another interesting challenge to science as the only guide to reality is fairly simple: **There is no proof that the scientific method works** because there is no way to test it. How can we? It's illogical to use science to prove itself, but based on our observations and experience, science appears to "work." There is no test for it except for the scientific method itself. However, it is illogical to rely on science to prove itself. You can't rely on an unproven method to prove the method works. This is philosophically similar to Gödel's theorem in mathematics, which oversimplified means that you cannot prove or define a system from within the system itself; you have to be able to step outside of the system to see it truly objectively. Again, this is paraphrased and oversimplified, and mathematicians would likely cringe at my explanation.

All this being said, I fully support science and believe it is a very effective tool based on our experience. I love science, especially subjects like chaos theory and quantum physics, neither of which I am competent to discuss. I, however, do not believe science is 100 percent infallible, and neither do most scientists. However, it's the best tool we have to study the material world. As we discover more, old understandings need to be refined and, in some cases, thrown out. Galileo, for example, was wrong about his heliocentric model, although he was righter than the geocentric model which placed Earth as the center of the universe. Science works best when it proves current understandings wrong. It doesn't mean that science was "wrong," it just shows that we are learning more. Science provides us with enough knowledge to press on to further discovery. As does faith.

Like many scientists and Christians, I believe that science is compatible with faith in God, as it provides us with a reasonable method for examining and learning about God's creation. It is another revelator of truth, which cannot conflict with other truths. Truth is truth, regardless of the source. Such conflicts are an indication that some of the facts we hold on to may not be that factual. As we discussed in the prior chapter, **we need to stop believing that somehow our thoughts and beliefs about God are inerrant** and that we need to guard them. As Peter Enns writes,

> We think true faith is dependent on maintaining a particular "knowledge set" and keeping a firm grasp on a tightly woven network of nonnegotiable beliefs, guarding each one vigilantly, making sure they all stay above the water line no matter how hard the struggle—because if what we "know" sinks, faith sinks right down with it.[23]

This same principle holds to science as well, where it is sometimes exhibited as *confirmation bias*, which is the tendency for humans (scientists are humans, too) to try to prove what we already believe to be true. One thing that science has proven about science is that confirmation bias does exist within science.

MATERIALISM AND METAPHYSICS

Another issue in the tension between science and faith is materialism, the belief that only the physical, material world exists. While the word "science" simply means "knowledge" (*Merriam-Webster* uses the example, *"the science of theology"*), that's considered an archaic use by many dictionaries. I think most of us would use the *Oxford English Dictionary*'s definition, *"The intellectual and practical activity encompassing the systematic study of the structure and behaviour of the physical and natural world through observation and experiment.*"

That is, science studies the observable world of matter. Scientists of all kinds, atheist to Christian, would generally agree with this definition. As Jesus said, however, "*God is spirit, and those who worship him must worship in spirit and truth*" (John 4:24). God and his realm are, by definition, outside of the physical, material world. To describe the realm of things outside of the material world, we use words like spiritual, metaphysical, or supernatural. Materialists might prefer the term "imaginary." Science can't study the metaphysical because it's imaginary. Belief through definition.

It is fine to simply say, "I choose to believe that the material world is all that exists." That, in my analysis, is simply a Kierkegaardian leap to faith in that belief, and I have no issue with that logic. We all make leaps to belief based on our assessment of the information we have (and our own confirmation biases). Again, materialists may cringe at this analysis but that's up to them.

A larger problem arises, however, when they make claims about proving that the material world is all that exists. For example, let's take the mythical Bigfoot. Can you prove that a Bigfoot doesn't exist? How do you observe something that you haven't seen? Even if you scour every inch of the forest, all you can claim is that you didn't find him. You can make a reasoned conclusion, but that's all. It is unlikely, but not to the same extent that we know we'll see the Sun again.

Now, let's consider science, which by definition is limited to what we can observe in the material world. You can study the psychological and physical responses to belief, but you can't prove whether the beliefs are true or false. You have no tools to either observe or measure God and no method to arrive at a conclusion about the existence of God. Your options are to:

1. Conclude that God doesn't exist because you don't believe in anything outside of the material world. This, of course, is a circular argument: Essentially, you don't believe in God because you don't believe in God.
2. Conclude that God doesn't exist because science cannot prove that he exists. This is another illogical argument, as we discussed above.
3. Conclude that God does exist because you can't prove he doesn't, which is also illogical.
4. Conclude that the question of God is not something science can address, which is the only reasonable conclusion.

Atheism is not a very certain position. There is no proof that God doesn't exist, except that you haven't experienced him firsthand (that you know of). You can't prove he doesn't exist, because we have no way to prove it—our best methods are limited to the physical world. And philosophy is debatable, but it is a belief system and is valid to the extent that you have enough information to make that leap.

THE BIBLE AS SCIENCE TEXTBOOK

Okay, this heading is a bit deceptive; I don't believe that the Bible was ever designed to teach science, or history, for that matter. This is something we'll get to shortly in more detail, but for now I will just mention my belief that Genesis was not written to provide a scientific, factual account of creation. The Jewish scholars didn't believe that, and neither did the early Christians (notably, Augustine). You can't even reconcile Genesis 1 and 2. Which is factual? They can't both be. But when you look at the point Genesis is making, do they need to be? I believe that we need to stop trying to make the Bible be things it isn't meant to be. It is not a modern text.

The bottom line is, let science be science, and let the Bible be the Bible. If anything, scientific discoveries should promote a greater sense of awe and wonder. As the late astronomer Carl Sagan wrote:

> How is it that hardly any major religion has looked at science and concluded, "This is better than we thought! The Universe is much bigger than our prophets said, grander, more subtle, more elegant?" Instead they say, "No, no, no! My God is a little god, and I want him to stay that way." A religion, old or new, that stressed the magnificence of the Universe as revealed by modern science might be able to draw forth reserves of reverence and awe hardly tapped by the conventional faiths."[24]

Sagan, too, saw the issue of having a god that was too small. Religion has God all boxed in (to a tiny, little box). Creation is in a box, the Bible is in a box, and God is in a box. Science opens the box, but only so far. To experience God, we have to also look beyond science, as I mentioned above. Replacing a small box with a bigger box is not the answer, although admittedly sometimes it's the best we can do. We're human, after all.

A REASONABLE FAITH

It is possible to have reasonable faith without losing any of the mystery of faith. To do so, I believe that we must begin to recognize when our beliefs conflict with what we experience with our five (or more) senses. This is not as easy as it might seem, as I have already discussed. And, it can be a lonely journey, as it is definitely the road less traveled. We can make "faith leaps" based on total insanity, or we can "look before we leap." The thief on the cross had very little information, but it was enough. Saul/Paul needed to be knocked off his horse before he had enough to make the leap. Both were wise leaps. We are all different, in different situations, and we must all decide for ourselves what we need to leap, and when we should do so.

CHAPTER 4

TAKING THE BIBLE OUT OF THE BOX

"So the Bible is the Word of God, right?" you question. "Why can't we just read the Bible and get all we know? Why do we need pastors, preachers, and books like this? Shouldn't things be simple?"

"You're absolutely right," I agree. *"Christianity has become way too complicated, like the rest of life. It seems that it's just something humans do. With a little understanding of why things are the way they are, we can try to unravel the tangled web we've woven and see if we can make things simple again."*

"You promise?" you ask.

"I'll try my best," I cautiously respond.

WHAT IS THE BIBLE?

Trying to logically discuss a topic as large and complex as Christianity, even now that we have laid some groundwork, presents a problem: Where does one begin? We could just start at the beginning. Both the Old Testament in our modern Bibles and the Gospel of John in the New Testament start with the phrase, "In the beginning . . ." But, before we get to those beginnings, we should talk about the source(s) of this information, which is the Bible. Or is it?

Attempting to explain the Bible is in itself a Herculean task, as this collection of books written over a thousand or more years by numerous authors is many things to many people. As Amy-Jill Levine and Douglas Knight write in the introduction to *The Meaning of the Bible*,

> *For some readers, the Bible is inerrant, perfect, and the source of all knowledge. For others, it is a repository of a people's culture or a brilliant collection of stories with varying degrees of historicity. For some, it is the source of hope and inspiration; for others, it is a text of colonialism, conquest, slavery, misogyny, and homophobia.*[25]

From the Holy Word of God to an ancient book of myths and morality tales, there are countless ideas of what the Bible is and even more ideas about what it means. Before we get into that, let us take a look at what the Bible, as a physical object, is. I was taught that the Bible is a collection of 66 separate "books." There are thirty-nine Old Testament books, written before the birth of Jesus, and twenty-seven New Testament books, written after Jesus' death and resurrection. But wait! There's more! (Or sometimes less!)

Not only are there hundreds of different translations, there are different Bibles with different books (some more, some less), organized in different orders, in different languages.[26] The Jews have a Bible, but as Amy-Jill Levine explains, Judaism does not have an "Old Testament."

Instead, it is called the Tanakh, an acronym. The T stands for Torah, a Hebrew term for the first five books of the Bible; N is for Nevi'im, the term for "prophets"; and the K stands for Ketuvim, or "writings" (the remaining books, such as Psalms, Proverbs, Esther, and Job).

In the academy, the common term for this collection is "Hebrew Bible," a descriptive rather than confessional name. It generally designates only the books in the Tanakh . . .[27]

For the Christian, we refer to some of the Jewish writings as the Old Testament, and of course, have added the collection of Apostolic writings as the New Testament. Both the Eastern Orthodox and Roman Catholic Bibles include several books identified as the Apocrypha, written in the time between the Old and New Testament periods and not included in the Tanakh. Also, the modern Christian translations into English include some fragments found in the Dead Sea Scrolls that the Jewish Bibles do not. For these reasons, we must be careful to designate to which documents we are referring. For our purposes, I will continue to use the common Christian terminology and identify the translations I am referencing, but I will use "Tanakh" to refer to the Jewish version of the OT.

Our modern English Bibles have consistent chapter and verse designations, which were not added to the text until roughly the 1600s, and these do not necessarily match those found in the Tanakh. While these numbering systems are helpful, in many cases, they hinder understanding, as they add artificial divisions amid a single thought. Also, the Tanakh only contains twenty-four designated "books," as they do not split

Chronicles, Samuel, or Kings, and they combine Nehemiah and Ezra, as well as combining the minor prophets (so-called as they are quite short) into one book. So, keep in mind that the chapters and verses (or the names and order of the books) are not in themselves "holy" or inspired.

PHILOSOPHICAL VIEWS OF THE BIBLE

Even if you want to, you just can't get away from philosophy. If you do, you will still have a philosophy, you just won't know what it is—it will be whatever was given to you by the authorities in your life. I like to choose my own. In this section, I am talking specifically about the philosophy—the overall set of assumptions that one has—of how to read and interpret the Bible. Is it the dictated Word of God, or was it produced by men, or is it a combination of the two? What was its purpose? Do we read it as a lawbook, a history book, or a book of moral stories? Is it the very thoughts of God, or God's thoughts as interpreted by men? Or men's thoughts projected on God? (Before anyone freaks out, I should point out that anyone with real faith will have no problems asking these questions.)

Traditionally the Bible has been read in different ways for different purposes—it can be read meditatively, allegorically, literally, in a historical context, and so on. The Jewish scholars used these different biblical approaches, as did the early Christian Church, and as many Christians do today. Augustine, for example, wrote two commentaries on Genesis for different purposes, one being allegorical. There are a few models—broad assumptions—that people impose on the Bible that can control how we understand what we read.

These are different than the contexts just mentioned; these models are all boxes that we can put the Bible in that force interpretations in one direction or another. These include a **flat** model, in which every word in the Bible is considered to have equal authority (except for those words we want to ignore), a **progressive revelation model** (where all the words accumulate in a crescendo of consistent truth), and a **Christocentric view** (where Christ is the pinnacle of revelation, and every word must finally submit to him)."[28] I tend to lean toward a Christocentric view, as that seems to be how the New Testament authors treated the Old Testament books.

For years, many post-Enlightenment people have defaulted to reading the Bible from a modernist, "flat" viewpoint, which means to view history as history, references to scientific topics as science, and so on, reading the Bible as if it were a modern text, critiqued by modern standards. The universe was created in six literal days, the Ark is hidden on Mt. Ararat, and so on. (Even still, there are exceptions, such as the Sun circling the Earth.) For many people, the historical context, as well as the historical understanding of the Bible text, are of little interest. Words are words, after all, and facts are facts. Six days are six days. These aspects are all read literally except when allegorical, and the Bible is presumed to be inerrant, or without error in everything it says (again, with a few exceptions).

There is a rather obvious parallel between the conservative evangelical approach to the Bible and the conservative approach to interpreting the Constitution:

> *Originalism requires that a judge ask questions such as "What was the writer's original intent?" and*

"What would reasonable people at that time have understood this text to mean?"... Justice Antonin Scalia defined it this way: "The Constitution that I interpret and apply is not living but dead..."[29]

In Hebrews 4:12 we read, *"For the word of God is living and active, sharper than any two-edged sword..."* (ESV). If the evangelical position is that the Bible is the Word of God, in taking a flat, literal view, they are not treating the Bible as "living and active," but as a dead document. Holy, but dead. This also allows evangelical scholars more power to control the Bible's meaning, which I suspect is precisely the point. As the author of the above quote goes on to say, *"As soon as words of life are treated as fixed and unchanging, doctrine and dogma become substitutes for a faith intended to fruitfully engage with a changing world."*[30]

This strictly modern approach to the Bible seems to make sense to many, as most of us were raised in this strictly modern environment, and often have had no exposure to anything else. I have heard it expressed that if God created the Bible for our benefit, we should be able to read it and get "the plain meaning" without needing to research history or understand the original languages. It is just too much to presume that God would require an ordinary person to study history or the original languages to "be blessed" by the Bible. This view seems to ignore many facts about the Bible and the many known changes in translation down through the years.

Plus, Western modernism is inherently arrogant and supremacist in everything that it touches, presuming itself to be superior to any pre-modern or Eastern understanding. We tend to view everything as if it was written not for first century believers but for us twenty-first century (First World) believers. This results in a very shallow—and often inaccurate—reading, not getting into the various other and often better ways it can be interpreted. Arrogance is not the same as faith, and reading the Bible through a modern lens is in effect keeping the Bible in a box. It's time to let it out and breathe. As Meredith Riedel has said,

> God doesn't just fit within the narrow confines of your denominational origins. And studying history, particularly the history of the church, ought to lead us to greater humility, so that we don't think "my way is the best way, the only way the true way, the only way that's ever been true or has ever been faithful."[31]

The problem we have today is that we are inherently modern—we have no choice, as the entire Western world thinks in modern terms. Due to thinkers like Descartes, in the 1600s the Western world changed. These changes have become "so fundamental to modern consciousness that it is hard not to regard them as part of the natural property of the human mind."[32]

I am myself a modernist to the core. This makes it difficult for me to bridge the chasm between contemporary thinking and that of the Bible, which is certainly not a modern text. When I was quite young, probably still in elementary school, a missionary from Hong Kong came and spoke to our Sunday School class. I can remember being quite offended when she told us that people in Hong Kong can understand the Bible better than we ever will because the Bible was written by Eastern minds. I came to realize that she knew what she was talking about. Western modernist arrogance is a difficult animal to tame.

So what are we to do? First, we must acknowledge our handicap and try to set aside our natural framework to see beyond our default lenses. It is difficult, and sometimes nearly impossible, but with practice it is possible to at least partially overcome the handicap.

THE BIBLE IS NOT A MODERN WORK

Pay attention to this: The Bible is not a modern work and cannot be judged according to modern standards. Let me put it this way: **The Bible is not a modern work and cannot be judged according to modern standards.** It is an ancient book and should be evaluated by ancient standards. That does not mean that you cannot use modern methods to study and analyze the Bible, it just means that you must study it knowing what it is: ancient literature that does not follow modern guidelines. You can use modern methods to study pre-modern writing if you critique the texts by pre-modern standards, appropriate to the genre. That is, poetry is poetry, allegory is allegory, and apocalyptic literature is apocalyptic literature, according to the styles of the time. Furthermore, ancient history is *not* modern history. To the ancients, the meaning of history is more important than the facts of history. Likewise, stories in the Bible do not contain anything related to modern science. So, don't try to make it so.

Most of us understand that when the Bible talks of the sun rising and setting, it is not meant to be a scientific explanation, it is what we call *phenomenology*—describing what we see rather than what is technically happening. Look at the weather app on your phone and it will still tell you when sunset and sunrise are, even knowing these terms are technically incorrect. Are our phones accurate? Yes, when viewed from a proper perspective. That is just the way we talk. It is harder for people to grasp ancient historical standards, which are not as concerned with facts as we claim to be today. I say, "claim to be," because, well, you're likely on social media, so you should understand. We have all been inundated in recent years with "alternative facts" and "alternative to alternative facts," and have figured out that history is often what someone claims it is.

When I was in elementary school, we were taught that Columbus was a great guy, we were kind to the Native Americans, and the Black Wall Street massacre never happened. It wasn't until much later that we learned about the raping and massacring and the Trail of Tears and that "all men are created equal" only referred to Anglo-Saxon males. As someone once said, "History is written by the victors," meaning the ones left standing tell the story from their perspective and who generally paint themselves in the best light. Now, however, the losers can concurrently publish their version of history.

An interesting fact about the Bible is that the above adage is proven wrong: both Testaments were written by a conquered people—by the "losers." This is not a victor's story, it is the writing of the oppressed and exiled that has much in common with slave narratives and spirituals, the more modern Jewish Holocaust narratives, as well as those of refugees around the world. It does not have that much (i.e., anything) in common with white Americanism (although we've historically interpreted it that way).

It seems less than fair to hold biblical stories, many of which were handed down orally before their being written, to a standard of factualness when we can't even expect that of our recent history. We now know

that much of early American history is basically mythology meant to preserve power in the hands of white
landowners.

> *The mythology relies on Americans living passively
> and accepting the stories they are told, the narratives
> that place the Founding Fathers and figures like
> Abraham Lincoln as secular saints, and that portray
> our abuses and crimes as well-meaning attempts
> to make the world safe for democracy and freedom.
> These are fairy tales. Intentionally simplified stories
> that allow Americans to continue playing a role in
> exploiting people here and abroad for their own
> comfort and profit.*[33]

It is especially ironic when we, as modern historians, claim to value facts and evidence in contrast to the
ancient historians, for whom the meaning of the story
outweighed the facts. This is important—the specific
facts of a story were not important. Which mountain?
Which sea? Which king? In what order? All these questions were not necessarily the questions that ancient
writers were interested in answering. Rather, they were
more concerned with questions like: Who is God? Who
are we? What is our place in the world? How should we
live? There's some indication that they may have even
retold existing and well-known stories to make a new
point. Being "inspired" does not necessarily mean that
a text stands up to modern expectations. Neither did a
"literal" telling of a story mean literal in the sense that
we use. As much as we'd like the Bible to be a modern
book, it simply won't adapt to our way of thinking. David Lambert had this to say on a recent *The Bible For
Normal People* podcast:

I think the direction to go in is the direction that certain parts of the field of biblical studies have gone in. Which is simply to say—if we want to look at the Bible, let's look at it through the ages. Let's not pretend that we're the only ones, let's not coronate ourselves, you know, as who decides what this means. And instead, let's look at the totality of how this text has been read in different communities. And when you do that, and when you experience the differences, you realize not just how this is a matter of different individuals having different ideas, but how this text is taken to be something fundamentally different in different places at different times. And at the same time, you start to learn the history of how it came to be viewed in the way in which you today view it. And what I always tell my students is, the way they grew up reading the Bible is a legitimate part of its history. It's part of what the Bible came to be in certain places at certain times. And they should understand that, but they should also be able to enter into a dialogue with what the Bible's been in other places and other times, that might differ from their own perspective.[34]

The Bible is not a modern book, and we need to know how it has been understood over time. As we continue to explore and uncover new facts, we see that some stories don't seem to match up with what we know of history from other sources, but others do. While much of the early biblical history (the Torah or Pentateuch) may be largely mythic (favoring meanings over facts), it is my understanding that the histories recorded after the Davidic Kingdom was in place have proven to be quite accurate and matches other records and archeological finds, although the "spin" is likely to be favorable towards the Jewish nation. It should be noted, though, that it is also often quite—and some-times brutally—honest about their failings.

MYTHICIZED HISTORY

Bible professor and author Peter Enns, in a short video called *A Technical Term that Will Change Your Life Forever*, explains a bit about "mythicized history," which is where stories that have a historical core are *"overlaid with mythical tones and mythical categories, which is how ancient peoples told their stories of great significance."*[35] Again, the story and moral of the story were more important than the underlying facts (which likely would have been forgotten or misremembered). That is not to say that these stories didn't happen, necessarily, but that they were embellished to make a point. This was not only typical, I suspect that this was also expected.

The Flood/Noah's Ark story is a great example, especially as it seems to be a universally held story. That is, other cultures also have a flood story—the most well-known is the epic tale of Gilgamesh, which existed in written form pre-dating the written Old Testament. The Epic of Gilgamesh was likely influenced by an even earlier Mesopotamian story, the Epic of Atrahasis. All these tales are likely based on a true event, as there is geological evidence of a major flood in that area (which would have represented the whole world to them, taking place likely between 3,000 and 4,000 BCE. It is expected that a shared historical event would show up in the myths of various cultures. While these stories have several common elements, Enns writes,

> . . . the Israelite version is aimed at saying something distinct about its beliefs, not simply relaying some meteorological information.[36]

He continues,

> Like the story of creation, Israel's flood story is a theological expression of self-definition. Like all of the other Mesopotamian versions, it answers the question, "Why did this massive flood occur?" But the answer it gives is different because it presumes a different idea of who God is as creator.[37]

In other words, the Israelite author(s) of Genesis may have retold this bit of common mythicized history but distinguished between the flawed Mesopotamian gods and the one true God of Israel. A constant theme throughout these retellings is the faithfulness of the God of Israel, who has chosen them and who is faithful to save them from the wickedness around them. This point is more important than the fine details that we might record today (and lose the meaning in the process). Using stories to preserve meaning seems more inspiring to me, rather than merely documenting on which mountain the ark was parked.

There are plenty of people who will hold to the literal forty days and forty nights details, as well as the precise measurements of the Ark, etc. That's fine. However, I don't believe that those precise details must be 100 percent accurate for the essence of the story to be true. The size of the ark changes nothing, in my mind. I will likely never refer to any number of cubits for any purpose, nor will I ever teach about which day the first dove was sent out. This may have relevance to someone, but I haven't found any yet.

In this way, we can see as the Old Testament progresses how the Israelites' view of their God developed as they reinterpreted the facts and narratives in the context of their current circumstances. The theme that starts with Noah is that of being chosen specifically by God, and that "chosen-ness" extends to Noah's family. God chose a group of people, as he did later with Abraham and his descendants, Moses and the Israelites, Judah, and into the New Testament. God has a people chosen for a particular purpose, not always a preferred role. As Tevye says in *The Fiddler and the Roof*, "*I know, I know. We are Your chosen people. But, once in a while, can't You choose someone else?*"

A turning point in Old Testament history was the Babylonian exile, which had a major impact on Israel's view of God and of their place in history, which is evidenced in the OT histories. This and other moments of national crisis explain numerous things, such as why later Old Testament books disagree with earlier books, both in stating the Law of Moses, and in telling the same history. New versions update, or perhaps correct, the old and history from the Northern kingdoms disagrees in perspective from the South, written later.[38]

But then, you ask, how can it all be **inspired** and **inerrant**? Hold that question.

CHRISTIANS AND THE BIBLE

For most of Western Christianity, everything comes back to the Bible. It is the source of all authoritative information about God, life, the universe, and everything. A "good" Christian will likely respond to any issue with, "The Bible says . . ." and then lay out a verse or three from whatever translation they like the best.

Most conservative evangelicals will hold that the Bible is both inspired (God-breathed) and inerrant (without error), although these terms, too, mean different things to different people. Even the most liberal Christians, who may doubt the veracity of some things, hold the teachings of the Bible in high regard.

While most Christians believe and respect the Bible, I expect that many have no real concept of how the Bible originated, they just take it on faith that the Bible we have is the Bible God meant for us to have, regardless of seemingly contradictory passages and differences in translations. I would tend to agree that the Bible we have is the one God wanted us to have. However, I believe that *the Bible we have is not necessarily the one that many Christians think God wanted us to have* or the Bible they imagine that we have. Again, the Bible is *not* a modern book, it is, and always will be, an ancient book, written by or through ancient people who had ancient worldviews and understandings.

In my reading, I came across a letter that C. S. Lewis wrote in response to someone who asked if the Bible was infallible. Lewis responds,

> *It is Christ Himself, not the Bible, who is the true word of God. The Bible, read in the right spirit and with the guidance of good teachers will bring us to Him. When it becomes really necessary (i.e. for our spiritual life, not for controversy or curiosity) to know whether a particular passage is rightly translated or is Myth (but of course Myth specially chosen by God from among countless Myths to carry a spiritual truth) or history, we shall no doubt be guided to the right answer. But we must not use the Bible (our fathers too often did) as a sort of Encyclopedia out of*

which texts (isolated from their context and not read without attention to the whole nature & purport of the books in which they occur) can be taken for use as weapons.

It has been my experience in several decades of church life, that many Christians don't worry about the odd little quirks of the Bible, nor do they understand that the New Testament as we know it wasn't assembled as such for the first three centuries (although copies of the books were handed around from church to church). As various people have pointed out over the years, the earliest martyrs had no New Testament; they simply had "the gospel," or what is referred to as the "Rule of Faith," a simple belief statement. In 1 Thessalonians 2:13, Paul writes, "*you received the word of God that you heard from us,*" clearly referring to oral teaching.

"Bible study" was a luxury that very few had, and detailed knowledge of any of the NT books was probably quite rare. If most early Christians had tried to explain theology in detail, they likely would have been heretics. Obviously, that's okay. The only time the nuances of theology become important is when we start asking questions and trying to figure things out further, which is also a good thing although there is always a risk of "over-defining" God (putting God in a new box) or of putting God in the wrong box completely. That is precisely what the early Church did—trying to walk that fine line—as we can see from the writings of the Church Fathers. As the Bible became bound in book form and reprinted, thanks to the invention of the printing press, it eventually took on an almost magical status and became "the Word of God," rather than that phrase referring to either Jesus or the gospel message. We'll come back to this.

I was still quite young when I learned that there was historical evidence for the Bible; I had thought that it told stories that were so old (like the stories that began, *"Once upon a time . . ."*) that it was simply accepted for what it said. Finding out that it was set in "real" history kind of took away some of its mystique. However, it also made the Bible more real, clearly distinct from the "Once upon a time" tales. This was a good thing, but that was the start of my deeper thinking about things, trying to put things in order. I was perhaps a little obsessive in that way, always needing to organize colors in rainbow order, and so on. And yes, I organized my M&Ms by color as well. Thus began my lifetime of asking questions and trying to make sense of Christianity.

OLD TESTAMENT ORIGINS

I believe it is generally accepted that the oldest books of the Bible are the first five—Genesis, Exodus, Leviticus, Numbers, and Deuteronomy—known as the Books of Moses, the *Pentateuch*, or the *Torah*. The title "Books of Moses" is somewhat telling, as tradition holds that Moses himself authored these five books. Many sources today will state unequivocally that Moses was the author, although this claim is not made in the books themselves and is questionable for several good reasons. Richard Friedman, a scholar of both the Bible and Hebrew, writes:

> But the tradition that one person, Moses, alone wrote these books presented problems. People observed contradictions in the text. It would report events in

a particular order, and later it would say that those same events happened in a different order. It would say that there were two of something, and elsewhere it would say that there were fourteen of that same thing. It would say that the Moabites did something, and later it would say that it was the Midianites who did it. It would describe Moses as going to a Tabernacle in a chapter before Moses builds the Tabernacle.[39]

Friedman also points out something that I had noticed myself some time ago. One of the books, Deuteronomy, records Moses' death (Deuteronomy 34:5), which Moses likely did not write himself. As well, Genesis 36 references kings who were not yet living at the time of Moses. You could, I suppose, theorize that God revealed the future to Moses, but there doesn't appear to be any basis for that. So, why invent traditions that we do not need?

ABOUT COMMON SENSE AND THE BIBLE

It is common in evaluating theories of negligence to use the "reasonably prudent person" standard, the standard by which a reasonably prudent person would act or think. (I mentioned earlier that I was an insurance claims examiner for many years, which fits with my tendency of trying to make sense of things that do not seem to line up.) Remember, employing this standard essentially entails a "common sense" approach to determine how a person with average intellectual abilities and information would act. It is my opinion that if someone with no prior knowledge of the authorship issue of the Pentateuch read these five books, they would assume that someone other than Moses was the author. There is some value in tradition that dates back over 2,000 years, but when the books do not claim authorship, and include things that Moses could not have written, I am satisfied at least considering that they were authored by some unknown person at a later date. Here are three specific excerpts from Deuteronomy that would indicate that at least these verses were written long after Moses:

> Then Moses, the servant of the LORD, died there in the land of Moab, at the LORD's command. He buried him in a valley in the land of Moab, opposite Beth-peor, but no one knows his burial place to this day. (Deuteronomy 34:5,6)

> Never since has there arisen a prophet in Israel like Moses, whom the LORD knew face to face. (Deuteronomy 34:10)

> ... He brought you out of Egypt with his own presence, by his great power, driving out before you, nations greater and mightier than yourselves, to bring you in, giving you their land for a possession, as it is still today. (Deuteronomy 4:37b-38)

As Pete Enns explains, for these verses to make sense, some considerable time must have passed, after the Canaanites had been driven out, likely after 1000 BCE.[40] This seems to be the simplest and most common-sense understanding of these verses.

I think of the original Bible manuscripts akin to the collection of notepads and slips of paper on my desk. Even though I sit behind two keyboards and multiple computer screens, I still take notes from meetings on legal pads, smaller notepads, and the backs of envelopes.

Imagine someone a thousand years from now trying to recreate what I wrote. Most of the time I can't even remember what I meant. There is no punctuation, words are misspelled or abbreviated, and important points are rephrased to make sense to me at the time. This is essentially what biblical translators had to work with.

The various fragments that became Genesis, for example, may have been bundled together for centuries before they were organized into the book we know as Genesis, which is perhaps why Chapter 1 differs from Chapter 2, etc. As new "scraps" are found, like the Dead Sea Scrolls, they are compared with existing manuscripts to see what the differences are, and how they help clarify the meanings. Some manuscripts and fragments may have been copies of earlier texts and pieced together with newer writings to make a more cohesive narrative. This, by the way, is the same way all ancient texts are reconstructed and translated.

The old view that the Torah, or the "Books of Moses," was all written by or at the direction of Moses is no longer the reigning view of scholars. In the 1900s the documentary hypothesis model was developed, in which it is thought that these five books were compiled from four specific sources, known as J, E, P, and D, each with their unique characteristics such as vocabulary, style, and theological perspective. J, for example, calls God Yahweh (Jehovah), E refers to God as Elohim, P stands for what is called Priestly material, and D refers to the primary author of Deuteronomy.[41] Considering that these four presumed documents can be logically reconstructed gives weight to this theory.

Some of you might be wondering, "What difference does it make who wrote them?" In my opinion, very little. Using real people as pseudonyms was not an uncommon practice, and it was not considered un-ethical. If the stories were inspired, the human hand doesn't matter, correct? Doubting the authorship of these first five books of the Bible does not question anything in the Bible; rather, it just questions some traditional thinking, which is often the problem of trying to make sense of Christianity. Again, not be-lieving Moses to have authored these five books is not the same as not believing the veracity of what the books say. And the acceptance of all these writings by the Jewish people indicates that they represent the collective wisdom of Israel regardless of authorship.

BACK TO SQUARE ONE

If you have never sat down and read the first two chap-ters of Genesis in one sitting, I suggest you do that now (although you likely won't, as I likely wouldn't if I were reading this as I am simply too lazy and arrogant to follow directions). Most of us are at least familiar with the six days of the creation narrative. However, know-ing what you do about what makes day "day" and night "night," does this make any sense? Seriously—I am not trying to be facetious. The Sun is not even created until day four, when three days and nights have already come and gone. The fact is that the order of creation does not follow any reasonable pattern to be completely factual.

Now, let's turn to Genesis 2:4, which starts a com-pletely different creation narrative. Here, Adam is created *before* any vegetation. Then, God creates the other animals and has Adam name them. What should we make of this situation? If the Bible is supposed to be without error, which version is correct?

I think we can suggest a couple of different possibilities. First, and I think likely, these are two different retellings of the creation narrative from different authors—i.e., different fragments, which were both included in a compendium that became Genesis. Second, these different versions likely had different purposes. The obvious point of Chapter 1 is that God created everything, and he pronounced it "good." The second chapter deals with man's place in the world and sets the stage for the serpent fiasco.

As I've said, many people have suggested that these early books were compilations of writings from different sources which were valued because they provide a broader view of Israel's history. There was no such thing as books as we know them today; there were likely numerous scrolls and pieces of parchment (and a stone tablet or two) that were collected as a sort of scrapbook. Friedman thinks that this may explain the numerous duplications (with sometimes conflicting information) found in the Old Testament:

Even in translation it is easy to observe that biblical stories often appear with variations of detail in two different places in the Bible. There are two different stories of the creation of the world. There are two stories of the covenant between God and the patriarch Abraham, two stories of the naming of Abraham's son Isaac, two stories of Abraham's claiming to a foreign king that his wife Sarah is his sister, two stories of Isaac's son Jacob making a journey to Mesopotamia, two stories of a revelation to Jacob at Beth-El, two stories of God's changing Jacob's name to Israel, two stories of Moses' getting water from a rock at a place called Meribah, and more.[42]

ORIGIN STORIES

Whether the Bible began with Moses or was compiled sometime later, we can be sure that the earliest stories were passed down orally, because that is the way things were done. Until modern times, oral tradition was considered just as authoritative as the written word. Oral tradition belonged to the people, not just to one person, so it was the entire community passing down these stories from generation to generation, using a sort of collective fact checker. Again, these were inspired but were still ancient stories.

We also know that God's people—like the Bible—did not originate in a vacuum. When God started over with Noah, God picked Noah out of the existing culture, such as it was. Likewise, when it came time to start creating his chosen people, he did not find someone who worshipped God the way the Israelites did later, but he picked someone who lived in a polytheistic culture and moved him to a new place where a new relationship could begin. Between Noah and Abram (who later became Abraham) a lot of water had gone under the bridge and belief in many gods was the norm for that area as other historical documents have shown.

Abram, the Bible tells us, came from Ur of the Chaldees. This is likely true, as Ur had begun at least by 4000 BCE, and by Abram's day (second century BCE) was perhaps the largest city around. However, the Chaldeans did not conquer the city until a few hundred years after Abram, which is another clue as to when things were written down. At the time the story was written, people likely would recognize the location as being Chaldean (like today, we might say Abraham was born in Iraq). It was, at the time of Abram, a Babylonian city. God picks

Abram and leads him on a journey away from his family (he took his wife and Lot with him), eventually winding up in Canaan which God reveals will be his descendants' land. You can likely find maps of Abram's journeys in some Bible maps, or multiple places online.

The point is, a significant time passed between Noah and Abram, and we know little of what happened during that period, except that the people of the area believed in many gods. Again, numerous writings from that period of Babylonian history tell us what their religious life was like in that area.

It is easy, reading through Genesis from our modern point of view, or even from the point of view of the later Jewish people, to assume that Abram grew up with knowledge of God (as opposed to the Babylonian collection of gods). However, we do not know that and don't know who Abram thought the god who spoke to him was, other than what God revealed to him along the way. And throughout the Old Testament we see indications that until late in the game, the Jewish people believed that there were other gods, even though they only worshipped YHWH.

This is how Abram was raised, and we can only assume that Abram and his family also believed in many gods, even after he was contacted by *the* God. I think a lot of us just assume that God always had a faithful remnant of true believers (I know I did), but that does not appear to be the case. There may have been a small group who continued to follow the God of Noah, but there is no indication that any sort of religious group existed until God chose Abraham. The only lead-in to the calling of Abram in the Bible is a very brief family history at the end of Genesis 11, which tells us they had moved as a family to Canaan. Chapter 12 starts with the call, seemingly out of the blue:

> Now the LORD said to Abram, "Go from your country and your kindred and your father's house to the land that I will show you. I will make of you a great nation, and I will bless you and make your name great, so that you will be a blessing. I will bless those who bless you, and the one who curses you I will curse, and in you all the families of the earth shall be blessed." (Genesis 12:1-3)

There is no introduction—as we see later with, *"I am the God of Adam or Noah"*—it is simply, *"Go."* What we see in the story of Abraham is how this Babylonian (likely) polytheist grows in the knowledge of the God of Israel.

The story I find most intriguing is the offering of Isaac, found in Genesis 22.

> After these things God tested Abraham. He said to him, "Abraham!" And he said, "Here I am." He said, "Take your son, your only son Isaac, whom you love, and go to the land of Moriah and offer him there as a burnt offering on one of the mountains that I shall show you." So Abraham rose early in the morning, saddled his donkey, and took two of his young men with him and his son Isaac; he cut the wood for the burnt offering and set out and went to the place in the distance that God had shown him. (Genesis 22:1-3)

Most of us know the story: Abraham is obedient and puts Isaac on the altar, but before Abraham can kill him, God provides a lamb to sacrifice instead. This story is taught with all kinds of super-spiritual meanings, and about how it is a foreshadowing of Jesus' sacrifice. That is all well and good, but it is still a horrific story. How could Abraham think that God would actually require him to sacrifice the child he promised Abraham, who was to be the source of Abraham's descendants? In fact, how could Abraham believe that God would require him to kill his son?

Just a few chapters earlier, God alerts Abraham that he plans to destroy Sodom and Gomorrah because they are wicked beyond saving, and Abraham starts negotiating with God to save them (Genesis 19). But here, with his son's life on the line, Abraham seemingly makes no effort to save Isaac. What's up with this? As a parent, I have big issues with this story. Over the years, I have come up with a couple of thoughts that help explain what is going on. (As always, they could be wrong.)

First, in keeping with the current thoughts about Abraham's background of polytheism, it is probably not out of the question that the "other gods" would require human sacrifices from time to time. Perhaps it was generally accepted that this is the way things go. Abraham has already seen God wipe out two large cities, so Abraham knows he means business. Second, perhaps Abraham misunderstands, and God watches to see what Abraham does.

Regardless of whether either of these thoughts are on the mark, I think these two stories were told in the way they were to make very different points. Remember, the concept of historical "fact" did not exist at that time, but historical "truth" did. Genesis 19 tells a different kind of story than Genesis 22. Perhaps Abraham did throw a major fit over the Isaac thing, but that detail does not help the story so that part was dropped along the way. We all leave out details that we do not think are important, or that do not contribute to the point we are making. I don't believe that the Bible was written just to record history, but to inform the current readership of important ideas about who God is and about who they (Israel) are. And sometimes, I believe that the authors reveal that they still did not understand God, either.

The point is, we need to look at what the stories are actually telling us. As James McGrath writes, *"At some point it is appropriate to stop trying to force the Bible to tell the story we think it should and instead listen to the story it actually tells."*[43]

BIBLICAL ARCHEOLOGY

How does one (or any number of people) go about dating the various books of the Old Testament? This is another of those fascinating subjects that I could lose myself in, had I enough time. Unlike most books published in the last few hundred years, there are no copyright dates, publication dates, or any other dates in the writings themselves that tell us specifically when a book (or portion of a book) was first written. At best, we have tidbits like Isaiah 6:1, *"In the year that King Uzziah died . . ."* Estimates are that King Uzziah lived and died in the 700s BCE, which happens to coincide with evidence of a major earthquake that is mentioned during his reign.

As we discover more documents like the Dead Sea Scrolls and other artifacts, including those from other neighboring cultures, experts can narrow down some dates about when things happened, if not when the books were written, which may have been significantly later.

But other clues help in dating the documents, especially the languages themselves. As with English, the biblical languages evolved. For example, if you are reading a story that makes regular use of phrases like "groovy" and "far out," you can place the origin as the late '60s or '70s. Terms like "social media" and "Google" definitely put you in a contemporary period. Now, go back and try to read the original version of *Beowulf*. Or *The Canterbury Tales*. Or, jump ahead and read Shakespeare. Shakespeare, by the way, is considered to be at the beginning of the modern English period. Even modern English has changed significantly. What about the *King James Bible* as compared to the *New International Version*? By keeping track of the evolution of the English language, you can become more competent at placing various writing in the proper period.

The same is true for the Old Testament languages, Hebrew and Aramaic. The earliest documents were written in Hebrew. Once in Babylonian captivity, the Jews over time adopted Aramaic, which was the language Jesus would have spoken. These were not static languages, either. And there are stylistic differences between authors. When you're reading along and all of a sudden, different words are being used—as one author refers to bubbly drinks as "soda" and all of a sudden, it's being referred to as "pop" or "Coke"—it's a clue that some editing was done, somewhere, including potential "mash-ups" of different documents as it made sense to do so.

Likewise, if you're reading a book and come across the word "colour," you can assume the writer was British, or perhaps from a former British colony. And if the author refers to a "walkabout," you can further suspect that they are Australian. Then, if you find a section written in French, you have a new mystery—obviously, we now have a second source from a different region, and perhaps even a different time.

This is the work of those creating a new Bible translation. Suppose you have 200 different scraps of the same verse with some copies using a word like "mountain," but other scraps using a word like "hill." Still others say "mound." Similar, but with some different connotations. Which word do you use? These are choices that have been made over and over throughout the years.

These changes are not apparent in our translated versions, or even in the Greek Septuagint, which was likely the Bible used by the Jews in the first century. In a sense, the translations "laundered" the original languages. For example, if Stephen King were to write a modern English version of *Sir Gawain and the Green Knight*, it would probably sound a lot like Stephen King. This is why discoveries like the Dead Sea Scrolls or other fragments are so important; by identifying the earliest copies of various writings, we can better identify and date the OT documents, as well as see how various edits were done along the way to clarify or emphasize points, or to correct outdated viewpoints.

I was taught years ago that the scribes whose job it was to make copies of the OT writings were so careful not to change God's words that they would even replicate spelling errors. This may have been the case on occasion, but the review of thousands of remnants of OT writings shows that this was not always the case. Sometimes there were significant changes in the texts to keep up with contemporary viewpoints.[44] Political correctness is by no means a new phenomenon.

Then, when the Hebrew and Aramaic texts were translated into Greek beginning a couple of centuries before Christ, there were a lot of interpretive decisions made. If you've ever compared New Testament quotes from the Old Testament, you might have noticed that sometimes they are not the same at all. But perhaps they were in the version they were reading—or perhaps the exact wording wasn't all that important to them.

Another issue that we need to deal with in the evolution of the Old Testament is that in the original languages, there was not only no punctuation, but there were no vowels. Seriously. The original manuscripts were long lists of consonants without spaces, forcing the reader to make a lot of decisions about where to split words and what vowels to insert. So, was it the Red Sea, or the Reed Sea? (Obviously, I'm using an English example to make a point.) The words "Jehovah" and "Yahweh" are two different guesses at pronouncing the four letters used in the Hebrew: YHWH. Which is right?

All these things come into play when trying to draw the most relevant meaning out of the Bible. Or you could just decide that the King James Bible was inspired and stop thinking about it, as some still do. Which is a great segue to the next section.

INSPIRATION, AUTHORITY, AND INERRANCY

I have an immense respect for the Bible, and I always have. I have never been able (even though I've been tempted) to take verses out of their obvious context or "bend" them to fit whatever point I would like to make, although such teaching is all too commonplace. Preachers whose strengths are topical sermon series often cherry-pick verses to fit their message, and some whose style is more expository often go off on tangents verse-by-verse that lose the context altogether. I can't count how many offensive sermons I've heard as the Bible is made to say things that were not intended, or even contrary to the intended point of the passage. McGrath writes, *"It is possible to honor the Bible with one's words, praising it and emphasizing its authority, while insulting and mistreating it by how one interprets it."*[45] On the other hand, I have had pastors who have been careful to teach verses in context and with respect, which is quite refreshing.

It is one thing to use a biblical story as a parallel to a point we're making; we do that often with historical stories. Sometimes just mentioning a name or place will recall entire stories that serve as a pattern or type that helps explain a current situation. This practice was common among the Jewish writers, and there are examples in the New Testament. However, it's another thing to twist words and take things out of context to make points that are actually contrary to Scripture. Being "biblical" does not necessarily mean "right."

In my readings and listenings over the past few years, which have included a few Jewish scholars, I have learned that there is a long Jewish history of reading entirely new meanings into the Scriptures to fit current situations or to make points that are completely foreign to the original passages, a method known as *midrash*. Several such examples can be found in Paul's writings, as well as in the teachings of Jesus. These are not cases of misinterpreting the Bible, but rather using biblical stories and passages as analogies to make various points, reading certain passages prophetically (applying them to current situations), or even reinterpreting the meanings of passages.

To modern eyes this may seem "liberal" or "progressive", but it is only recognizing how Scripture has been read and understood down through history, including by Jesus and the New Testament authors. It seems that a lot of what modern evangelicals view as new is rediscovering what the modernists have chosen to forget or ignore from the past.

Before we get into a few examples, I wanted to take a bit of time to discuss the common words that people throw around when talking about the Bible.

FIRST KEYWORD: INSPIRATION

> *All scripture is inspired by God and is useful for teaching, for reproof, for correction, and for training in righteousness, so that the person of God may be proficient, equipped for every good work. (2 Timothy 3:16, 17)*

Most of us have heard this verse countless times; it is the primo biblical affirmation about itself. Or is it? I think I have pondered this verse as much as any in the Bible because it raises so many questions. I almost hesitate to say this as it will be so easy to take out of context, but I don't think this verse is nearly as important or meaningful as many seem to think. Here are two basic questions that come to mind:

1. *What does "inspired" mean?*
2. *What is Paul referring to when he says "Scripture?"*

"Inspired" is more literally interpreted as "God-breathed." So, what does that mean? Or better, what does that imply? Theories range from the Bible as being sort of "spirit writing" where God takes over the person and bypasses the person's mind and hand to being a quiet nudge to write what was on their heart. It could be a mix of both and everything in between. Phillip Cary has opined that the more a person becomes like Christ, the more their thoughts and words are those of Christ. I think this is a valid theory and could fit the bill for being "inspired."[46]

There are enough personality differences in the Bible to say that not everything was dictated word-for-word, not to mention the factual disagreements found in both the Old and New Testaments. The dictation theory makes it harder to account for the internal discrepancies. It seems to me that to insist on having been dictated word for word by God forces you to adopt a very dishonest way of reading the Bible (as many Christians do). As Pete Enns has explained, he believes that God lets his people tell their stories in their own way.[47] Since God has given us free will and power in the world, this seems to be a fair assessment.

Does this mean that the Bible is not "God-breathed?" I don't believe so. Suppose God lays it on David's heart to write a Psalm about his situation. Or Paul is suddenly "inspired" to lambast the Galatians. If God knows what is on David's or Paul's heart (or David's heart reflects that of God), doesn't that make perfect sense? It was, after all, the people of God who collectively chose what was inspired and what was not. I can imagine the Church looking at the Gospel of Thomas and going, "No, I don't think so." Which is, of course, what happened. In my opinion, down through the ages God has trusted his people way more than I would have. Seriously, just think about it: God gave humans the power to create life. And not just any life, but *created-in-God's-image-with-eternal-souls* life. And he lets seriously unprepared humans raise and train these lives. So, do you think that God might just trust humans to write inspired letters, poetry, and history? We must stop using our human limitations and tendencies to decide what God will or won't do, and instead start looking at what God has already done.

The Orthodox Church, which again is the only church that can trace its roots and teaching directly to the first Century, believes that "the entire Bible is inspired by God," which means that it "contains no formal errors or inner contradictions **concerning the relationship between God and the world**" (emphasis mine),[48] which provides a good distinction lacking from evangelical thinking, which we'll address more below.

So, yes, I believe that the Bible is indeed "God-breathed." I do not believe it was dictated word for word. Even if the original text was dictated word for word, as we don't have those copies and the variations we do have show that God wasn't as concerned with making sure the copies were all identical.

And now, we come to the second question: What does Paul mean when he says "Scriptures?" The Greek word there is *graphe*, which means "writing." All writing? So, let's look at the prior verse, where he talks about Timothy's devotion to the "sacred writings." So, that clarifies it a bit. But is Paul referring to his own letters and those written after he wrote to Timothy? Even Revelation? The stock evangelical answer is, of course, "yes," as they're all contained in the same black leather-covered book. McGrath points out, "It should go without saying that a verse in the Bible cannot be used to prove the status of the entire Bible as God-breathed, inspired, authoritative, inerrant, or anything else."[49]

However, I really do not argue with saying that the whole Bible is inspired, keeping in mind that some of the books have continuously been questioned down through the years, such as Revelation and Hebrews. And of course, the authorship of some of the New Testament books has been questioned for various reasons. Bottom line, I am fine with calling our Bible "inspired."

But when we try to narrow down what Jewish Scriptures Paul was referring to, we have other questions, as they were not yet formed into any sort of Canon.

> To speak of the Tanakh in the time of Jesus would be anachronistic—there was no agreed-upon, three-part Bible to which all Jews then subscribed. Beyond the Torah or Pentateuch, the first five books in all traditions, the order and selection of the books that communities held sacred differed; nor was the text of the various books yet uniform.[50]

At the time of Jesus, there were the original Hebrew and Aramaic scriptures and the Greek Septuagint, which changed several things from the original languages. Isaiah 7:14 in Hebrew, for example, refers to a young woman (not necessarily a virgin) who may be, or may soon be, pregnant, whereas the Septuagint calls her "a virgin who is also pregnant," a clear change in meaning.[51] Many Christians have chosen to accept the Septuagint as inspired even though the translation changes the meanings of some texts from the original. Some consider only the original writings to be inspired, even though we may not even possess copies of the original writings (which I've always thought was a great little loophole).

So, it could be that Paul was referring to literally "all" of the Jewish writings, whether or not they eventually were included in the Tanakh. He could also have included various scholars' notes on the Oral Torah, a tradition that was at the time forbidden to be written down, aside from these notes. It eventually was written down in the second century as the *Mishnah*. (I should mention that I try to find Jewish sources for this information. There is an abundance of Christian sources that love to opine on all things Jewish, but to be honest, I don't trust them. I've found that many if not most Christian theologians don't understand Judaism, although they are arrogant enough to presume to understand Judaism. Thank God for Jewish scholars. If you want to know what the Jewish community thought—or thinks—about a subject, look to them.)

Where the modernist, evangelical approach to biblical scholarship is to use the Bible to create modernist "boxes," the original Jewish approach to scripture is to take it out of the box, discuss it, *argue* about it, and see what kinds of meanings could be drawn from it. Paul was certainly creative in how he used the Jewish Scriptures, which you might have noticed.

SECOND KEYWORD: INERRANCY

Inerrancy is the belief that the Bible contains zero errors. This is not a historical belief—if it had been, later writers and translators wouldn't have made editorial changes, and, for example, John wouldn't disagree with the other Gospel authors about the timeline of the crucifixion. When there are discrepancies, logic tells us everything can't be inerrant. Logic, of course, is how the doctrine of inerrancy came about. If the Bible is the actual word of God, and God doesn't lie, then everything in the Bible must be true.

In 1987, a group of about 200 evangelical Bible scholars developed a statement on biblical inerrancy[52] that went far beyond Paul's declaration about inspiration. As far as I can see, it provided a bright line that distinguished who is, and who is not, a real evangelical (read "Christian"). Whatever. They essentially took the Bible and forced it into a new box labeled "Evangelical," which was a lot smaller than it should have been, so the Bible has been stifled by these new rules. Having never considered myself an evangelical, their little rules have no impact on me, other than to clarify what people mean when they insist on inerrancy. (However, there are other definitions of "inerrancy," as we shall see.)

This document, the Chicago Statement on Biblical Inerrancy, begins with a preface and five main points followed by nineteen articles of affirmation and denial and an exposition. The evangelical Bible box is very well-defined. The opening five points are:

A SHORT STATEMENT

1. God, who is Himself Truth and speaks truth only, has inspired Holy Scripture in order thereby to reveal Himself to lost mankind through Jesus Christ as Creator and Lord, Redeemer and Judge. Holy Scripture is God's witness to Himself.

2. Holy Scripture, being God's own Word, written by men prepared and superintended by His Spirit, is of infallible divine authority in all matters upon which it touches: it is to be believed, as God's instruction, in all that it affirms, obeyed, as God's command, in all that it requires; embraced, as God's pledge, in all that it promises.

3. The Holy Spirit, Scripture's divine Author, both authenticates it to us by His inward witness and opens our minds to understand its meaning.

4. Being wholly and verbally God-given, Scripture is without error or fault in all its teaching, no less in what it states about God's acts in creation, about the events of world history, and about its own literary origins under God, than in its witness to God's saving grace in individual lives.

5. The authority of Scripture is inescapably impaired if this total divine inerrancy is in any way limited or disregarded or made relative to a view of truth contrary to the Bible's own; and such lapses bring serious loss to both the individual and the Church.

For those who accept this position, it creates a new "house of cards" belief, requiring an absolute belief that every little thing in the Bible is accurate. If one little thing is wrong, it casts doubt on the whole Bible and everything comes crashing down. Belief in Jesus becomes dependent on belief in the scientific accuracy of the Bible. For example, in the 2014 HBO documentary *Questioning Darwin*, Pastor Peter LaRuffa states, "*If, somewhere within the Bible, I were to find a passage that said 2+2=5, I would believe it, accept it as true, and then do my best to work it out and understand it.*"[53]

Bible professor Dr. James F. McGrath had this to say in response:

When pastor Peter LaRuffa recently said that he would believe the Bible even if it said 2+2=5, he probably thought he was standing up for biblical inerrancy. In fact, he was undermining it, showing it to be meaningless . . . What pastor LaRuffa was actually saying is that he would prefer to believe nonsense that he does not understand rather than allow evidence to show his doctrine of biblical inerrancy to be false.[54]

Dr. McGrath then essentially echoes Augustine when he goes on to say,

No Christian should think that this horrific way of thinking about the Bible, math, science, history, and rationality is anything but a disgrace, one that brings shame on Christianity by being associated with it.

To me, this is a modernist error of categories. There shouldn't even be a discussion about whether the Bible is inerrant or errant because that distinction is a modern category that doesn't even apply to ancient literature like the Bible. Inerrancy implies that certain standards must be adhered to when these standards never existed when the Bible was written. Trying to claim that God inspired an inerrant book specifically to satisfy modern readers is a bit too arrogant, even for modernists. Modern inerrancy is simply the wrong category/box to try to fit the Bible into because it has no respect for the authors or the general worldviews of the time in which the books were written. Inspired? Yes. True? Yes. Inerrant? Not necessarily. It depends on how you define "inerrancy."

Because there are errors and discrepancies, the evangelicals cleverly defined "inerrant" to only apply to the original, autographic writings.[55] That is, those in Paul's or John's handwriting. Meaning, of course, that we don't have any of these autographic texts, and chances are no one ever did have a whole inerrant Bible. This is an unprovable proposition, based on wishes and dreams rather than on anything the Bible claims about itself.

The Eastern Orthodox view of inerrancy (that is, the traditional, historic view of the Church) is that the Bible contains no formal errors or inner contradictions concerning the relationship between God and the world. Orthodox scholar George Cronk further explains, *"Many Orthodox scholars believe that the Bible may contain 'incidental inaccuracies of a non-essential character.'"*[56]

This is a realistic position, as there are in fact "incidental inaccuracies" that do exist, as I've already discussed. I think that modern inerrantists simply mistake inerrancy for truth. They want the Bible to be true *in their modernist, categorical way,* even though their own logic prevents this from being possible. However, we know that there are many ways for something to be true. I find it highly presumptive for some trifling Bible scholar to claim to know what God's intent was when Genesis or any other book was written.

This brings me back to my earlier thoughts in Chapter 2 about wonder. When I take the Bible out of the box and see the amazing ways God's thoughts have been transmitted to us, I am just floored. As I've researched this chapter, I have bought and read countless books that have opened my world wider, while growing my faith deeper: *". . . for the letter kills, but the Spirit gives life"* (2 Corinthians. 3:6).

In my mind, the Evangelical Bible Box limits the Bible's potential. The Bible doesn't have to be without any errors in the original texts or otherwise, *because it's bigger than that!* I see the evangelical view of inerrancy as a modern golden calf—a substitute for the real thing which is living and active and bigger than any theological box.

THIRD KEYWORD: AUTHORITATIVE

"Authority" is one of those slippery words that can hold different meanings for different people. When we talk about the authority of the Bible, or say that the Bible is authoritative, what people often mean is that their *interpretation* of the Bible is authoritative, in whatever way they want it to be. For some, that means that when Genesis says the universe was created in seven days, the Bible has more authority over any scientific claim. Oddly enough, the Bible doesn't seem to be authoritative when it comes to the operation of churches or the behavior of pastors and elders. (Apparently, the Bible has loopholes that apply to divorce and remarriage, adultery, greed, gluttony, abuse, and so on.)

N.T. Wright has this to say:

> *The meaning of "authority," then, varies considerably according to the context within which the discourse is taking place. It is important to realize this from the start, not least because one of my central contentions is going to be that we have tended to let the word "authority" be the fixed point and have adjusted "scripture" to meet it, instead of the other way round.*[57]

In the early days of the Church, authority was found in the Apostles and the gospel message. In the later first and second centuries, this became the writings of the Apostles, along with the oral traditions that they set in place. In the Eastern Churches, Tradition (with a capital

"T") is still considered to have authority and includes the decisions of the early Ecumenical Councils, which is where the creeds developed and where the biblical canon was agreed to. Again, the choice of the books in our Bible depends on church Tradition.

As most of us know in the West, the Roman Church made the Pope the authority, which led to all kinds of heresy and evil. Then comes Martin Luther, who declares *Sola Scriptura* (Scripture alone)! I don't believe Luther intended to completely erase hundreds of years of Church authority, but once the cat was out of the bag, so to speak, the reformers and their followers more or less took the Bible and ran with it. Some of this was good, putting the Bible in the language of the people, but it also had its downside as interpretations of Scripture were all over the map.

Going back to the Chicago Statement, Article One says, "*We deny that the Scriptures receive their authority from the Church*," forgetting, perhaps, that it was the Church who agreed which books should be included in the New Testament in the first place. You could even say that the Bible got its authority from the Church. If the Table of Contents ("the cannon") is inspired, it would have been the Church that was inspired to choose the right books. I could go on and on, but I think my point is made. The Bible, which has been authoritative in the Church, is not the inerrant original autographs that no longer exist, but a Bible which has been copied and translated and passed around for years before it took its present shape.

It is my opinion that the added qualifications and necessary new beliefs have turned the inspired texts into a "flat" or "dead" text which now must conform to modernist standards. It is okay to believe things in the

Bible to be inerrant/true; in fact, I think that is a good default position. But don't confuse truth with fact. Just understand that if you find something in your Bible that is inaccurate (e.g. 2+2=5), that doesn't mean that the message of the Bible is not inspired and true.

AUTHORITY–WHAT IS IT GOOD FOR?

This brings us to another issue—what is biblical authority for? The Bible is certainly not a rulebook or a "how-to" book. In the Bible, you can find "authority" for killing people, for not killing people, for sacrifices, for no sacrifices, and so on. No one in a Christian church follows Leviticus, aside from a few choice verses that serve their prejudices. They don't even follow the Ten Commandments, although some like to post them in public as if they do.

And what about correct doctrine? A few will be quick to respond Yes! but just try to sit down with a Baptist, a Lutheran, and a Pentecostal and see what kind of correct doctrine you can all agree to. There is no list of proper or necessary beliefs to be a Christian. If so, we wouldn't need so many denominations, and churches wouldn't need to develop their bylaws and statements of faith—these would all be redundant. We have been given *"all things that pertain to life and godliness,"* (2 Peter 1:3 ESV). Peter does not point to the Bible as the source, but in the knowledge of Jesus.

It would seem that we are back to square one: just what is the authority of the Bible good for? I believe that the gospel message—the original "Rule of Faith"—is the only real authority (besides God himself) in the Church, but we can't even get all Christians to agree to that. As Paul told the Galatians, if someone preaches any different gospel, let him go to hell (Galatians 1:6-9 my paraphrase). The Bible itself does not claim "authority." Paul wrote, *"All scripture is inspired"* (2 Timothy 3:16), not "all scripture is authoritative." The only book that seems to claim authority is Revelation, which just happens to be the book most in question.[58]

I believe that the authority of Scripture must be mediated, or interpreted, by the entire universal church. It must be carefully reviewed and interpreted and then we must ask what the application is and then seek out contrary positions. Is God's authority revealed clearly? God began his revelation by speaking to and through humans, and it seems that he continues to speak to and through humans, even in applying the Bible's authority.

Next, let's open the Bible and see what we've got.

CHAPTER 5

OPENING THE BIBLE

"Clever title," you state. "I presume you're talking about something more than just how to open a Bible."

"Thanks," I humbly respond. *"And you're right. I could have called this chapter, 'How the Bible Really Works,' but that's kind of already used. My goal here is to look at just that: how the Bible works, as opposed to what it is."*

"Here's hoping . . ." you reply.

A LITTLE INTRODUCTION

I want to start this chapter by giving credit to my main influences, as I will likely say a great many things that I have assimilated over the years without any knowledge of exactly where I "borrowed" them. I try my hardest to give credit where it is due, and I've spent countless hours trying to track down thoughts and ideas that I've stored away in my cranium and give specific references where I can. However, these are my general sources and influences: Besides being raised on the Lutheran Catechism, I have found some more "evangelical" sources to be helpful, especially

J. Sidlow Baxter's *The Strategic Grasp of the Bible*, and James Buswell's *A Systematic Theology of the Christian Religion*, as well as various readings by people like John Stott when I was in Bible College for a [short] spell. I also read a lot of C. S. Lewis. My education took a slight turn toward the East when I was introduced to Orthodox thinking and theology by a friend who had converted to Greek Orthodox, and I have been influenced by traditional Orthodox writings as well as by authors like Peter Gilchrist and Robert Webber. I've also learned a lot from secular sources like Bruce Feiler and Thomas Cahill.

Since then, my views on Scripture have been heavily influenced by N.T. Wright (an Anglican theologian), Ken Blue (evangelical), Peter Enns (evangelical), Amy-Jill Levine (Jewish), and Bradly Jersak (Orthodox). As you might guess, these folks would not agree with each other on many points, but each adds a unique perspective not unlike the unique perspectives found in the Bible itself. I am nothing if not eclectic (some would say confused). I have, however, been excited to discover that many of the concepts I've taken from these folks have fit together quite nicely. And my thinking on several things has continued to evolve as I've written these last two chapters, which is what happens when you read a lot.

One of the first things I learned from Baxter's book is that there is a reason for how some of the books are arranged and it's not chronological, a fact which causes some issues in understanding. As I mentioned in Chapter 4, the Jewish arrangement of the Old Testament books is arranged differently than the Christian versions, but still not necessarily chronologically. The bottom line, the Table of Contents is not inspired, and neither are the chapter and verse designations. So basically, it is what it is because of convention (i.e., tradition).

SOPHIA

One of the great things about a Greek Orthodox church service (The Divine Liturgy of Saint John Chrysostom) is when you hear the chant *"Sophia!"* This has nothing to do with a woman of that name; *Sophia* means "wisdom" in Greek, and it is an announcement that the Bible, either from the Epistles or the Gospels, is to be read aloud to the congregation. If the Liturgy is done in English, the chant is "Wisdom!" The chant is not "Law!" or "Prophecy!", it is "Wisdom!" The Bible is, foremost, a book of wisdom, and it needs to be read with wisdom.

Peter Enns discusses at length how the Bible functions as a book of wisdom because *"The Bible isn't a book that reflects one point of view. It is a collection of books that records a conversation—even a debate—over time."*[59] He continues,

> *Adaptation over time is baked thoroughly into the pages of the Bible as a whole and as such demonstrates that the Bible is a book of wisdom, demanding to be adapted again and again by people of faith living in vastly distant cultures and eras—including our own, removed by as much as two millennia from the time of its completion.*[60]

Somewhat later in the book, Enns revisits this thought:

> *This process of needing to adapt over time—as I will not tire of emphasizing—is part of the biblical fabric, baked into its pages, and a crucial yet overlooked*

aspect of the Bible's character as a book of wisdom rather than a once-for-all book of rules and static information. The Bible in that respect is more like a living organism than a carved tablet.[61]

This brings me back to a question I posed earlier: Is the Bible a living document, continually inspired by the Holy Spirit, or is it a fixed, "dead" document, only to be read forensically?

THE WORD OF GOD

Before we go any further, I'd like to throw a little monkey wrench into your thinking with this quote:

The Word of God is inspired, inerrant, and infallible. And when he was about eighteen years old, he grew a beard.[62]

The Gospel of John, of course, opens with the statement, *"In the beginning was the Word . . . And the Word became flesh and dwelt among us, and we have seen his glory, glory as of the only Son from the Father, full of grace and truth"* (1:1, 14).

"The Word of God" is also used several times in the New Testament, but never to refer to the Scriptures, *per se*—it always refers to the gospel message, the testimony concerning Jesus, the living Word of God. What makes the Bible the Word of God is the Holy Spirit speaking through the text (John 16:13), giving testimony to Jesus. As Jesus himself said,

"You search the scriptures because you think that in them you have eternal life, and it is they that testify on my behalf." (John 5:39)

This statement by Jesus introduces the proper way for Christians to approach the Bible, called the "Christocentric view," where Christ is the pinnacle of revelation, and every word must finally submit to him.[63]

> *Jesus is the Word of God. And any Scripture that claims to be a revelation of that God must bow to the living God when he came in the flesh. "No man has seen God at any time, but God the only Son, who was in the bosom of the Father—He has made him known."[64]*

A key passage supporting the Christocentric view of the Bible is Hebrews 1:1-3:

> *Long ago God spoke to our ancestors in many and various ways by the prophets, but in these last days he has spoken to us by a Son, whom he appointed heir of all things, through whom he also created the worlds. He is the reflection of God's glory and the exact imprint of God's very being . . .*

The implication here is clear—**the prophets presented an inspired but human-relayed view of God, but now, finally, God speaks to us through Jesus, who is the exact representation of God.** That is, where the Old Testament view of God differs from Jesus, it's wrong (did I just say that out loud?), or our understanding of the text is wrong. God hasn't changed, and Jesus is not the "good" version of God—he's the **exact** image of God (to believe that there is any moral difference between Jesus and the Father is heresy). The written and handed-down message must now be submitted to Jesus. One of the main reasons for misinterpreting the Old Testament is to read it without Jesus, something that Christians seem to do quite often when it works to their benefit (like when it's time to condemn someone or to justify their questionable actions). Martin Luther had this to say:

> "*The true touchstone for testing every book is to discover whether it emphasizes the prominence of Christ or not. All Scripture sets forth Christ, Romans 3:24f. and Paul will know nothing but Christ, 1 Corinthians 2:2. What does not teach Christ is not apostolic, not even if taught by Peter or Paul. On the other hand, what does preach Christ is apostolic, even if Judas, Annas, Pilate, or Herod does it.*"[65]

For the Christian, the Bible never supersedes the witness of Jesus and is not even on the same level as Jesus, who is the authentic Word of God.

WWJD?

What this means in practical terms is that whenever you read something in the Old Testament that says God did this or God told the Israelites to do that, ask yourself, "Is this what Jesus would do? How does this line up with what Jesus taught?" If not, you must then ask yourself how to reconcile this disparity. How can you explain how the God of the Old Testament appears to be different from the God of the New Testament? The answer is hinted at in Hebrews 1—the prophets, as good as they were, were not Jesus. They did not have the complete revelation of God. This is not my idea, this is from the author of Hebrews. There used to be a transmission problem between heaven and earth, but there isn't anymore. If you have any doubts about the standing of Jesus, here are a few verses:

- Whoever has seen me has seen the Father. (John 14:9)
- He is the image of the invisible God, the first-born of all creation. (Colossians 1:15)
- For in him the whole fullness of deity dwells bodily. (Colossians 2:9)
- He is the reflection of God's glory and the exact imprint of God's very being, and he sustains all things by his powerful word. (Hebrews 1:3)

Now, let's practice. Read this passage from Numbers:

The LORD spoke to Moses, saying, "Avenge the Israelites on the Midianites; afterward you shall be gathered to your people." They did battle against Midian, as the LORD had commanded Moses, and killed every male. They killed the kings of Midian: Evi, Rekem, Zur, Hur, and Reba, the five kings of Midian, in addition to others who were slain by them, and they also killed Balaam son of Beor with the sword. The Israelites took the women of Midian and their little ones captive, and they plundered all their cattle, their flocks, and all their goods. Moses, Eleazar the priest, and all the leaders of the congregation went to meet them outside the camp. **Moses became angry with the officers of the army, the commanders of thousands and the commanders of hundreds, who had come from service in the war. Moses said to them, "Have you allowed all the women to live?** *These women here, on Balaam's advice, made the Israelites act treacherously against the LORD in the affair of Peor, so that the plague came among the congregation of the LORD. Now therefore, kill every male among the little ones, and kill every woman who has known a man by sleeping with him. But all the young girls who have not known a man by sleeping* *with him, keep alive for yourselves." (Numbers 31:1-2, 7-9, 13-18, emphasis mine)*

So, WWJD? Does this line up with anything that Jesus said? "Love your enemies," etc.? No, to me, this sounds like Moses reading a whole lot into what he was told by God. Either that or the story was embellished quite a bit after the fact for dramatic effect. After all, this story was likely written down many generations later, and this little embellishment is perhaps not unlike being told that your favorite football team wiped the field with the opposition. Either way, I don't believe we can blame this on God, who is love, and who doesn't change.

The other day I picked up a new book by an Orthodox author whose position was that Jesus is not as gentle as many would like to think, that he, in fact, is that same OT God. He essentially was claiming that Jesus would wipe out little children if he had to. As you would expect, this author also believed the OT was inerrant as written. So, there are opposing viewpoints, even among the Orthodox. Sorting through these things is where wisdom comes in.

Look again at the words of Moses and try to picture Jesus saying this: *"Have you let all the women live? . . . kill every male among the little ones, and kill every woman who has known man by lying with him. But all the young girls who have not known man by lying with him keep alive for yourselves."* Or, does wisdom tell you that Moses (or someone later) may have put words in God's mouth? Keep reading . . .

Here are a couple of examples where the Bible itself shows that the Israelites may have misheard—or invented—some things. Take these, for instance:

You need make for me only an altar of earth and sacrifice on it your burnt offerings and your offerings of well-being, your sheep and your oxen; in every place where I cause my name to be remembered I will come to you and bless you. (Exodus 20:24)

The LORD spoke to Moses, saying, "Speak to the Israelites and say to them: When you come into the land you are to inhabit, which I am giving you, and you make an offering by fire to the LORD from the herd or from the flock—whether a burnt offering or a sacrifice, to fulfill a vow or as a freewill offering or at your appointed festivals—to make a pleasing odor for the LORD. (Numbers 15:1-3)

Pretty straightforward, and not unexpected, from what we know of the OT law. But I've always wondered about these psalms by David:

Sacrifice and offering you do not desire,
but you have given me an open ear.
Burnt offering and sin offering
you have not required.
Then I said, "Here I am;
In the scroll of the book it is written of me.
I delight to do your will, O my God;
Your law is within my heart."[66]

You do not delight in sacrifice, or I would bring it; you do not take pleasure in burnt offerings. (Psalm 51:16, emphasis mine)

Does David know something we don't? And if that's not enough, listen to what God tells the prophet Jeremiah:

Thus says the LORD of hosts, the God of Israel: Add your burnt offerings to your sacrifices, and eat the flesh. For in the day that I brought your ancestors out of the land of Egypt, **I did not speak to them or command them concerning burnt offerings and sacrifices.** *But this command I gave them, "Obey my voice, and I will be your God, and you shall be my people; walk only in the way that I command you, so that it may be well with you." Yet they did not obey or incline their ear, but, in the stubbornness of their evil will,* **they walked in their own counsels** *and looked backward rather than forward. (Jeremiah 7:21-24, emphasis mine)*

He said what? Jeremiah lived about 500 years after King David, and long after the laws of Moses were put in place. Is God suggesting that the Laws regarding burnt offerings and sacrifices did not originate from him? This is certainly something worth considering. We know many today project their own views on God; is it possible the Old Testament writers did so as well? What does wisdom tell you?

To probe a bit more, we also know that there are conflicting laws, especially when they are restated in Deuteronomy (which as we discussed in the last chapter, is likely written by a different author than the other four books in the Torah). And, the histories found in First and Second Chronicles differ significantly from the same stories in the earlier books like Kings and Samuel. There is a ton of material available on these discrepancies from people trying to discredit the Bible, as well as "explanations" from literalists trying to defend their viewpoints. However, what if we don't need to? What if the Bible is okay just the way it is?

Once more, with feeling: **What if the Bible is okay just the way it is?**

YOU'RE OK, THE BIBLE'S OK

I have learned over the increasing number of years I have lived that I have no need to defend God or the Bible and that God himself does not feel the need to defend himself or the Bible. Assuming (as I do) that the Bible is inspired, I sometimes think that God could have inspired a more consistent set of writings. I am a post-enlightenment, modern thinker by default, and I often have wished God were a bit more modern as well. But I presume that this was not his point—a Bible like that could have easily become a static, dry, lifeless rulebook, not requiring anyone to depend on the Holy Spirit (wisdom) for understanding. This explains a lot of evangelical error, I think, for those who do try to use it as such a rulebook. Evangelicals tend to want the Bible to be a modern, perfect set of rules and guidelines to fit their modernist theologies, as well as to be able to argue away the parts that they do not agree with.

This reminds me of a great article I came across somewhere around 1975, called "Frontier Theology." It compares two types of Christians, identified as Pioneers and Settlers. My favorite part has to do with the Holy Spirit, and why the Settler Christians tend to shy away:

> IN PIONEER THEOLOGY—the Holy Spirit is the buffalo hunter. He rides along with the wagon train and furnishes fresh, raw meat for the pioneers. The buffalo hunter is a strange character—sort of a wild man. The pioneers never can tell what he will do next. He scares the hell out of the settlers.[67]

Depending on the Holy Spirit for guidance and wisdom, even in understanding the Bible, is risky. You could, for example, discover that you were wrong about some things. And imagine—you could even discover that the Bible does not condemn the same things you like to condemn, but that it does condemn judgmentalism. What? Literalists spend a lot of time trying to remove any such risk. But where's the adventure in that? Why be afraid of stepping out of your box and discovering that God is much bigger than you were aware of?

Peter Enns, in his book *The Sin of Certainty*, talks about how both fundamentalists and modernists are searching for certainty in the Bible, both making grave errors as they refuse to let the Bible be what it is.

> *I believe that the Bible does not model a faith that depends on certainty for the simple fact that the Bible does not provide that kind of certainty. Rather, in all its messy diversity, the Bible models trust in God that does not rest on whether we are able to be clear and certain about what to believe.*[68]

God could have given us a Bible where everything was neatly spelled out, so we would have a very clear theology and guidelines for how we should live as Christians. The fact that there are hundreds of denominations and arguments about literally everything tells us that this is not the Bible that we have. So, either God failed, or we must assume that God gave us what he wanted us to have, a Bible that we must engage with in order to grasp. The fact that Jesus spoke in parables that even the disciples found confusing tells us that God is very happy with not giving us easy answers.

I believe that the reason is for faith. God wants us to need and rely on him, not some instruction book.

THE GREAT MEN OF FAITH

Just think about those people in the Old Testament—Moses, David, and so on. What did they have to rely on? The Israelites carried on for years without any written documents that we know of, and even with some, they were not always used. Moses led the people for forty years before he got the stone tablets. I always found it interesting when King Josiah found the scrolls and said, "Hey, why is no one reading this stuff?" (2 Chronicles 34:21 my paraphrase). Since there were only a few copies of the scrolls, I imagine it was not unusual for many people to have never held or even seen one. Josiah realized the value of actually reading them. Without having any inspired writings for various long periods, the only certainty the Israelites had was that of oral tradition. And they, apparently, did okay. Just read the list of the great people of faith named in Hebrews 11—most of them lived before Moses, so they had no scriptures at all!

Certainly, these Old Testament folks made a lot of mistakes—terrible mistakes. *And it's all written down for us to learn from, both good and bad* (2 Timothy 3:16)! You may have heard the humorous line, "What if the purpose of my life was to serve as a warning to others?" Well, the Old Testament is full of people to whom this seems to apply. People like Abraham, Jonah, David, and Elijah are not presented as perfect, by any means. Even the "great men of faith" present a list of highly defective individuals, who did a lot of great things as well as a lot of terrible things that serve as illustrations of actions that should be avoided. And what about the twelve disciples? Often, they acted more like the Keystone Cops[69] than serious followers of Jesus. When reading Bible passages, sometimes the lesson to be learned is "don't do that!"

It is clear from the biblical history itself that faith in God does not require a written book, much less a perfect book that doesn't require us to seek wisdom from God. This reminds me of the Garden scenario: Trust in God, or eat of the tree of the knowledge of good and evil? And again, think of Jesus's warning not to look in the Scriptures when Jesus is right there.

ONCE AGAIN, I BELIEVE THE BIBLE IS INSPIRED

I have to keep repeating this because I am not trying to discredit the Bible in any way; I am just trying to put it in its historical context, so we can appreciate it properly. Treating it like a textbook is not treating it properly.

Many of you might be familiar with the concept of an "unreliable narrator," a literary device in which the narrator does not tell you the truth of the story, often because the narrator's point of view is skewed by his or her own errant thinking, such as Holden Caufield in *The Catcher in the Rye*. Consider that some of the Old Testament narrators—especially in the earliest stories that were handed down for generations—had a very limited understanding of who God was, often seeing him in the same light as the other gods of their neighbors. Just as Abraham grew to know God better throughout his life, so did the Jews after him. This could be why the stories that are retold in First and Second Chronicles, which are much later books than Kings and Samuel, vary so much from the earlier tellings. Several hundred years of perspective make a difference.

This is not to say that the Old Testament writers were not being honest, just that they could only relate to the best of their understanding. They are reliable narrators according to ancient standards, *but they are unreliable narrators by modern standards.*

While many Christians continue to deny that there are discrepancies in the Bible, the truth is that they exist, and no amount of denial will make them disappear. Creative translation can hide some of them, but that's a dishonest way to read the Bible (and then, what's the point?). Paul told Timothy that the Scriptures are "inspired and suitable for teaching," not that they were 100 percent accurate or that you should necessarily follow the example of Israel's mistakes. If the Bible is a book of wisdom, "living and active," illuminated by the Holy Spirit, then we must continue to allow the Holy Spirit to illuminate them for us, not treat them as dead manuscripts. My suggestion is to loosen your grip on the Bible, and let it breathe life as a living document should.

DISCLAIMER

Now, a great many intelligent, well-educated scholars do indeed believe that the Bible is without error and should be read as literally as possible, and I do not claim to be as smart or as well-educated as they are. However, being smart and well-educated does not always make you right (we can learn that from the Bible, too). Many other smart, well-educated scholars have approaches that I have found much more faith-building, that accept the Bible as-is and try to understand how it points to Jesus. I invite you to do more reading and decide for yourselves. After all, you have been given *"all things that pertain to life and godliness, through the knowledge of him who called us to his own glory and excellence."* (2 Peter 1:3)

THE BIBLE AS WITNESS

> *"And the Father who sent me has himself testified on my behalf. You have never heard his voice or seen his form, and you do not have his word abiding in you, because you do not believe him whom he has sent.* **You search the scriptures because you think that in them you have eternal life, and it is they that testify on my behalf.** *Yet you refuse to come to me to have life." (John 5:37-40, emphasis mine)*

There is one important thing to keep in mind when reading anything in the Bible, either Old or New Testaments: **Everything in the Bible functions as a witness to Jesus**, and I think most Christians will generally agree. As Bradley Jersak writes, *"To speak of the Bible as 'inspired' is to affirm its role as a faithful witness to the Word and his gospel."*[70] This, of course, is not to say that there are no other valid ways to read the Bible, but that for Christians, the primary function of both the Old and New Testaments is to point to Jesus, and that it is not improper to read Jesus into the Old Testament. The Eastern Orthodox view is that "the historical writings of the Old Testament point toward the incarnation of God the Son in Jesus Christ. The Old Testament as a whole is a foreshadowing of the New Testament revelation."[71]

As quoted earlier, Martin Luther said (in German, of course), *"Christ is the Master; the Scriptures are only the servant. The true way to test all the Books is to see whether they work the will of Christ or not. No Book which does not preach Christ can be apostolic, though Peter or Paul was its author. And no Book which does preach Christ can fail to be apostolic, although Judas, Ananias, Pilate, or Herod were its author."* While this is true for the New

Testament, the same principle pertains to the Old as seen from a Christian, New Testament perspective.

Amy-Jill Levine is a New Testament scholar and writer who happens to be Jewish. As she and her co-author Marc Brettler explain:

> *The Old Testament and the Tanakh are not, today for Christians and Jews, self-standing books. Christians read their Old Testament through the lens of the New Testament, and Jews read the Tanakh through the lens of postbiblical Jewish commentaries.*[72]

This is not unusual; in fact, it is to be expected. Jewish readers will read the Tanakh through the eyes of a particular Rabbi, and they would expect Christians to do the same through *their* Rabbi (Jesus). They also explain that to Jews, the Scriptures themselves are not as important as the interpretation of the Scripture. Shortly we will take a look at how both Jesus and New Testament authors reinterpreted the Old Testament in ways that were completely foreign to other Jewish readers.

There are many Christians who read Isaiah 53 as an obvious prophecy of Jesus, but it's only obvious once we know about Jesus. No Jewish scholar before Jesus' death and resurrection may have ever understood this to be a future prophecy of Jesus, but that's okay. The death and resurrection of Jesus is the lens that opens up the Old Testament in new ways. This is what Jesus did when he joined the two men on the road to Emmaus:

> *Then beginning with Moses and all the prophets, he interpreted to them the things about himself in all the scriptures. (Luke 24:27)*

Jesus, in effect, rewrote the Old Testament, inserting himself into the narrative. This is fitting, of course, as he was present in a very real way, from creation on. Levine and Brettler continue,

> As the early followers of Jesus, reflecting on the proclamation of his resurrection, turned to books such as Isaiah, Jeremiah, and Psalms more fully to understand their risen Lord, they found throughout the ancient sources new meaning. Instead of asking what the texts meant in their original contexts, they asked what the texts meant to them, in their own lives centuries later. Jews throughout the ages have done the same.[73]

LET ME PREACH FOR A MOMENT . . .

So yes, it is perfectly legitimate to read new interpretations into the Old Testament, *but the only valid Christian way is to make sure it points to Jesus.* That is, you can't just read things into the Bible for your personal benefit, or to support your personal biases (judgments). Historically, the Bible has been interpreted to support war, capital punishment, racism, slavery, misogyny, nationalism, greed, homophobia, and even adultery, if you can believe that. Reading through the Gospels, you cannot find anything that would suggest that Jesus would support any of these things. These kinds of interpretations are meant to steer the Bible *away* from Jesus, not toward him. A good way to self-check your interpretation of any Old Testament passage is to read Jesus into it and see if he fits. If it agrees with Jesus, you're likely okay; if not, it's a clue that further examination is necessary. This is not "whitewashing" the Old Testament, it's reading it as Jesus himself modeled.

Allow me to toss in a folksy illustration of my point. When I was quite young growing up in the country, I discovered something odd when plotting a path from point A to point B. The clearest, easiest path rarely looked the same from both sides of the path. Often, once I arrived at my destination and looked back, I saw that the clear path back was not at all the path that I had initially taken. I guess a short version of this is "hindsight is 20/20." So, we cannot necessarily fault the first century Jews for not making what to Christians are obvious assumptions about the Old Testament, and neither can we fault contemporary non-Christians for not accepting a Christian reading of any Old Testament passage. We should welcome the different viewpoints and use them to build bridges.

I would expect that it would be natural for many Jewish people to think that Christianity has stolen and perverted the Tanakh. However, we can learn to appreciate various Jewish perspectives and also be able to explain how we see Jesus in those same scriptures. We have a big God, and the Bible is a big, inspired book. I find Jewish interpretations of the Tanakh to be interesting and often enlightening, as well as valid. The fact that they do not see Jesus does not nullify the fact that we do, and the differences could present a very good topic of conversation, as long as we don't try to nullify their insights. Again, God is big enough.

This is mind-expanding stuff, people.

HOW JESUS USED THE BIBLE

Now let's turn to some of the ways that Jesus used the Tanakh. The first instance we have (chronologically) is shown in Luke 4. First, Jesus and Satan play a little

Bible battle, and then Jesus heads to Nazareth, where he volunteers to read in the synagogue.

> When he came to Nazareth, where he had been brought up, he went to the synagogue on the Sabbath day, as was his custom. He stood up to read, and the scroll of the prophet Isaiah was given to him. He unrolled the scroll and found the place where it was written:

> "The Spirit of the Lord is upon me,
> because he has anointed me
> to bring good news to the poor.
> He has sent me to proclaim release to the captives
> and recovery of sight to the blind,
> to set free those who are oppressed,
> to proclaim the year of the Lord's favor."

> And he rolled up the scroll, gave it back to the attendant, and sat down. The eyes of all in the synagogue were fixed on him. Then he began to say to them, "Today this scripture has been fulfilled in your hearing." (16-21)

So, what are we to think about this? First, we can compare this to the original passage and see that Jesus left out the last line, "and the day of vengeance of our God." Next, we must look at the context of these verses. Christians raised hearing this story will automatically assume that Isaiah was prophesying about Jesus—but this is not necessarily how the Jews understood it. For one thing, it's usually been assumed that Isaiah was referring to himself; the Spirit of God had authorized him to proclaim a time of Jubilee that would come for Israel. This was certainly the context of this section of Isaiah. But all of a sudden here's this local kid claiming that *he* was the anointed one, as well as bringing the time of Jubilee. This is just not how things were done, and no one wanted a carpenter messiah, even if he could turn water into wine.

While various Old Testament texts certainly spoke of messianic figures, there was no clear understanding of who this figure—or figures, as the passages didn't necessarily line up to point to the same person—was. It is only through looking at these passages from within the context of Christianity do they point to Jesus. Finally, we go back to the missing line. The first century Jews *wanted* vengeance. They wanted a messiah who would lead them to victory over Rome, which was what they thought of as the essence of God's favor, not someone who would merely bless everyone. However, Jesus was never shy about inserting himself into the Scriptures and he began his ministry by setting this pattern of reinterpreting Scripture.

Turning now to one of my favorite passages, John 10. There's just so much great theology in this chapter. In the first section, John records Jesus' teaching about being the good shepherd, and so on. Then, Jesus goes to Jerusalem for the Feast of Dedication, and "the Jews" (weren't they all Jews?) cornered him and asked him point-blank if he claimed to be the Christ, to which he replied, *"The Father and I are one."* So, "the Jews" picked up stones to chuck at him. A rowdy bunch, these Jews. Chapter 10 continues,

> Jesus answered, "I have told you, and you do not believe. The works that I do in my Father's name testify to me, but you do not believe because you do not belong to my sheep. My sheep hear my voice. I know them, and they follow me. I give them eternal life, and they will never perish. No one will snatch

them out of my hand. My Father, in regard to what
he has given me, is greater than all, and no one can
snatch them out of the Father's hand. The Father and
I are one." The Jews took up stones again to stone
him. Jesus replied, "I have shown you many good
works from the Father. For which of these are you
going to stone me?" The Jews answered, "It is not
for a good work that we are going to stone you but
for blasphemy, because you, though only a human,
are making yourself God." Jesus answered, "Is it not
written in your law, 'I said, you are gods'? If those to
whom the word of God came were called 'gods'—and
the scripture cannot be annulled— can you say that
the one whom the Father has sanctified and sent into
the world is blaspheming because I said, 'I am God's
Son'? If I am not doing the works of my Father, then
do not believe me. But if I do them, even though you
do not believe me, believe the works, so that you may
know and understand that the Father is in me and I
am in the Father. (25-38)

Did you follow this conversation closely? I have read
this over many times, and to be honest, I still have to
stop and scratch my head at Jesus' argument. If I read
this correctly—and I always allow some room to be
wrong—Jesus is playing word games with them and using their own version of literalism against them. Now, I
don't believe that God told the Jews that they were gods
in the same sense that He was God. The "Jews" also understood that. But Jesus pins them to the wall with "and
Scripture cannot be broken." In this literal context, Jesus'
use of "Son of God" is technically correct, although it is
clear he means something far different. This is not how
I was taught to use the Bible—although, I figure Jesus
has that right. I won't draw any more conclusions about

the mentality of Jesus, because I don't have any. But I do find Jesus' argument with the "Jews" something very interesting to ponder. The older I get, the more okay I am with leaving things unanswered. Sometimes I am only left understanding what is not true, rather than what is.

Now, here is another interesting discussion between Jesus and some Pharisees.

GOD, OR MOSES?

Let's look at this passage from the OT Law:

> *Suppose a man enters into marriage with a woman but she does not please him because he finds something objectionable about her, so he writes her a certificate of divorce, puts it in her hand, and sends her out of his house; she then leaves his house and goes off to become another man's wife. Then suppose the second man dislikes her, writes her a certificate of divorce, puts it in her hand, and sends her out of his house (or the second man who married her dies): her first husband, who sent her away, is not permitted to take her again to be his wife after she has been defiled, for that would be abhorrent to the LORD, and you shall not bring guilt on the land that the LORD your God is giving you as a possession. (Deuteronomy 24:1-4)*

We all know—or presume—that the Old Testament law was given by God through Moses. When we refer to the "Law of Moses," we don't mean to suggest that Moses made up these laws himself. But let's look at this conversation from the book of Matthew:

Some Pharisees came to him, and to test him they asked, "Is it lawful for a man to divorce his wife for any cause?" He answered, "Have you not read that the one who made them at the beginning 'made them male and female,' and said, 'For this reason a man shall leave his father and mother and be joined to his wife, and the two shall become one flesh'? So they are no longer two but one flesh. Therefore what God has joined together, let no one separate." They said to him, "Why then did Moses command us to give a certificate of dismissal and to divorce her?" **He said to them,** *"It was because you were so hard-hearted that Moses allowed you to divorce your wives, but from the beginning it was not so. And I say to you, whoever divorces his wife, except for sexual immorality, and marries another commits adultery, and he who marries a divorced woman commits adultery." (19:3-9, emphasis mine)*

Here the Pharisees first attribute the law regarding divorce to Moses rather than claim it was a command of God. Jesus does not dispute this in response but instead appears to confirm it by stating that it was indeed Moses who allowed for divorce, rather than God ("from the beginning it was not so"). What are we to make of this exchange? What, if anything, are the implications regarding the rest of the law in Deuteronomy? It would appear that Jesus is at least distinguishing this portion of the law and the commands of God.

Jesus says a few other things of interest concerning the Law of Moses, which you may be familiar with. Matthew 5 records what is typically referred to as the "Sermon on the Mount." The first several statements are the Beatitudes: *"Blessed are those who*

. . .", and so on. Starting at verse 17, he starts teaching on the Law:

> "Do not think that I have come to abolish the Law or the Prophets; I have come not to abolish but to fulfill. For truly I tell you, until heaven and earth pass away, not one letter, not one stroke of a letter, will pass from the law until all is accomplished. Therefore, whoever breaks one of the least of these commandments and teaches others to do the same will be called least in the kingdom of heaven, but whoever does them and teaches them will be called great in the kingdom of heaven. For I tell you, unless your righteousness exceeds that of the scribes and Pharisees, you will never enter the kingdom of heaven." (Matthew 5:17-20)

Then Jesus continues with, "You have heard that it was said to those of old, 'You shall not murder . . .'"—not, "God wrote on the stone tablets . . ." or "Moses taught . . ."—but, "You have heard that it was said." Then, he follows with, "But I say to you that everyone who is angry with his brother will be liable to judgment . . ." (21-22).

This is one more place where I don't know what Jesus was suggesting regarding the Ten Commandments, only that he switched the focus from actions to the heart. He then used the same sentence forms to deal with adultery and lust, swearing oaths, revenge ("an eye for an eye"). Finally, he says, "You have heard that it was said, 'You shall love your neighbor and hate your enemy . . ." but love your enemies, too (42-43). In each case, he goes further than what the Law stated, retooling the Law (what they had "heard it said"). This section seems to contradict Jesus' statement in verse 17 (above), but I have a hunch that it is not contradictory at all, but that "fulfilling" the law has to do with moving from legalism to attitudes of the heart.

To top this off, Jesus seems to reference Deuteronomy 28 when he says, *"But I say to you, love your enemies and pray for those who persecute you, so that you may be children of your Father in heaven, **for he makes his sun rise on the evil and on the good, and sends rain on the righteous and on the unrighteous"** (44-45, emphasis mine). However, that is not what Deuteronomy 28 says; rather, there we find that God will send rain to the faithful, but he will curse the wicked. Is this a change of heart, or is it a correction of teaching about the heart of God? Who do we trust, Jesus, or some possibly unknown ancient author?

A small-minded person would deny any contradictions and present a clear answer to this question, but I—another small-minded person—am fine with leaving this unanswered for now. If God needs us to know, I'm sure he can clarify it.

BUT WHATABOUT DAVID?

Moving ahead a few chapters, we come across this little incident:

> *At that time Jesus went through the grain fields on the Sabbath; his disciples were hungry, and they began to pluck heads of grain and to eat. When the Pharisees saw it, they said to him, "Look, your disciples are doing what is not lawful to do on the Sabbath." He said to them, "Have you not read what David did when he and his companions were hungry? How he entered the house of God, and they ate the bread of the Presence, which it was not lawful for him*

or his companions to eat, but only for the priests?"
(Matthew 12:1-4)

By itself, Jesus' response sounds a lot like "what-aboutism." But let's continue:

"Or have you not read in the law that on the Sabbath the priests in the temple break the Sabbath and yet are guiltless? I tell you, something greater than the temple is here. But if you had known what this means, 'I desire mercy and not sacrifice,' you would not have condemned the guiltless. For the Son of Man is lord of the Sabbath." (Matthew 12:5-8)

Jesus could be "pulling rank" here, essentially saying, "Hey, I'm God, so . . ." But I believe he's once again getting at something deeper. I think Jesus is making the point that keeping the Law is not about rules, but about the attitude of the heart. This is why his quote from Hosea 6:6, *"For I desire mercy, not sacrifice"* (NIV) fits the context of the discussion. Consistent with Hosea's prophetic criticism of Israel's focus on rule-keeping and judgment rather than on mercy, Matthew's Jesus is consistent in pointing out that the law was never about keeping rules. And because he is, after all, "lord of the Sabbath," he should know.

JESUS PUSHES THE ENVELOPE

Immediately following this passage we read in verses 9-12:

He left that place and entered their synagogue; a man was there with a withered hand, and they asked him, "Is it lawful to cure on the Sabbath?" so that they might accuse him. He said to them, "Suppose one of you has only one sheep and it falls into a pit on the Sabbath; will you not lay hold of it and lift it out? How much more valuable is a human being than a sheep! So it is lawful to do good on the Sabbath."

Jesus is a bit more direct here, pointing out the apparent "emergency" loophole in the Sabbath rules, then states clearly that yes, it is okay to do good on the Sabbath. On one hand, we have Jesus dismantling the Old Testament Law despite saying earlier that he was not doing that, and on the other hand, teaching that the whole law is actually about love and mercy, siding with the later prophets' challenge to the earlier focus on rule-keeping. There is a tension in the Old Testament between the earlier writings and the later writings, as I've already mentioned, and Jesus now adds his authority to the latter view.

One more verse to finish out this thought, this time from Mark:

One of the scribes came near and heard them disputing with one another, and seeing that he answered them well he asked him, "Which commandment is the first of all?" Jesus answered, "The first is, 'Hear, O Israel: the Lord our God, the Lord is one; you shall love the Lord your God with all your heart and with all your soul and with all your mind and with all your strength.' The second is this, 'You shall love your neighbor as yourself.' There is no other commandment greater than these." Then the scribe said to him, "You are right, Teacher; you have truly said that 'he is one, and besides him there is no other'; and 'to love him with all the heart and with all the understanding and with all the strength' and 'to love one's neighbor as

oneself'—this is much more important than all whole
burnt offerings and sacrifices." When Jesus saw that
he answered wisely, he said to him, "You are not far
from the kingdom of God." After that no one dared to
ask him any question. (12:28-34)

Here we have the scribe expanding on Jesus' statement of the two most important commandments, adding
that these are *"much more than all whole burnt offerings*
and sacrifices," with which Jesus agreed. Once again, love
and mercy trump offerings and sacrifices.

Through these verses, we can see that Jesus did
not necessarily use the Old Testament the way many
modern readers do, which is not surprising. As I have
already discussed, the Jews in general did not use the
Scriptures the way modern readers do. Secondly, Jesus
was the full revelation of God, and we can see where
God's focus is. Unfortunately, there are way too many
Christians who still use the Bible to judge rather than
learn from Jesus that "mercy triumphs over judgment."
(James 2:13)

OLD TESTAMENT QUOTES IN THE NEW TESTAMENT

There are many, many OT quotes found in the rest of
the New Testament, and I'm not going to elaborate on
each one of them (to your relief, I am sure). I just want
to point out that many of these quotes are from the
Septuagint, the translation of the Old Testament into
Greek. This was not a strictly word-for-word translation or even a concept-for-concept translation. The
Septuagint contained many editorial changes to the
original texts, meant to clarify as well as occasionally
to update or reinterpret certain sections to make sense

to contemporary Jewish readers. The use of these "up-dated" scriptures didn't seem to bother any of the NT authors. Even the Pharisees never argued "But you're not reading from the Hebrew!"

Paul's use of the Old Testament is of particular interest, as he brought a completely new understanding of Jewish history and God's purposes, which we will get into in a later chapter as we discuss Paul's theology.

The key takeaway is that for Christians, the point of the Old Testament is to point to Jesus as the full revelation of God. This is how the New Testament authors used the Old Testament, and how the Orthodox Churches still view the Old Testament. While many in evangelical circles have separated the OT from that "Jesus context," I think it crucial that we regain that understanding so as not to be drawn away from the gospel itself into various forms of legalism.

CHAPTER 6

THE GOD QUESTION

"So now," you ask, "are you going to prove to me that God exists?"

"Nope," I respond.

"Why not?" you ask incredulously.

"Because," I answer, *"I don't think it's possible. What I will do is present a few ways people try to prove that God exists, then we'll talk about God, assuming that he/she/they exist."*

"Why assume that God exists?" you wonder.

"Because why talk about someone you assume doesn't exist?" I smile. *"For the purpose of this book, I'm going to assume that the God of the Christian Bible exists, rather than some other god, simply because that's who I believe in, and I think it's reasonable to do so."*

I Believe in God the Father Almighty, Maker of Heaven and Earth.

So begins the Apostles Creed, one of the earliest belief statements of Christianity. The Nicene Creed (more accurately, the Nicene-Constantinopolitan Creed, being amended in Constantinople in 381) expands this statement somewhat, *"I believe in One God, the Father Almighty, Maker of Heaven and Earth, and of all things visible and invisible."* These beliefs echo the first verse of Genesis, *"In the beginning, God created the heavens and the earth."* This belief is not unique to Christians but is shared with Jews and Muslims as well as various offshoots. One God. Almighty (all-powerful). Creator of all things, both material and nonmaterial.

I said early on in this book that I was raised knowing that God knew me, was watching me, and that he loved me unconditionally. I can only speculate that this belief was based on revelation mixed with knowledge of who God was. No matter how I felt about myself or how anyone else felt about me, I knew that I was loved and accepted by God. It was a great way to grow up, and I am sad for people who didn't have this advantage. I can't imagine growing up being afraid of God. A lot of how you respond to a belief in God has to do with the theology you were raised with. Is God primarily a God of wrathful judgment (as many of my friends were raised), or is he a God of mercy and love? Or is God merely a fairy tale, so no worries? To move forward with Christianity, this is a foundational question. Too many people who have been raised with the judgmental God have walked away from religion altogether, seeing life with no God as a better option (and they could be right about that). To invert a Bible verse, if God is against us, who can be for us? That indeed is a terrible way to live.

THE FIRST QUESTION

Before we talk about who God is, we should address the most basic questions: Is there a God, and how can we know?

For the record, if you happen to be an atheist, I will not hold that against you. I have several friends who are atheists, and I value their friendship and insights. I believe it's a good thing to have some atheists as friends, as they are the ones who can ask the tough questions lest we get lazy in our beliefs. And no, I am not worried about them ending up in hell (more on that later). I suspect that God has a soft spot for atheists. I once read a quote from some unidentified Rabbi that said atheists are the best examples for those who believe in God, for an atheist does moral acts not out of fear of punishment or the promise of heaven, but because it's the right thing to do. In some ways, God's people should act more like atheists (including not being afraid to ask questions). An honest atheist is a lot better off than a deceptive believer, in my opinion.

So, my answers to the above questions are 1) Yes, there is a God, and 2) I don't know. Now you know that I'm being honest—I am not going to make up answers to make you feel better or to make myself seem smarter than I am. I have some friends who believe that they have logical proofs that establish God's existence. However, they have never convinced me, even though I already believe what they're trying to prove. I have a habit of playing devil's advocate. When I read or hear these arguments from the evangelical experts, my response is typically, "Wait, no, that's just not convincing because—." If these logical proofs only convince people who already believe in God, they're not much good.

Many, if not most, atheists are unimpressed by these kinds of arguments, and I find them embarrassing to Christendom in general.

I do believe that there is circumstantial evidence that can lead us in the direction of belief, but I am a firm believer in Kierkegaard's[74] "leap to faith." Evidence and logic will only get us so far, then we must choose which direction to leap. That's right, it's your responsibility. Even to believe in a purely materialistic world (what many people think of as "science") takes a leap of faith, or leap *to* faith. Let's talk about that for a moment longer. (Yes, I know—more philosophy.)

David Hume was an eighteenth-century Scottish philosopher who seems to have laid some of the foundation for Kierkegaard's thinking. Hume is perhaps best known for his treatise arguing that you cannot objectively prove that a miracle has happened, something that a few atheists like to throw around claiming that miracles can't exist (which isn't really what Hume argued, and which can't be proven either). Hume, however, also argued—quite convincingly—that causation cannot be proven, only implied. Just because something happened in the past does not mean it will happen that way next time. Not really, it's just a matter of probability based on experience. People have been trying to disprove Hume's logic for a couple of hundred years, but so far they have found nothing to prove causation. With this, the whole foundation of science is challenged—the fact that you can observe something happen 1,000 times does not mean that it will happen next time. Causation is merely implied, and to rely on it for any future action requires a belief in the probability that causation exists (my incredible oversimplification).

The bottom line is that every belief system—even a reliance on science—requires a kind of faith. I know scientists who will try to argue semantics to avoid using the word "faith" (they define it as "blind faith," which is a different animal), but it comes down to the same thing. It's a chosen belief. You have faith that your car's brakes will work, that jet planes will fly, and that gravity will keep us from floating off into space. This is based on our experience and is an informed choice to believe in predictable causation. People believed in gravity before it had a name—due to experience. Likewise, whatever we believe about God requires a leap from the implications of the information we have to a belief that God does or does not exist.

So, back to my answers to the big questions. I am convinced that God exists. This belief is based on personal experience and logic that supports my experience—or, you could say, personal experience that supports my informed choice to believe. Either way, it's non-quantifiable and unprovable, but I have what I need to make an informed belief choice, and no reason whatsoever to doubt that belief. When it comes to belief in God, science and logic are simply not good enough. So yes, I believe God exists, because I have chosen to believe that God exists based on the knowledge and experience that I have. It's not a random choice, or "blind" faith, but rather it is an informed belief. Either God exists, or I am delusional and crazy. And even if that is true, it still doesn't mean that God doesn't exist. God isn't Tinker Bell, and doesn't require belief to exist, or for any other reason. But centuries of God telling humans that he does indeed exist would add weight to my belief.

ARGUMENTS FOR THE EXISTENCE OF GOD

I find the facts about how the universe, and our planet in particular, appear to be specifically designed to support life to be quite compelling. There are millions of tiny details that had to be put in place for things to work as they do. The probability that all these things evolved at the right time and in the right order is astronomical, and that still doesn't explain the existence of life and human intelligence, such as it is. The multiverse theory[75] is one explanation for improving the odds of randomness, but it still doesn't answer all the questions, especially those concerning the existence of intelligent life. There are, of course, some very sophisticated arguments on both sides of this issue, and I have read some of them. To be honest, I haven't been that impressed with most of the arguments on either side (except for the *appearance* of design argument) and suspect that they do more to reinforce already-held beliefs than change anyone's mind. Still for me, as the Bible says, "*the heavens declare the glory of God*" (Psalm 19:1). Creation connects me to God.

Suppose on some archeological dig, a very advanced machine is discovered. No one would propose that "it just happened." If there are signs of design, the most logical assumption is that there had to have been a designer, perhaps some past civilization or some visiting aliens. Is there proof of either scenario? In the absence of finding an owner's manual or manufacturer's logo, probably not. However, is anyone going to hold on to the belief that it just appeared naturally? Again, I am not claiming that the appearance of design is absolute proof of anything; however, it does strongly suggest a designer. It is a commonsense belief. The appearance of design is so apparent that it is occasionally suggested that we exist in a computer simulation, like that in the movie *The Matrix*, or merely exist in some being's mind. To me, it doesn't matter how we exist—it's apparent that we do, and that there is a designer for whatever existence we have. In the end, pragmatism rules.

A related argument is called the nomological argument, which argues that merely the existence of laws implies a design. Why are there any consistent laws at all, regardless of whether they're fine-tuned or not? As far as I know, there is nothing that says the laws of nature have to exist at all. Why is centripetal force a thing? Why isn't the world simply flying off into space rather than hanging around the sun? Why is the Earth's rotation constant? Why does math work? "Because" is not a very satisfactory answer.

Another argument for the existence of God is the need for a "first cause." The proposition is that everything that begins to exist has a cause, thereby implying the need for a first cause, which would be God. I find this to be a rather weak argument; it just brings us to, "Where did God come from?" To say that God always existed opens the possibility that the universe always existed in some form. At the risk of offending some of my apologist friends, close but no cigar. I believe that God was the first cause of creation and also exists outside of time itself, but that's a belief, not a proof.

Many God-proofs fail because many Christians ask too much of them. That is, they believe these arguments are undoubtable proofs, which they are not. They are relying on modernist thought to prove someone outside of the realm of modernist logic. They just need to get over it, in my opinion. The bottom line is that I don't believe that the existence of God can be proven, except from first-hand experience (which is still subjective). Someday, I think, we'll all have that first-hand opportunity. But for now, all we get are hints.

MORE ARGUMENTS FOR THE EXISTENCE OF GOD

Theologian N.T. Wright has a marvelous little book called *Simply Christian: Why Christianity Makes Sense*, in which he makes a very different argument. He suggests four basic human longings that he refers to as "echoes of a voice":

1. *Justice*

2. *Spirituality*

3. *Relationship*

4. *Beauty*

These (aside from perhaps relationship) have seemingly no evolutionary value, but they are universally innate drives in humans that Wright suggests point to "something beyond" itself. We will put ourselves at personal risk for each of these. Lately, I have read arguments that there must be some evolutionary benefit to religion, or we wouldn't have the need for it, which only reinforces the fact that spirituality is a recognized universal human drive. Again, none of this proves there is a God, but they are clues not only to the existence of a God but about the nature of that God.

Many of our American founding fathers believed in a god, but they were *deists*—they believed in a nonpersonal creator god. This is more or less a belief in a "safe" god, one who created a good world but pretty much leaves us alone. It's the next best thing to having no god at all, except perhaps that god would keep the world going for a while. Rejecting the notion of a personal, interested god, deism also rejects any notion of supernatural revelation.

Christianity is without apology a Theist religion, believing in a God who is not only involved in creation but who participates in our lives, and who became one of us about 2,000 years ago. This is the God we will be taking for granted as existing, and who we'll be discussing from here on out.

BACK TO THE BEGINNING

What we know about God we learn from the Bible (as the recorded history of God revealing himself to humankind). Now, I've just referred to God as "himself," which is simply a traditional convention going back to the first translation into English. God is a spirit and is neither male nor female. However, Jesus refers to God as "Father," so I'll continue to use the male pronoun, even if it's not technically correct. Also, after more than sixty years of referring to God as "he," it's hard to break that habit. I do sincerely apologize if this bothers some of you. I am quite aware and sensitive to the sexist (anti-female) history of theology and am attempting to avoid sexist language and thought to the best of my ability.

To my knowledge, every culture has what is called a "creation myth," a story about where we came from. Most cultures developed some belief in God, and some even share some of the Old Testament stories, like the Great Flood. This is to be expected, presuming God exists, etc. Did they borrow stories from one another, or were the stories passed down from the true story in different ways? Either way, we shouldn't find this commonality surprising. What we understand from the Bible is that God chose people—Adam, Noah, Abraham, The Jews—to reveal himself to and to be a beacon of truth to the world. Whether you believe it or not, the Jews did, and this has been the focus of their message down through the Ages: God is one God, and we are his people. Christianity has carried this forward.

So, first from what we know is that in the beginning, God created the heavens and the Earth. God is identified in Genesis as the "first cause." As we've discussed earlier in the book, Genesis gives two different perspectives on how creation came about. I don't feel like I need to know exactly how creation came about, but my own belief is that it is not the literal six-day creation some talk about, as the days are not in a logical order, and the order differs in Chapter 2. For one thing, in Genesis 1, the Earth seems to exist as "formless and void," "and the Spirit of God was hovering over the waters," and there was night and day, long before the sun and the moon were created.

As is usually the case, there have been several theories down through the years as to how creation came about. One theory, more or less consistent with the Big Bang theory, is that God created everything out of nothing. One minute there was nothing, the next there was. I am fine with this theory, however, I do believe that the Earth provides evidence that creation took longer than a few days. I'm fine with that, too. I don't believe Genesis 1 was attempting to present a scientific explanation of creation, but rather just present a short version to make a few points. Creation combined with evolution doesn't bother me either;

it changes nothing, except for some questionable theology about sin and death and blood, which we'll talk about in a later chapter.

Another theory, presented centuries ago by some Muslim philosophers (Muslims have a rich philosophical history)[76], is that God is creative by nature, and has always been creating. This fits nicely with the formless and void earth, etc. For all we know, God could have had a prior creation, another idea coming from an Islamic theologian. For example, the angels could have preexisted our universe, along with the "waters" mentioned in Genesis 1. Again, it doesn't bother me. However God chooses to operate is fine with me. In all these discussions, we need to look for the "bottom line," or the take-away. The important point in all of this is that God is our Creator, of all that we see and experience, and I believe he created everything intentionally. He is the first cause. I don't spend time wondering where God came from (okay sometimes I do, just a little), because I know I can't answer that no matter how hard I try. We also learn from Genesis that God is happy with creation and that he continues to be involved and has revealed himself to humankind. I believe these things wholeheartedly, regardless of the creation method used. The "how" is inconsequential. The "now" is much more important.

It is interesting as we go on in the early Genesis stories that God appears somewhat limited in knowledge, not knowing where Adam and Eve were hiding, or when he asks Cain where Abel was. I have always interpreted that to mean that God was asking rhetorical questions to prompt responses from Adam, Eve, and Cain. Some believe that God doesn't know everything and learns along with us. This is called open theology, and I don't buy it. It's going back to a "small god" concept.

In any event, God appears intimately involved not only with humans while in the Garden, but afterward as well. However, this same level of interaction does not seem to have continued in the same fashion, as later revelations are presented in more of a "godlike" manner—voices from above, visitations of angels, talking animals, or whatever. I attribute this perception change to a growth in understanding about just how big God is. We don't know what we aren't told, so any additional communications are merely guesswork.

ABSOLUTELY EXISTENTIAL

Most of us are familiar with the story of Moses encountering God in the burning bush, or at least we have heard it used metaphorically. One day, Moses encounters a bush on fire, but the bush is not consumed. It turns out to be God, who tells Moses he is to go lead the Israelites out of Egypt. Moses, somewhat wary of the project, asks God his name so he can tell the Israelites who sent him: *"God said to Moses, 'I AM WHO I AM.' He said further, 'Thus you shall say to the Israelites, "I AM has sent me to you."'"* (Exodus 3:14) **This is the most existential statement I can imagine.** Descartes said, *"I think therefore I am,"* but God says, *"I am because I am."*

Earlier in the conversation, he did identify himself as the God of Abraham, etc., but when asked point-blank who he is, he responds by essentially saying "I am pure existence," which goes well with the concept that the universe exists and continues to exist, because of God. This is the all-powerful, one-of-a-kind God. But more than that, this God reveals himself and carries on conversations with humans and has taken a special interest in the Jewish people. All-powerful and relational, a God with a plan that relies on human cooperation, such as it is.

A GOD WHO LISTENS

Backing up just a bit, we see God revealing himself to Abraham, Sarah, and Hagar, showing that not only does God reveal himself to individuals, but he also listens to what they have to say. He even allows Abraham to negotiate with him over the destruction of Sodom. Moses, too, negotiated with God in the burning bush. Now I am no expert on other gods of the time, but I kind of doubt that these were the kind of gods people negotiated with, much less have them communicate. Even back then, statues were not known for their communication skills. But here is a God who not only talks to individuals but listens to the concerns and ideas of individuals.

God also shows his power. While he was hanging out with Moses on top of the mountain, the Israelites witnessed a terrifying display from below that so freaked them out they made a golden idol. Not a wise move, but they likely thought Moses was toast and needed a backup plan of some sort. It turns out that God wanted a relationship with all of them, but they ended up getting a bunch of laws to follow instead. A few millennia later, people are still choosing laws over relationships. Go figure.

NO OTHER GODS

When Moses finally comes down with the stone tablets, the first statement identifies God, just so there is no confusion: "*I am the* LORD *your God, who brought you out of the land of Egypt, out of the house of slavery . . .*" (Exodus 20:2) As you can see, this is a statement, not a commandment. God begins with "I am," and connects himself to their history. One God, their savior. He then goes on,

> ...you shall have no other gods before me. You shall not make for yourself an idol, whether in the form of anything that is in heaven above or that is on the earth beneath or that is in the water under the earth." (3, 4)

JUST BECAUSE I'M NOT HIDING ANYTHING . . .

Some might notice that I didn't finish verses 5 and 6, which say "*You shall not bow down to them or serve them, for I the* LORD *your God am a jealous God, punishing children for the iniquity of parents to the third and the fourth generation of those who reject me but showing steadfast love to the thousandth generation of those who love me and keep my commandments.*" These verses would indicate that not only is God a jealous God, but that he holds a grudge. However, we must be careful of taking verses out of the context of the entire Bible. It's possible that whoever wrote this law down did a little embellishing to make a point, as somewhat later God himself puts an end to this kind of thinking:

> *The word of the* LORD *came to me: What do you mean by repeating this proverb concerning the land of Israel, "The parents have eaten sour grapes, and*

the children's teeth are set on edge"? As I live, says
the LORD God, this proverb shall no more be used by
you in Israel. (Ezekiel 18:1-3)

This chapter in Ezekiel goes on to clarify that God does not punish children—or anyone else—for someone else's sin. (Keep this chapter in mind later when we talk about the so-called "sin of Adam.") Jesus clarified this further in this story from John's Gospel:

As he walked along, he saw a man blind from birth.
His disciples asked him, "Rabbi, who sinned, this
man or his parents, that he was born blind?" Jesus
answered, "Neither this man nor his parents sinned;
he was born blind so that God's works might be
revealed in him." (9:1-3)

The disciples repeated the common belief that one's suffering was due to some sin, even ancestral sin. (Sadly, you still hear this kind of nonsense from Christians today.) However, Jesus makes it clear that this is not the case.

So again, the bottom line is that there is one creator God, and no other gods (imaginary as they might be). The God of Genesis is the God of Abraham, the God who led the Jews out of Egypt, and who set them up in the promised land, *and* the God we talk about today. We see that the Israelites believed many things about God, not all of which were accurate, as God corrects them in later revelations, as we've just seen. We also remember his earlier correction, *"I never wanted your sacrifices . . ."* (Hosea 6:6) And as we'll see, once Jesus comes, God corrects even more misunderstandings.

THE PROBLEM WITH DEFINITIONS

Another subject that I find quite interesting is the power of language. Because we need language to communicate our ideas with one another, language is inexorably tied to our thinking, not just to express our thinking but it also determines how we think in the first place. The words we have access to determine the categories we use to classify things. This is probably less true today than it was even a few decades ago because ideas have become more globalized. There is more cross-over of languages, and with it, ideas. For example, the word *gestalt* is a German word that means "whole," but signifies the concept of the whole as something more than just its assembled parts. The word now has meaning for us English speakers that isn't captured by simply saying "whole."

The problem we have in trying to define God is that we don't have words to describe concepts that are outside of the human imagination and experience. To say, for example, that God has existed "forever" references the concept of time as we experience it. If God created time, as I believe he did, then we have no word for a being who exists outside of time that has any real meaning. Terms like "timeless" or "non-temporal" (we don't even have a good antonym for "temporal") are inconceivable ideas.

The result is that **trying to define God by using terms we understand means that we are always wrong in describing God.** In trying to put God into our linguistic categories we become heretics to some extent. The more we try, the more heretical we become. This is why the Orthodox call their theology **apophatic**, basically meaning "negative." It is easier, and safer, to talk about God in terms of what he is not. Saying that God is "non-temporal" is apophatic, as it is saying that he is not limited by our concept of time. It's the best that we can do.

However, there are a few words and concepts that are pretty safe to use, as they come directly from the Bible with enough context to be understood. For the sake of throwing in another new word, this is known as **cataphatic** theology.

THE SAME YESTERDAY, TODAY, AND TOMORROW

As we touched on a moment ago, we believe that God is **eternal** and **unchanging**, based on many verses in both the Old and New Testaments. The two concepts often go together, so we will continue with that overlap. As "eternal" is more or less beyond our comprehension, we'll simply go with that; but here are a couple of verses to back that up:

> Have you not known? Have you not heard? The LORD is the everlasting God, the Creator of the ends of the earth. He does not faint or grow weary; his understanding is unsearchable. (Isaiah 40:28)

> "I am the Alpha and the Omega, the First and the Last, the Beginning and the End." (Revelation 22:13)

Again, I don't tend to discuss things like "where did God come from" because I don't have a clue, and neither does anyone else. I'm happy just going with that.

I think the important aspect here is "unchanging," as it has real-world significance. Many people look at God in the Old Testament and then see Jesus in the New, and figure that God has changed. We've already looked at some of those verses, where it wasn't God that changed, it was humanity's view of God that changed. One of my favorite verses about God's consistency is Malachi 3:6, *"For I the* LORD *do not change; therefore you, O children of Jacob, have not perished."* This says two things about God: One, he hasn't changed. Two, the implication is that he has always been gracious and merciful and isn't about to start being mean now. Therefore, when it seems he was being vengeful in the past, it must have been a misperception. It happens.

Another verse from the New Testament says the same thing: *"Every generous act of giving, with every perfect gift, is from above, coming down from the Father of lights, with whom there is no variation or shadow due to change."* (James 1:17)

One of our issues in trying to understand God is our tendency to be **anthropomorphic**, seeing God with human characteristics. People use terms like "angry" to refer to God, and all we can imagine is human anger. Also, there are places in the Old Testament where God is said to have changed his mind, or even "repented." However, we have this from one of the Pentateuch books: *"God is not a human being, that he should lie, or a mortal, that he should change his mind. Has he promised, and will he not do it? Has he spoken, and will he not fulfill it?"* (Numbers 23:19) In both the Old and the New Testaments, God is referred to as being unchanging, so I believe it's safe to describe God that way. (Hint: So, when Jesus reveals what God is really like it's the way he's always been.)

HERE, THERE, AND EVERYWHERE

God's **omnipresence** (being everywhere at once) is an interesting concept, and our understanding has changed over the millennia. The earliest writings tend to show God as being in specific localities, and not being able to see everything at once. However, through most of Jewish history, God has been known to be present everywhere. In Jeremiah 23:23-24, God says, *"Am I a God near by, says the* LORD, *and not a God far off? Who can hide in secret places so that I cannot see them? says the* LORD. *Do I not fill heaven and earth? says the* LORD.*"*

Psalm 139:7-10 reinforces this:

Where can I go from your spirit?
Or where can I flee from your presence?
If I ascend to heaven, you are there;
If I make my bed in Sheol, you are there.
If I take the wings of the morning
and settle at the farthest limits of the sea,
even there your hand shall lead me,
and your right hand shall hold me fast.

And Proverbs 15:3 states, *"The eyes of the* LORD *are in every place, keeping watch on the evil and the good."* The New Testament appears to take this for granted, with God seeing every sparrow fall and counting the hairs on our head, and the promise to always be with us.

An associated concept is that of **omniscience**, meaning that God knows everything, as you can see from the above verses. As I mentioned earlier, recently there have been proponents of something called "process theology" and an "open" view of God who believe that God does not know everything, especially not the future. These people believe that God responds to events and learns along with us (and changes accordingly). This kind of thinking seems to place God *within* time and subject to it, meaning he is not all-powerful. While

I understand the philosophical difficulties of believing in a God who knows the future while allowing us to have free will, I have no problem accepting that. Some find it impossible to believe that God knew, for example, that the Holocaust would happen and still allowed it to happen. This problem is tied in with the belief held by many today, that everything that happens is God's will. The thinking is that as God's will is supreme and he is all-powerful, everything that happens is to be foreordained or predestined by God. This is where we can start getting into heresy, by trying to fit God into our puny human philosophical boxes.

"So why does God allow bad things to happen?" we ask. But seeing as how God gave control of the world to Adam and Eve, he should be asking us "How *we* can allow bad things to happen?" Rather than God fixing everything in real-time, he has an ultimate redemptive plan that will save the whole of creation. And, I have to believe that a short time of suffering on Earth will not compare to an eternity of something much better.

We in the Western, post-enlightenment world like to fit everything into categories. We get extremely uncomfortable with anything for which we have no comprehendible category. "Time" is a big, important category. If you don't believe me, watch *Doctor Who*. Trying to grasp the concept of being outside of time is mind-blowing. The "problem" of a God who knows the future is resolved when we understand that God is outside of time and can view all of time in one glance. Second Peter 3:8 tries to explain it this way: "*But do not ignore this one fact, beloved, that with the Lord one day is like a thousand years, and a thousand years are like one day.*" If you think of time as linear—like a classic time-line—just picture God sitting off the line, being able to see the beginning or end of the line (which is finite, although outside of our range). God drew the line, and he can show up anywhere along the line, in any direction, without having to direct everything if he chooses not to.

For that matter, some physicists have theorized that all of time—the whole timeline—exists now, so the future is happening, just further down the timeline. Think of it as a highway: your starting point and your destination exist coincidentally, but you only experience the exact place you occupy.

Time to move on.

As I have just mentioned, Christians (as well as Jews and Muslims) believe that God is all-powerful, or **omnipotent**. There are many verses attesting to this, which I won't bother to list here. It's pretty obvious that as the Creator of the universe, as we know it, he'd be more powerful than anything he created. Only man is silly enough to do something like that. Okay, here are a couple of verses, both speaking specifically of Jesus in the context of his being God (we'll get to that, too):

- He himself is before all things, and in him all things hold together. (Colossians 1:17)
- He is the reflection of God's glory and the exact imprint of God's very being, and he sustains all things by his powerful word. (Hebrews 1:3)

OMNIPOTENCE AND THE ATTRIBUTES OF GOD

The problem with cataphatic theology, as we've seen and will continue to see, is that it quickly leads to heresy and just downright stupidity at times. Western evangelical Christianity, especially of the Reformed variety, is particularly fond of listing the **attributes** of God. Some of these we've just mentioned, such as omnipotence and infinite. However, many lists are just meant to build a box for God, becoming just as prescriptive as they are descriptive. Many lists include terms such as holy, love, gracious, and merciful, as well as terms like sovereign, just, jealous, and wrath. It doesn't take long before we start to think that God may have sort of a split personality. On one hand, God is loving, gracious, and merciful, and on the other, he is bound by his sovereignty, justice, and wrath. Calvinists tend to emphasize these last three, saying that God has to send some folks to hell because he is just, he has to defend his sovereignty, etc.

Wait . . . God *has to?* What about God being all-powerful? Are God's attributes in control of God's behavior? Can't God choose to save everyone, or is he powerless to do so? Can you imagine God telling someone, "I love you and would like to save you, but you know, I'm sovereign and wrathful and there's this just thing I have to do—."

So is God in control, or not? Who put him in this attribute box?

The moral of this mess is that it is dangerous to try to define the indefinable. You always end up a heretic. So, let's continue trying to explain God without becoming heretics ourselves.

SPIRIT

The Bible says, *"God is spirit, and those who worship him must worship in spirit and truth."* (John 4:24) First off, this is a mite confusing. Seeing as Jesus, who is God as well as human, is saying this. But, I've always taken this to mean God the Father, as Jesus referred to God, who his listeners would have understood God to be. And as Jesus is now in what I expect is some spiritual realm (he's no longer physically present on Earth), and the Holy Spirit as "spirit" in its name, we can say that all of God is spirit. The Gospel of John puts it this way: *"No one has ever seen God. It is God the only Son, who is close to the Father's heart, who has made him known."* (1:18) Taking my own great advice, I am not going to try to explain this apparent contradiction further.

However, here's another way of looking at this. The universe as we know it and experience it is **material**. We can see it, feel it, measure it, and so on. We can use the scientific method to study it. Matter was created by God. God is outside of the created universe and is not made from matter, and therefore cannot be scientifically studied (which drives some scientists crazy). When Jesus was on Earth with a physical body, he made the invisible, immaterial God known (visible and material). This is also true—perhaps even more so—regarding making known God's character and nature. This concept of becoming material is referred to as **incarnation**, which is a very important word we will discuss in the next chapter.

GOD IS LOVE

Based on a human understanding of love, this might be understood as a character trait rather than an existential trait, but the Bible talks about love as if it is essential to who God is. In the first letter of John, we read,

> *Beloved, let us love one another, because love is from God; everyone who loves is born of God and knows God. Whoever does not love does not know God, for God is love. God's love was revealed among us in this*

way: God sent his only Son into the world so that we might live through him. (1 John 4:7-9)

A moment ago, I talked about those who define God with words like "righteous," which carries with it connotations of having to punish the unrighteous. While I believe God is indeed righteous, if defined properly—if God is love, then it goes without saying that what he does is out of love, and, by definition, this is also right. It also means that God responds to unrighteousness with love as well, because God is love. Psalm 116:5 says, *"Gracious is the LORD, and righteous; our God is merciful,"* and this ties God's righteousness to his being gracious and merciful.

John stated clearly that "God is love," so I am perfectly fine defining God this way. No verse says God is wrath. I also don't believe that God has any kind of insecurity requiring him to defend his glory. My God is not that small. These are non-perfect, human (anthropomorphic) traits projected on God. So, we keep this in mind when we think about God: God is in essence, love. If we see something about God that doesn't seem like love, then we need to stop and ask if this is God, or if it's someone's mischaracterization of God.

The words we use to describe God are just that: descriptive. Again, some have started to believe that these words are *prescriptive*; that is, they determine what God must be. The idea is completely ridiculous. Don't fall for this kind of game-playing.

JESUS–THE FULL REVELATION OF GOD

Jesus is where the rubber meets the road, so to speak. Some Christians think that they need to balance what they see in Jesus (the good God) with the God they think they see in the Old Testament (the God of wrath), but that's because they haven't realized the implications of Jesus's comment: "*You search the Scriptures because you think that in them you have eternal life; and it is they that bear witness about me . . .* " (John 5:39) Jesus does not need to be "balanced"—he is the crux, the heart, the point of the Bible.

John introduces Jesus this way:

> *In the beginning was the Word, and the Word was with God, and the Word was God. He was in the beginning with God. All things came into being through him, and without him not one thing came into being. What has come into being in him was life, and the life was the light of all people. The light shines in the darkness, and the darkness did not overtake it.* (John 1:1-5)

John is identifying Jesus as being God. The Greek word translated as "word" is *logos*, from where we get the word "logo." It basically meant "picture," but has a bit more meaning in Greek philosophy, as "divine reason" or the creative, organizing force of the universe. So, there's a lot of meaning in those verses. John then goes on in verse 14 to say, "*And the Word became flesh and dwelt among us, and we have seen his glory, glory as of the only son* (or "one") *from the Father, full of grace and truth.*" To drill this in a little further, we see in John 14:9 that Jesus says, "*Whoever has seen me has seen the Father.*"

So, Jesus is the full representation of God, in the flesh. Or as theologians like to say, Jesus is God **incarnate**. The God-who-is-spirit has become flesh and blood, matter, the stuff of creation. Imagine the creator of a video game finding a way to become part of his game, making himself subject to everything he programmed. Jesus was not stepping in and out of the game when he felt like it; he was in for the duration, subject to hunger, thirst, and even death. But he still acted with the full nature of God. He could say without hesitation, "You see me, you see God."

The author of the book of Hebrews (whoever he was, he was a great writer) introduces Jesus this way:

> Long ago God spoke to our ancestors in many and various ways by the prophets, but in these last days he has spoken to us by a Son, whom he appointed heir of all things, through whom he also created the worlds. He is the reflection of God's glory and the exact imprint of God's very being, and he sustains all things by his powerful word . . . (Hebrews 1:1-3)

The author does a lot in these opening lines. First, he sets up a hierarchy of sorts of God's revelation of himself: A long time ago, God spoke through prophets, etc. Now, God speaks to us directly through Jesus, **who is also the Creator**, who is the **exact imprint of God's nature**, and who upholds the universe. That's quite a resumé.

The Nicene Creed, the Church's first real attempt to define God, has this to say about Jesus:

> We believe in one Lord, Jesus Christ,
> the only Son of God,
> eternally begotten of the Father,
> God from God, Light from Light,
> true God from true God,
> begotten, not made,
> of one Being with the Father;
> through him all things were made

For us and for our salvation
he came down from heaven,
was incarnate of the Holy Spirit and the Virgin
Mary
and became truly human.
For our sake he was crucified under Pontius Pilate;
he suffered death and was buried.
On the third day he rose again
in accordance with the scriptures;
he ascended into heaven
and is seated at the right hand of the Father.
He will come again in glory to judge the living and
the dead,
and his kingdom will have no end.

The odd phrasing at the beginning, "eternally begotten, etc.," is a reference to a main issue at the Council of Nicaea where this was formulated. There was a rather large group who were teaching that Jesus was created by God and was not God. Saint Nicholas (of Santa Claus fame) is rumored to have gotten into a fistfight with the main proponent of this teaching, although it was the argument of Athanasius that swung the vote. I don't know what "begotten" means, and I doubt anyone does, only that Jesus was not created, and we believe he is God in the same way as God is God.

I suspect that this definition may not be totally accurate, because we after all are only human. But I believe it works for now, in much the same way as we explain to our young children that gravity means that everything falls. It's not perfectly accurate, but it's true enough. The point is that Jesus is 100 percent God, while also being 100 percent man. You can't separate the two realities of Jesus.

One thing that really blows my mind is to think that for most of eternity up until recently, Jesus existed without his human body. Once he became incarnate, he was grown from an infant into an adult male, *for all time.* He didn't just say, "Well, I don't need this body anymore" and go back to his pre-human state. He did trade in his decaying body for a new, eternal one (apparently similar to what we will have someday), but still with the wounds in his hands, feet, and side (John 20:27).

Don't ask me to explain it further, because I can't. I don't find it important for the here and now, but someday I will no doubt find it fascinating. I still find the "nots" to be more correct in defining who Jesus *wasn't*—he wasn't created, he is without beginning or end, he did not stop being God to become a man, and he didn't stop being a man to go back to the Father. He was not magic, he was not impervious to pain or hunger, and he had human emotions.

While some theologians believe that Jesus was a myth, I believe there is compelling evidence to show that he was indeed a real, historical figure, and also that he was executed and rose from the dead. Anthony Flew, a formerly atheist philosopher, came to that same conclusion shortly before he died. Even many people who are atheists will have to admit that there is evidence that Jesus was a real person. As far as ancient documents from all sources go, the New Testament documents are highly reliable.

What can we believe about Jesus? Considering that the Gospels were not written in a vacuum—that is, there were many, many witnesses to the events in the Gospels—there is ample reason to admit that the stories are true. So, I personally believe in the virgin birth of Jesus, that he performed miracles, that he was crucified, and that he was resurrected. I see no reason to doubt any of these things. Whether you believe in a "real" Jesus or not won't change reality; Jesus is not like Tinker Bell, kept alive by belief. Our beliefs do not affect reality, we just try to determine what reality is for our benefit.

THE TRINITY

You won't find the word "trinity" in the Bible, which is a big talking point for Jehovah's Witnesses (who deny that Jesus was God). It doesn't matter that it's not in the Bible, it's just a descriptive word assigned to a concept about the nature of God that no one really understands. Other terms meaning the same thing include "the triune God" and "three-in-one." We often pray in the name of the Father, the Son, and the Holy Spirit (or Ghost), naming the persons of the Trinity.

Christians describe God as one God in three persons. There are not three Gods, and yet the three persons are unique and distinct. Jesus is not the Father, the Father is not the Holy Spirit, and so on. Perhaps the best example of this is the baptism of Jesus.

> And when Jesus had been baptized, just as he came up from the water, suddenly the heavens were opened to him and he saw God's Spirit descending like a dove and alighting on him. And a voice from the heavens said, "This is my Son, the Beloved, with whom I am well pleased." (Matthew 3:16-17)

Here we have Jesus in the flesh, the Holy Spirit descending, and the voice of the Father coming from heaven—three distinct persons. So some would say "three gods," but the Bible also makes it very clear in both the Old and New Testaments that there is but one God. Furthermore, from the way the New Testament authors referenced "one God," it is obvious that this was a fact that was already assumed by the Church, like in James 2:19:

> You believe that God is one; you do well. Even the demons believe—and shudder!

And in Romans 3:29-30 Paul writes:

> Or is God the God of Jews only? Is he not the God of gentiles also? Yes, of gentiles also, since God is one, and he will justify the circumcised on the ground of faith and the uncircumcised through that same faith.

Because these kinds of references are almost off-hand, we need to look at the whole representation of the New Testament. For example, Paul writes in 1 Timothy 2:5, *"For there is one God, and there is one mediator between God and men, the man Christ Jesus,"* and then in Galatians 2:30 he clarifies, *"Now an intermediary implies more than one, but God is one."*

Jesus himself made the point that there is but one God and that he is one with God, as in these two statements:

> Jesus answered, "The most important is, 'Hear, O Israel: The Lord our God, the Lord is one.'" (Mark 12:29)

And,

> *My sheep hear my voice. I know them, and they follow*
> *me. I give them eternal life, and they will never perish.*
> *No one will snatch them out of my hand. My Father,*
> *in regard to what he has given me, is greater than all,*
> *and no one can snatch them out of the Father's hand.*
> *The Father and I are one."* (John 10:27-30)

The final words of Jesus as recorded in the Book of Matthew, name the three persons of the Trinity: *"Go therefore and make disciples of all nations, baptizing them in the name of the Father and of the Son and the Holy Spirit"* (28:19). Even if you try to make the case that this was an added comment inserted by Matthew or some later person, we can still attest that the existence of the Triune God was the belief of the early church.

The concept of God having multiple "persons," or *hypostases* in Greek, was not necessarily new to Christianity. This concept was also found in Jewish writings before the time of Christ, which suggested there were two hypostases, one that appeared in bodily form, and one that was unseeable.[77]

DEFINING THE TRINITY

As is usually the case in theology, whenever people start "legalizing" definitions, problems arise. As the Church grew, various opinions arose about several things, including the exact relationship between the Father, Son, and Holy Spirit. In the early fourth century, a priest named Arius was promoting the teaching that Jesus was subordinate (lesser than) God the Father, and that he was not "in the beginning." Another theologian, Athanasius, was a leader of those who held that the three persons of the Trinity were co-equal in every way. After Constantine legalized the Church, he wanted to unify the factions, so he organized what is known as the First Ecumenical Council of Nicaea, as I discussed above.

And along came Augustine (who we will be discussing at length in another chapter), a Latin-speaking Bishop, who had converted to Christianity after following a non-Christian religion as well as Neo-Platonism, both of which had a strong belief in dualism, the separation between the spiritual and the physical, the pure and the impure. He would have caused a major uproar had it not been for the fact that most of the Church did not read or speak Latin. It's a long, complicated story, but his teaching that the Holy Spirit was subordinate to both the Father and the Son led to a change in the Western wording of the Nicaean Creed and the eventual schism of the Church. Again, more on this later.

While we don't know exactly (or for that matter, even minimally) how the Trinity exists and functions, the standard Christian belief is that all three persons are co-equal and unified. As far as I know, the only distinctive difference between the three persons is that Jesus took on a human body for all time, which in no way diminished his godliness.

THE HOLY SPIRIT

Ah, yes, now we come to the Holy Spirit (last, and certainly not *least*). The Holy Spirit is a very mysterious sort, as Jesus explained, *"The wind blows where it wishes, and you hear its sound, but you do not know where it comes from or where it goes. So it is with everyone who is born of the Spirit"* (John 3:8). In the Greek, the same word is used for both "wind" and "Spirit." As I mentioned in the previous chapter, the Holy Spirit is very frightening to those Christians who prefer things ordered and legalistic and is the most controversial person of the Trinity, and teachings about the Holy Spirit have caused a great many divisions.

In the Old Testament, the Spirit of God inspired the prophets, indwelt kings, and so on, but is not generally seen as a person of a triune being. The Spirit was not thought to indwell everyone but would rest on those it wished to communicate through. The Jewish kings were "anointed" with oil (which represented the Holy Spirit) and God would send his spirit to indwell (or at least be with) the king.

The prophet Joel (thought to be perhaps one of the later prophets) prophesied a change that was to come regarding the Holy Spirit,

> "Then afterward
> I will pour out my spirit on all flesh;
> your sons and your daughters shall prophesy,
> your old men shall dream dreams,
> and your young men shall see visions.
> Even on the male and female slaves,
> in those days I will pour out my spirit."
> (Joel 2:28-29)

This was quoted by Peter in Acts 2 on the day of Pentecost when the Holy Spirit fell on the crowd and people started speaking in tongues, and so forth. Just that story is enough to scare many churches. From a Christian standpoint, the world changed on that day as the Holy Spirit did indeed come to everyone. This is also what Jesus promised his disciples:

"And I will ask the Father, and he will give you another Helper, to be with you forever, even the Spirit of truth, whom the world cannot receive because it neither sees him nor knows him. You know him, for he dwells with you and will be in you. These things I have spoken to you while I am still with you. But the Helper, the Holy Spirit, whom the Father will send in my name, he will teach you all things and bring to your remembrance all that I have said to you." (John 14: 16-17, 25-26 ESV)

At one end of the "Holy Spirit spectrum," we have those Christians who take a rather minimalist approach, where the Spirit's primary function is to convict of sin:

"Nevertheless, I tell you the truth: it is to your advantage that I go away, for if I do not go away, the Helper will not come to you. But if I go, I will send him to you. And when he comes, he will convict the world concerning sin and righteousness and judgment: concerning sin, because they do not believe in me; concerning righteousness, because I go to the Father, and you will see me no longer; concerning judgment, because the ruler of this world is judged." (John 16:7-11 ESV)

On the other end of the spectrum are those who view the Holy Spirit as the life of the party. Besides the spiritual gifts mentioned in 1 Corinthians 12 (which I won't discuss here), several churches "worship" to bring about various manifestations of the Spirit, including laughing, falling over, going into trances, shaking, having gold dust fall from the ceiling, and more I haven't heard about.

The things Jesus said about the Holy Spirit tell me these things:

1. He/She is to be a helper (some versions use the word "comforter").

2. The Holy Spirit brings truth.

3. The Holy Spirit is a continuing revelation of God.

This last point means that whatever the Holy Spirit does will be consistent with what Jesus taught and did.

A LITTLE WRAP-UP

So, we have one God, in three separate persons. This math is beyond me, but then so is E=MC². God is eternal and timeless (no beginning or end), omnipresent (everywhere), and is the Creator of all that exists. He doesn't change, in any way whatsoever. So, the God in the Old Testament is identical to Jesus and is identical to the Holy Spirit acting in our lives today. God is love (not "loving", but love itself), is Truth, and is merciful and gracious. He does not have humanity's imperfect characteristics (jealousy, anger, hate, etc.). He desires to set the world back to rights and is personally involved in creation.

I think the best way to end is with another of the Church's ancient creeds, the Apostles' Creed:

I believe in God, the Father almighty,
creator of heaven and earth.
I believe in Jesus Christ, God's only Son, our Lord,
who was conceived by the Holy Spirit,

born of the virgin Mary,
suffered under Pontius Pilate,
was crucified, died, and was buried;
he descended to the dead.
On the third day he rose again;
he ascended into heaven,
he is seated at the right hand of the Father,
and he will come to judge the living and the dead.
I believe in the Holy Spirit,
the holy catholic church,
the communion of saints,
the forgiveness of sins,
the resurrection of the body,
and the life everlasting. Amen.

The last five lines we will get to in due time.

CHAPTER 7

UNBOXING THE INCARNATION

"Okay, I think you're getting beyond me," you say.

"I don't think so," I reply. *"You seem pretty smart to me. And besides, I think I explain things pretty well."* I add, *"This is important stuff for Christians. Think of Christmas. Little baby, drummer boy, you know the story."*

"Drummer boy?"

"Just checking to see if you're still paying attention," I say. *"This chapter is about God coming to Earth and why. And in a later chapter, we'll talk about 'why' some more, because it's the whole point of Christianity."*

BIG WORD, BIGGER CONCEPT

And the Word became flesh and dwelt among us . . . (*John 1:14*)

We believe in one Lord, Jesus Christ, the only Son of God, eternally begotten of the Father, God from God, Light from Light, true God from true God, begotten, not made, of one Being with the Father; through him all things were made. For us and for our salvation he came down from heaven, was incarnate of the Holy Spirit and the virgin Mary and became truly human.[78]

Merriam-Webster defines incarnate like this:

incarnate **adjective** *in·car·nate | in-ˈkär-nət , -ˌnāt :*

~1 a: invested with bodily and especially human nature and form

~b: made manifest or comprehensible: EMBODIED[79]

Okay, big word, even bigger concept. God, through some process only God can understand, chooses to come to Earth in the most humble way imaginable, being born as an infant to an unmarried Jewish girl. We don't know for sure when Mary and Joseph were officially married, but we know that she became pregnant before being married, and as we are told, before having sex. The point is that Jesus—both God and man by birth—was born as a completely helpless infant and raised as a normal Jewish kid by a couple of very pious Jewish kids (Joseph was probably older than Mary by a decade or more).

The Creator of the universe is now present inside his creation, subject to the same experiences every other Jewish kid had. He was circumcised, and I assume that he cried. The God who created time now has to live inside of time, growing thirty years or so before he began his public life. Note that he didn't *have* to—he could have just appeared out of the desert, or whatever. But, he *chose* to experience everything as a fully human being, and all of you know how painful that process can be.

This is huge. To me, the big miracle is not becoming incarnate (a doozy in itself), the real miracle is not exploding the universe in the process. I mean, whoa . . . If you ever need something to meditate on, just sit and think about this. It's mind-blowing. Timeless all-powerful being crying in a cradle, having to listen to some kid play a toy drum (yes, that's a joke).

Paul lays this out in his letter to the Philippians, to give them a lesson on humility:

> *Let the same mind be in you that was in Christ Jesus, who, though he existed in the form of God, did not regard equality with God as something to be grasped, but emptied himself, taking the form of a slave, assuming human likeness. And being found in appearance as a human, he humbled himself and became obedient to the point of death—even death on a cross. (Philippians 2:5-8)*

Note that Paul isn't providing a technical explanation here but making a point. This, by the way, is the rule of thumb when reading Paul, something that many people miss. He refers to Jesus and God separately, not to imply that they are distinct beings, but rather to distinguish between the person of God who exists as spirit and God who exists as the man Christ Jesus. I know, it is a bit sci-fi. Then we add the Holy Spirit into the mix, which is how we end up with what we call the Trinity. One God, three persons. We've just talked about this. Many people have tried to explain it, and my hunch is that all the explanations are a bit (or a lot) wrong. Some are outright heretical. But, as we will see, this is not a new concept dreamt up by Paul. The Jews had already surmised that God existed in different *hypostases*, or forms. The New Testament writers just made the connection to Jesus as God, now incarnate.

This thesis regarding the integrity of the Incarnation, however, is not adequately expressed by saying that God's Son assumed human nature. It must say, rather, that the Son assumed the full human condition; He entered into and experienced history, not in a general and abstract way, but by the organic insertion of His personal being into a determined time and specific circumstances. Otherwise it would not be the case that "in all things He had to be made like His brethren." (Hebrews 2: 17)[80]

When we put the information about Jesus together, we have God Jesus who is identified as the creator of the universe, living on Earth as a real, down-to-earth (pun) man who was still God at the same time. He could have held on to all his power but chose to set it aside ("empty himself") to become a poor itinerant preacher in a country under the control of a government that believed their leader was God. (Shows how human they thought their gods were.) He even let them execute him and forgave them all as he was dying.

So, this is the complete representation of God, right here. I find it very hard to consider anyone who asserts their power over another—or seeks that power—a Christian. There's no room for white supremacy, manifest destiny, America (or any other country) first, or most of what we think of as success. Jesus spoke several times about humility, putting others first, and serving others, and demonstrated those throughout his ministry.

So, feel free to ask, "What would Jesus do?"

Then ask yourself, "Do I like this God?" And, "Is this the God that my church teaches?"

HOW DUALISM RUINED CHRISTIANITY, PART ONE

One of the problems with understanding the incarnation is the teaching of dualism that was inserted into Christian theology by Augustine of Hippo. Augustine, born in 354, was an early bishop of the Church in what is now Algeria. He first belonged to a religion known as Manichaeism, then later adopted a Neoplatonist philosophy. He converted to Christianity in 386, but unfortunately carried over some ideas from his earlier life, especially the concept of dualism. Manicheans held to a dualistic worldview in which there was a good spiritual world in battle with the evil material world. Spiritual good, physical bad. Platonism also held to a similar sort of dualism where an invisible line separates the world of perfect ideas from the imperfect material world, below.

So, when Augustine adopted Christianity, he came with all kinds of philosophical baggage which he did not discard but folded into his new religion. My analysis is that Augustine never fully adopted what the Orthodox call their *phronema*, a Greek word that refers to the Orthodox mentality or mindset, which for the Orthodox is as important as their theology, if not more so.[81] While he was a Christian, he never became fully "Eastern." So armed with his non-Christian ideas of dualism, he saw the spiritual as good and heavenly, whereas the physical world was corrupt and evil. This, of course, has led to all kinds of terrible teachings and suffering as can be evidenced today in Western Christianity, especially Catholicism and evangelicalism. Since

Augustine wrote in Latin rather than in Greek as the other church leaders did, much of his wilder ideas were not discovered by the Church until sometime later. As a result, Augustine holds a rather unusual distinction in the Eastern Church: honored as a Bishop but dismissed as a theologian.

Fortunately, the Church had already decided that Jesus was of a dual nature, fully God and fully man, before Augustine came around, so the Nicene Creed was free from that kind of influence. Of Jesus's divine nature, it states that he was:

> *eternally begotten of the Father,*
> *God from God, Light from Light,*
> *true God from true God,*
> *begotten, not made,*
> *of one Being with the Father;*
> *through him all things were made.*

I can't tell you how accurate this is because we don't know the inner workings of God, and we don't have answers to questions like, "How can Jesus be eternal and still be begotten?" As I've said, I think that any time we try to describe God we are likely wrong to some extent, and that's to be expected. Based on the teachings of the Apostles and those other first and second generation Christians who passed on the earliest teachings of the Church, this is what they formulated.

Regarding the human nature of Jesus, the creed continues:

> *For us and for our salvation*
> *he came down from heaven,*
> *was incarnate of the Holy Spirit and the Virgin Mary*
> *and became truly human.*

The point here is Jesus is fully God in the same way God is God, and fully human as we are human. It is a case of one plus one equals one with two natures. It's wrong to say that Jesus's body was human and his spirit was God, as a dualist might be tempted to. We believe that Jesus was human, body, soul, mind, spirit, whatever and that he was God's body, soul, spirit, mind, whatever. To try to describe it further just invites heresy, more so than I probably have done already. As Bradley Jersak writes,

> *Christ was and is fully human and fully divine at all times. In fact, he must be fully human in order to experience our death, and fully divine in order to overcome that death. In the Incarnation, God the Son assumes (takes on) humanity, makes it his own, and in so doing, not only restores but perfects humanity.*[82]

As I have stated previously, the concept of God having multiple "persons," or *hypostases* in Greek, was not necessarily new to Christianity. This concept was also found in Jewish writings before the time of Christ, which suggested there were two hypostases, one that appeared in bodily form, and one that was unseeable.[83] Likewise, the *logos* or "Word of the Lord" was "understood as a divine Person who had appeared and spoken to the prophets in bodily form."[84] When John opens his gospel with " . . . *the Word became flesh,*" he is not creating a new metaphor but is directly introducing Jesus as hypostases of God. (If you don't read some Eastern Orthodox sources, you'll never learn some of this stuff. Many Western theologians, I'm afraid, tend to ignore things that mess up their preconceptions.)

While some believe that the concept of the Trinity— one God in three persons—was a later idea that formed over time, however, references to the Trinity are found in the New Testament, such as in 2 Corinthians 13:14: *"The grace of the Lord Jesus Christ and the love of God and the fellowship of the Holy Spirit be with you all."* Stephen DeYoung, who pastors an Antiochian Orthodox Church in Louisiana, writes,

> Far from revealing a primitive stage of Christian belief regarding Christ from which later dogmas regarding the Holy Trinity and Christology would evolve, St. Paul's writings reveal a Christology and Trinitarian belief already fully formed. These earliest of the New Testament writings were able to present such an understanding because St. Paul is interpreting the revelation of Jesus Christ in the flesh and the coming of the Holy Spirit through the lens of existing Jewish understandings of the God of Israel. Rather than struggling to concoct a middle ground between monotheism and polytheism, St. Paul reveals the true nature of the divine figures with whom his readers were already familiar through the tradition in which they had received the Scriptures.[85]

THE INCARNATION IS IT

While Western Christianity (and the whole Western world) is big on celebrating Christmas (our entire economy depends on it), they tend to gloss over the full impact of the incarnation itself. For me, the incarnation is the thing. It's the point. The incarnation is not the means to an end, it is an end in itself. The Eastern Church still considers the incarnation to be more important than Jesus's death and resurrection.[86] I would go so far as to say that the incarnation even includes Jesus's birth, life, death, and resurrection. It's a package deal.

It was one mission that Jesus undertook, and that mission was the main point of all of history. Or you could say it was the main point of time itself. I'll say it right now: The incarnation was the main point of time itself. The folks who started numbering the years even used the incarnation as the central focus—ground zero, as it were—of history (or at least attempted to—they may have been off a couple of years).

I believe this was God's plan from the beginning, as hinted in Genesis 3:15—"*I will put enmity between you and the woman, and between your offspring and hers; he shall strike your head, and you shall strike his heel.*" While somewhat obscure, I think it hints at a plan to put things right at some point in the future with an "offspring" of the woman. It's not a huge jump to suspect this is referring to Jesus.

Irenaeus, a second century theologian, believed that the incarnation was planned even before humanity was created. He wrote, "*Forinasmuch as He had a pre-existence as a saving Being, it was necessary that what might be saved should also be called into existence, in order that the Being who saves should not exist in vain.*"[87]

Irenaeus, by the way, was a bit more than just a random theologian. He was from Smyrna, the home of a guy named Polycarp. Polycarp knew John (of the Gospel of John fame) and was taught by John. Irenaeus was born and raised in the Church, and so was a student of Polycarp, and so had a lot of insight into what John knew. Fortunately, we have a rather substantial amount of Irenaeus's writings. On the incarnation, he writes:

> *For it was for this purpose that the Word of God was made man, and he who was the Son of God became the Son of Man: so that man, having been*

taken into the Word and receiving adoption, might become the son of God. For it was not possible that we could have attained to incorruptibility and immortality unless we had been united to incorruptibility and immortality. But how could we be joined to incorruptibility and immortality, unless incorruptibility and immortality had first become what we ourselves are? [And this was] so that what was corruptible might be swallowed up by incorruptibility, and what was mortal by immortality, so that we might receive adoption as sons.[88]

He also said more specifically that Christ *"became what we are in order to enable us to become what he is."* A couple of centuries later another famous theologian, Athanasius, put it more boldly: *"God became like us, so that we might become like God."* This concept is known in the Orthodox Church as *theosis*. No one takes this to mean that we become gods in the way that the LDS (Mormon) Church believes, but rather, as Irenaeus explained above, God came down and bridged the gap to become one of us so that we could have the kind of relationship with God that would enable us to become Christlike (a word Christians seem okay with).

Thomas Aquinas summarized the patristic teaching on this point when he wrote: In Christ each nature is united to the other in the person; by reason of this union the divine nature is said to be incarnate (natura divina incarnata) and the human nature is said to be deified (et humana natura deificata).[89]

Or, as Paul said, *"And we all, with unveiled face, beholding the glory of the Lord, are being transformed into the same image from one degree of glory to another."* (2 Corinthians 3:18)

This is more than simply becoming *like* Jesus, but the point is unity with God, as Jesus prayed: *". . . that they may all be one, just as you, Father, are in me, and I in you, that they also may be in us, so that the world may believe that you have sent me."* (John 17:21) The Buddhists have a concept known as *Nirvana* (not the band) which refers to the hoped-for result of the Buddhist life, a state of perfect peace, and no further sense of self. This is not the unity that Christians refer to. A place of perfect peace, yes, unity with God and others, yes, but no loss of self. Jesus's incarnation showed us that our bodies and our sense of self are important.

Now perhaps you can see why I say that the incarnation is "it." If God hadn't become created matter, he'd still be out of reach. He'd be spirit-God, beyond time, etc., and we'd be dust (evil dust, according to some). However, God said "I don't have a problem with dust. I created matter. I like matter. I have no problem becoming matter myself." He ate fish, he ate bread, he drank wine. He got tired. He cried. And when left, he said,

"And I will ask the Father, and he will give you another Helper, to be with you forever, even the Spirit of truth, whom the world cannot receive, because it neither sees him nor knows him. You know him, for he dwells with you and will be in you . . . In that day you will know that I am in my Father, and you in me, and I in you." (John 14: 16-17, 20)

It's all pretty cosmic, I know. But if you accept that there is a spiritual (nonmaterial) reality, you're halfway there. While on Earth, doing our day-to-day stuff, we can become more like God, with more godlike characteristics, and more godlike thinking (back to the Philippians 2 verse I quoted back a few pages). We will begin to see others more like God sees them. And, as my favorite gospel-writer John says,

> *Beloved, let us love one another, because love is from God; everyone who loves is born of God and knows God. Whoever does not love does not know God, for God is love. God's love was revealed among us in this way: God sent his only Son into the world so that we might live through him. In this is love, not that we loved God but that he loved us and sent his Son to be the atoning sacrifice for our sins. Beloved, since God loved us so much, we also ought to love one another. No one has ever seen God; if we love one another, God abides in us, and his love is perfected in us. By this we know that we abide in him and he in us, because he has given us of his Spirit. And we have seen and do testify that the Father has sent his Son as the Savior of the world. (1 John 4:7-14)*

RAMIFICATIONS OF THE INCARNATION

A major impact of having an incarnational theology (in which God inhabits his creation), is that God inhabits his creation. The fact that Jesus was completely human, having to eat, drink, go to the bathroom, and so on, means that matter is not evil. This blows the concept of dualism to shreds, especially where the material world is supposedly less holy than the nonmaterial world. Jesus did not have a pseudo-material body; he had a real one. It wasn't some kind of fake movie prosthetic body. There were no special effects. He didn't have a stunt double. God wasn't pulling a fast one on us. He became common, ordinary, human flesh, the same kind you and I have. His body died, just like ours will. So what conclusions can we draw from this? Simply that matter—the physical creation—is not "evil." Your physical body (kind of redundant) is not evil or unholy. God has no problem using matter, for any purpose he wants to. He can even indwell it!

> *Irenaeus reasoned, "Unless Christ is fully human, then He has nothing in common with Adam. And if He has nothing in common with Adam, He cannot be the new Adam. And if He is not the new Adam, then He cannot represent the fullness of humanity."*[90]

As Peter Enns points out, *"The Council of Chalcedon rightly concluded that if Christ only appeared to be human, then the death and resurrection are not real."*[91] This is an important point, and we'll get back to it.

The whole concept that has pervaded Christianity for years is that "spiritual good, physical bad" is hogwash. When Paul refers to "the flesh" he is not necessarily talking about something evil; sometimes he is merely talking about that part of us that returns to dust.

> *The "sinful flesh" (sarxs hamartias) of which Paul writes in Romans 8:2, the flesh assumed by God's Son, is the same flesh of which Paul complains all through the previous chapter. According to St. Paul, that is to say, the flesh assumed by the Son of God was identical to our own. Becoming like us (en homoiomati), He took on "the flesh of sin"—sarxs hamartias. In view of the New Testament's insistence that Christ was sinless—and that death, consequently, had no hold on Him—Paul's description of the Incarnation in this text of Romans seems unusually bold. It is valuable for its clear assertion that the Son, in the Incarnation, assumed our humanity with the weaknesses and disadvantages of its fallen state.*[92]

By God becoming common, ordinary matter, it shows that matter is not evil, or unholy, or something that we can dismiss out of hand. Creation was good then, and it's good now.

> . . . if the fact of the Incarnation means that the Word adopted the fullness of human experience— sin excepted, says the Epistle to the Hebrews— then nothing human can be excluded from the study of redemption. The Word, embracing our humanity, took possession of all of it in order to redeem all of it.[93]

He was, as they say, "all in."

Another ramification of the incarnation involves a crazy teaching that says God is too holy to look at sin, which is why Jesus had to come to stand in front of us so God can't see us directly. *What?* Unless you're saying that Jesus wasn't really God (which we've already dealt with, hopefully) we have Jesus who lived in the middle of sin for thirtysomething years. He was born in the middle of it, raised in the middle of it, and died in the middle of it. It seems to me that God looked at a whole lot of sin and loved the world despite it. And that great writer of Hebrews says that we now have the confidence to personally enter the Holy of Holies (where the presence of God dwelt) (Hebrews 10:19).

This "God can't look at sin" heresy eventually means that at the cross the Father has to look away; the Father and Jesus have to part ways, splitting God in two. This is a theological no-no. If Jesus is God, and he can look at sin, what does that mean for Jesus? And if Jesus takes upon himself the sin of the world, then the Father would have had to say, "Sorry, kid, you're on your own."

Neither of these scenarios are acceptable without questioning the nature of God.

Therefore, the material world is completely suitable for God to indwell, even in its current fallen state. Matter, the Earth, all creatures, and even you, are not evil or profane. Everything is holy. God is no longer "confined" (as if he ever was) to the Holy of Holies, and the Holy Spirit is poured out on all flesh.

Environmentalism, therefore, is also a Christian duty. I'd even say that it's a holy duty. We don't toss aside people (or we shouldn't), and we shouldn't *not* care about nature. It is not "all going to burn," as they liked to say in the '70s. Now I am not one of those panentheists who believe that God indwells all of creation (again, kind of like the Force). I do believe that God can use whatever matter he wants for any purpose, like talking through a burning bush or a donkey. There are good arguments for God to impart grace through physical things such as water for baptism or bread and wine for communion. I don't think it needs to "become" the body and blood of Jesus to serve its purpose. I just believe that God has shown that he is willing and able to use anything at all.

So, just forget any notion you may have had about your spirit being holy and your body being sinful. Just forget it.

THE CONSTRAINTS ON THE INCARNATION

Many people seem afraid to treat Jesus as a man, thinking they are not giving enough credit to his God-nature. So, Jesus becomes like some kind of superhero, a Superman walking around in Clark Kent glasses. He walked on water, after all, and did miracles. Do you think Peter ever gave Jesus a buddy-slug on the arm or did the Disciples all sit around and gaze at him in awe all day long? Chances are those who encountered him treated him as just a plain, ordinary Jew. Consider how the crowds treated him, and then think of how the Roman Soldiers treated him. He was pushed, shoved, and spit on. We do need to start thinking about the man Jesus as just that if we are to fully understand and appreciate the incarnation. Remember, the physical body is just as holy as anything else—ours as well as his.

The incarnation also means that Jesus was rooted in first century Israel. Whether or not he understood astrophysics (he was the Creator, after all) as a man is irrelevant. He would have been taught the first century languages. He spoke using first century ideas and phrases. We don't ever see him correcting inaccurate understandings of science or history. He *was,* from a first century standpoint, a first century Jew and shared in the community of first century Judea.

Another constraint of being incarnated as a first century Jew is that Jesus was not, and never will be, white. To say that Jesus was white is to deny the fact of the incarnation. If Jesus was just a spiritual construct, we could rewrite him as white, black, Asian, Hispanic, Native American, or whatever else to relate to him more fully, but that is to deny the reality of the incarnation. He is not *just* a spiritual construct, but lived in a specific place in a specific time and everything he did has to be seen as happening in that certain space and time.

So, then, this takes a little work for us non first century Jews (that means all of us, including present-day Jews), as we have to learn what place Israel had in the early first century. These were not the winners of the world, they were not the great Israel who could best any enemy, they were a long-conquered people, whose promised land had been under the control of others for many, many years. This means that Native Americans can relate to Jesus much better than white northern Europeans like me. Refugees can relate to Jesus better than me. You've got the idea. This is what the incarnation means. To ignore this reality is to ignore the incarnation.

WHAT THIS DOES *NOT* MEAN

This, however, does not mean that Jesus isn't everyone's savior or that he cannot relate to everyone equally. From a spiritual point of view, Jesus is indeed white, black, Native American, Hispanic, Asian, rich, and poor, and he is even female because in Christ there is no race nor class distinction nor gender: *"There is neither Jew nor Greek, there is neither slave nor free, there is no male and female, for you are all one in Christ Jesus"* (Galatians 3:28 ESV). Jesus also hinted at this lack of gender when he said, *"For in the resurrection they neither marry nor are given in marriage, but are like angels in heaven."* (Matthew 22:30 ESV) This does not mean we will *be* angels (whatever they are—I won't get into that), but they were understood by the first century Jews to be non-sexual. It's another off-hand reference that no one understands, so we can't make too much of that. The point is that Jesus, being a Jewish male, is not showing preference to Jewish males but pragmatism, seeing as how God had been working through the Jews for centuries. (Being God's "chosen" people does not necessarily make you more successful.) The bottom line for us today is that Jesus is *not* preferential to white males, as much as some people would like to think.

208 • ALDEN SWAN

Humanity—all people—are created in the image of God. I don't know exactly what that means, except that as hard as it is to imagine, humans are the closest thing to God besides himself. This is true regardless of race, gender identification, culture, education, social status, etc. From this standpoint, God is like us. Kind of.

Whoa, what?

Basic logic: if we are like God, then God must be like us, at least to a point. Never forget the first century Jewish Jesus because we need to understand him in context, but also know that God is also like you, whoever you are. You are all—everyone—created in God's image, and so reflect some aspects of God. I don't have any references for this, as this is just my thinking; I threw this in for free.

Another of my thoughts is that perhaps Jesus became the lowest of the low (a homeless Jewish man subject to Roman rule) in that he might relate to everyone. He had already had everything, as Paul mentions in Philippians 2, but he didn't consider that something to be held on to. Rather, he gave up everything to be a servant to all.

It may seem like I am contradicting myself, and perhaps I am to some extent. Such is the nature of trying to explain in an inexplicable. The bottom line, Jesus had a real Jewish man's body, but that does not limit him from relating to everyone.

OTHER RAMIFICATIONS OF INCARNATIONAL THEOLOGY

First, let me emphasize once again that when I talk about the incarnation, I am talking about the whole package from birth to death and back again. Modern thinking likes to break things down and examine their parts, looking at what was accomplished by Jesus's birth, what was accomplished at the cross, etc. I suppose that could have some benefit at times, but usually, it just fractures the storyline. I believe Jesus' mission was to be born, grow up, spend a few years teaching people about God and the Kingdom, dying to set us free from sin and death, resurrecting, and ascending into heaven, so to speak. Had all this not happened, Jesus wouldn't have completed what he was sent to do. Orthodox author Patrick Henry Reardon has a few thoughts on this:

> First, God's Son assumed our flesh in order obediently to die in that flesh. Second, His death in the flesh meant the destruction of the devil, "who had the power of death." According to Hebrews, then, God's Son took flesh in order to die, and He died in order to overcome death and the devil.[94]

> `Thus, Irenaeus writes of our Lord's birth, which the Word of God underwent for our sake, to be made flesh, that He might reveal the resurrection of the flesh and take the lead of all in heaven.[95]

And here he breaks the life of Jesus down in a manner, still emphasizing that, as he says, "the entire 'event' of Jesus was redemptive:"

> Thus, the threefold impediment (kolyma) to man's deification was overcome in three ways (tropoi): first, the Son's Incarnation, whereby He opened a path for man's return to union with God; second, His sacrificial death on the Cross, by which He vanquished the reign of sin; and, third, His Resurrection from the dead, by which He delivered us from that final enemy. According to this formulation, the entire "event" of Jesus Christ

was redemptive, beginning with His personal and permanent assumption of our human existence.[96]

Bradley Jersak has this to say:

> *While the Cross was truly a definitive event in our salvation, we must not forget or negate all that was accomplished for our salvation through the Incarnation, nor the essential elements yet to happen through Christ's resurrection from the dead, his descent into hades, his ascension into heaven and his final return in glory.*[97]

My goal here is to make the point that the incarnation, life, death, resurrection, and ascension of Jesus were redemptive. Furthermore, it was redemptive not only of select humans but of all creation.

> *. . . for the creation was subjected to futility, not of its own will, but by the will of the one who subjected it, in hope that the creation itself will be set free from its enslavement to decay and will obtain the freedom of the glory of the children of God. We know that the whole creation has been groaning together as it suffers together the pains of labor, and not only the creation, but we ourselves, who have the first fruits of the Spirit, groan inwardly while we wait for adoption, the redemption of our bodies. (Romans 8:20-23)*

Once again, Jesus became man to redeem all of creation. Not a small goal.

THEOSIS (AKA "DEIFICATION")

Okay, this is where many evangelical theologians lose their minds because it sounds too Buddhist or Mormon or something. The incarnation is important because, as the early Church Fathers put it, *"God became man so that man might become God."* This doctrine is known as *theosis*, a fairly acceptable term as very few know what it means. Another word is **deification**, which causes more than a few people to choke. One of the best explanations I have found is again from Brad Jersak:

> *This bold affirmation is no mere "New Age" drivel. It is the inspired revelation of the Psalmist (Psalms 82:6) and of Jesus Christ. (John 10:34) The early church theologians, including Irenaeus, Athanasius, and Augustine, echoed it unanimously. As a major Christian doctrine, it came to be known as deification or divinization or theosis.* **Not that we literally become God (as in the Trinity) or equal to God, but rather, as Peter said, "We become partakers of the divine nature."** *(emphasis mine, 2 Pet. 1:4)*[98]

We know that humanity (all of it) was created to be in a relationship with God and to exist in unity. This was Jesus's prayer:

> *"I do not ask for these only, but also for those who will believe in me through their word, that they may all be one, just as you, Father, are in me, and I in you, that they also may be in us, so that the world may believe that you have sent me. The glory that you have given me I have given to them, that they may be one even as we are one, I in them and you in me, that they may become perfectly one, so that the world may know that you sent me and loved them even as you loved me." (John 17:20-23 ESV)*

Paul echoes this in a slightly different way (again, emphasis is mine):

*All this is from God, who reconciled us to himself through Christ and has given us the ministry of reconciliation; that is, **in Christ God was reconciling the world to himself,** not counting their trespasses against them, and entrusting the message of reconciliation to us.* (2 Corinthians 5:18, 19)

I have heard it suggested (I really can't remember from whom) that the incarnation was not an afterthought or rescue plan put into effect after Adam sinned, but that this was the plan from the beginning, to create this unity between God and his creation. Until God took the first step to become one with man in the person of Jesus, there was no way for the creation to make that step. It was God who lowered himself so that he might raise us up.

And yes, while our salvation is from sin and death, our redemption also includes our deification: *"And we all, with unveiled face, beholding the glory of the Lord, are being transformed into the same image from one degree of glory to another. For this comes from the Lord who is the Spirit."* (2 Corinthians 3:18 ESV) We'll get into more of this in Chapter 8 when we discuss the topic of atonement.

At the danger of getting a bit mystical, the process of deification has already begun for those of us in whom the Holy Spirit is working. At the risk of sounding a bit heretical, I believe this process is also underway in at least some people in whom the Holy Spirit is at work without their knowledge. Quoting one of my favorite authors, C. S. Lewis,

"There are no ordinary people. You have never talked to a mere mortal. Nations, cultures, arts, civilizations— these are mortal, and their life is to ours as the life of

a gnat. But it is immortals whom we joke with, work with, marry, snub and exploit—immortal horrors or everlasting splendors."[99]

As Dietrich Bonhoeffer said, *"The Incarnation is the ultimate reason why the service of God cannot be divorced from the service of man."*[100] Or as Jesus put it, *"Truly, I say to you, as you did it to one of the least of these my brothers, you did it to me."* (Matthew 25:40)

The incarnation changed everything—everything you see and touch is sacred, and everyone you meet is holy and is, even more than, an emissary of God. (I am slightly overwhelmed by this thought as I write this . . .) The incarnation means that God is no longer somewhere else, or is something unreachable. There is no longer a need for a priest or intermediary to approach God. God's nature is already at work in us and in the world around us, even if we can't see it at the moment. The incarnation, once again, is "it."

Before we go, once more from the creed:

*For us and for our salvation
he came down from heaven,
was incarnate of the Holy Spirit and the
virgin Mary
and became truly human.*

CHAPTER 8

WHATEVER HAPPENED TO WESTERN CHRISTIANITY?

"Now we're getting somewhere," you say. "This is going to be good."

"Hopefully it is," I respond. *"More history, a bit more philosophy, and some theology. We're in for a good time."*

"You're weird."

ONE WORD–AUGUSTINE

While many would argue with me about whether Augustine messed up the Western Church or was the most brilliant theologian of all time, I think most would agree that for good or ill, Augustine was a turning point for Western Christianity. As Fr. Michael Azkoul writes,

> *So important a figure is he that his theology is ordinarily perceived to be the supreme articulation of the Christian Faith. Thus, an attack on Augustine is commonly taken as an attack upon Christianity herself; and to abandon Augustinianism is to abandon the Church.[101]*

His theological ideas are at the crux of many of the divisions between Eastern and Western Christianity and form the foundation for Roman Catholicism as well as Calvinism, Lutheranism (to a point), and modern evangelical churches. Augustine can be credited with the doctrines of original sin, predestination, and just war theory. And he laid some of the early groundwork for penal substitutionary atonement (PSA), although we can put most of the blame on Calvin for that.

My quest for a more unadulterated theology began when I started listening to a lecture series some years back on the life of Augustine. Until then, I was fairly content with a basic understanding of Lutheran theology and knew only that Augustine was a guy whom the Augustinians were named after (Luther had been an Augustinian monk). I soon realized that Mr. Augustine had some issues and that his theological innovations may not have been healthy. The more I learned, the more I realized just how deep his rabbit hole went, and began rethinking several things, especially penal substitutionary atonement (the teaching that God had to kill someone due to original sin, so he killed Jesus).

It is important to note that most people writing about Augustine have been raised in an Augustinian environment, so the default position is to look at him in a rather favorable light. Most non-Orthodox Christians accept the notion of original sin as "gospel." The reason that most of us today see Augustine's ideas as so reasonable is that we were either raised or converted into a belief system that accepted these ideas are true. How many would question the notion that the flesh is evil compared to the spirit, or that we are born sinful? It is these and later developments by those who came after Augustine that make up the basis for both Roman

Catholicism and evangelicalism, the two main wings of Western Christianity. Face it, we're Augustinian whether we like it or not. It takes real work to start to see around it.

It became obvious to me that to properly evaluate Augustine's theology I had to first get out from under it—escape the box, if you will—to view it objectively. There's a concept in mathematics called Gödel's Theorem which suggests that one cannot prove a system from within that system. I think that's often true about objectively critiquing a philosophical system as well. As there is no place to critique Augustinian theology from within Western Augustinian theology, I had to get to know pre-Augustinian theology as found in the early Church Fathers and the Eastern church which had largely ignored Augustine.[102] That's when the fun began, and I began to develop a more objective view of Western theology.

I already had exposure to Eastern Orthodoxy and discovered that some contemporary writings were quite helpful, both from Eastern writers as well as from Western converts who were more able to "translate" concepts from East to West. While I have appreciated and appropriated some Eastern theology, I have not converted to Orthodoxy as some of my friends have. There is a foundational mindset difference that the Orthodox would say is more important than mere theology; it is at this point that I must remain in respectful disagreement.

I should also mention that many of the same Western authors who write about Augustine know little or nothing of very early church theology or the Eastern/Orthodox church, even to the point of assuming that the Roman Church was the original church and that Augustine is considered a saint by both East and West.

Point to remember: most Western church historians have a very skewed understanding of church history, as it has been handed down through the Roman Catholics. Did I just say that church history is just as suspect as American history? Yes, I did.

AUGUSTINE'S BACKGROUND

By the way, my retelling of things will be skewed as well—it's the way things are. I've already revealed my take on Augustine, so just keep this in mind. Facts are facts; however, the contexts differ. I should and will mention here that the basic historical information in this section comes from Stephen A Cooper's little book, *Augustine for Armchair Theologians*.[103] I consulted several sources, finding some conflicting information, however, most sources agreed with Cooper's retelling of the basic facts.[104]

Augustine had an eclectic background which undoubtedly flavored his Christian theology. He was born in what is now Algeria, which was then an African-Roman state. He was raised a Christian by his mother, although he strayed early. For one thing, he couldn't accept the Christian teachings on sex and marriage and partied quite a bit with his friends. When at school at seventeen, he began living with a woman and fathered a child. He also got involved with a cult called the Manicheans, who believed that there are two ruling powers, one good and one evil, who live in the heavens as the sun, moon, and stars. To them, Jesus came to be a source of light but was not a savior, per se. Augustine also drifted into astrology for a time. Because he had studied astronomy in school, he eventually began to doubt this nonsense. During his later years as a Manichean, he started listening to the teaching of a priest named Ambrose who preached a figurative understanding of the Bible, which Augustine liked and began blending some Christianity in with his Manicheist beliefs.

For a few years, he held to an odd mix of Christian/ Manicheist beliefs, then he became a Neo-Platonist[105], adopting Plato's thoughts on the dual nature of reality. The light/dark dualism of Mani became a spiritual/ physical dualism, although there was still a good versus evil component. Spiritual became good, physical became sinful or evil. Neo-Platonism also added an element of mysticism to philosophy, teaching that we can experience higher levels of reality with the goal of becoming God. Augustine saw some parallel thinking to that of Christianity and at that time saw Jesus as a man who had achieved this.

Meanwhile, his personal life was still not stellar. At the coaxing of his mother, he sent his girlfriend away so that he could be engaged to a girl of his same social status. She was not yet old enough to be married (marriage age in the Roman Empire was about eleven or twelve) and so there had to be a two-year engagement. Augustine decided that he couldn't wait two years to have sex again, so he found a mistress to tide him over. (This background is important in understanding Augustine's views on sin, etc.)

Then, Augustine had some sort of revelatory experience by which he came to understand that God as the Creator is superior to all the universe, physical and spiritual, and he chose to convert to Christianity. He also decided to "subdue the flesh" and became celibate, ending his engagement and other activities. Augustine took his vows seriously, becoming a priest, and eventually became the Bishop of Hippo, another Roman/Algerian city.

He was a prolific writer, putting a lot of his thoughts on paper. His first major book is called *Confessions*, which is important for a couple of reasons. From a literature standpoint, this is the first real autobiography, in which he relays the above history in great (and often painful, in my opinion) detail. The other reason is that he reveals a lot about himself which helps us evaluate his later theology. A lot of his writings were to resolve various conflicts in the Roman branch of the Church, of which there were many—including some that were just political rather than theological. However, much of his theology came from his arguments against various teachings which he believed were erroneous.

Perhaps the most crucial issue he dealt with was that of Pelagius, who taught that God had given man the ability—without further help from God—to achieve that which he was called to do, including being saved. Where Pelagius thought that man could save himself, Augustine went to the opposite extreme, arguing that man had absolutely no ability to contribute to his salvation—it was by God alone. He also wrote books dealing with the Trinity (another source of heresy) and of course, his other well-known book *The City of God*, dealing with the Church in the context of secular society.

All his writing was in Latin, which kept him out of the mainstream of church theology, as the rest of the Church spoke Greek. While the Greeks knew Augustine at the time, they saw him as dealing mainly with African-Roman Church issues and didn't realize until much later the impact of his theology. He was quoted in the West over the centuries in dealing with various issues, but was noticeably absent in the East, even if other Western theologians were mentioned.[106] So, he was ignored in the East, and argued about in the West, for several centuries. He wasn't an authority in the Roman Church until the later Middle Ages.

NON-WESTERN VIEWS OF AUGUSTINE

In my continued research in writing this book (which causes me to be constantly rewriting what I've just written), I came across what turns out to be the source that I've been looking for for years. The only problem is that the book is now out of print. I did find a used copy for sale—for $264. Fortunately, I was able to find an archived copy online, for free. It can be found in a scanned format, as well as in several downloadable formats on the Internet Archive: Fr. Michael Azkoul - The influence of Augustine of Hippo on the Orthodox Church.[107]

Azkoul analyzes Augustine's theology from a clearly non-Western point of view in what I think is an even-handed manner. However, the same caveat applies when reading Orthodox critiques of the West, as you have to keep in mind a basic "you're wrong because you don't agree with us" mindset. Again, everyone has their own prejudices and contexts, and reading opposing viewpoints helps maintain an approximation of objectivity.

Azkoul, as well as other sources I have read, have made a point to mention that Augustine, besides being ignored in the East, was not even an authority in the West for several hundred years. The Roman popes (they used the Latin *pope* rather than terms used in the East) did not study Augustine, and he was not even one of the favorite Western theologians. His name came up on occasion and people debated some of his ideas, but it was not until the late ninth century that he became "the supreme patristic authority in the West."[108]

Again, he was virtually ignored in the East until the later thirteenth century (aside from having some historical note). He was never "sainted," he does not have an Orthodox feast day, and "simply no visible evidence of sanctity." While he was never named a heretic (there are benefits to being largely ignored), most of his major teachings are rejected by the Orthodox, most for good reason.

One of the major complaints that the Orthodox have about Augustine is his reliance on human reason in developing his theology. It is well accepted that he merged Christianity with secular philosophy and deviated in many ways from traditional Church (remember, there was only one church at that time) belief.

> . . . "Faith and reason" is the mantra and driving principle of Catholic theology. The foundation for this was laid by St. Augustine (d. 430), whose writings so dominated the Latin Church that they fundamentally changed Western thought. Augustine was trained and educated as a philosopher and rhetorician. Later, as a bishop of the Church, he tried to resolve theological questions by the application of reason and logical deduction. Lacking a formal theological education, Augustine relied on his philosophical training. He believed that truth could not conflict with reason because God is the source of both. Therefore, he concluded that deductive reasoning can be utilized in the service of theology.[109]

Personally, I don't think Augustine's use of reason was the problem—it was that his reasoning was tainted by his own personal issues and pre-Christian beliefs. Whereas Augustine practiced "faith seeking understanding" (a later term coined by Anselm), the Orthodox Church holds that faith is essentially all you need:

> The phronema of the faithful in general, and the theologian in particular, is an unshakeable certainty about the truth of Faith.[110]

. . . and that

> Purity of soul, not human reasoning, is the key to enlightenment.[111]

For the Orthodox, having an Orthodox mindset/ phronema is more important than having a proper theology, the basic concept is that with the right phronema, theology will work itself out through faith in and putting oneself under the authority of the Holy Traditions of the Church. Augustine was never, to my knowledge, a part of this kind of community, and likely never adopted this Eastern phronema. Therefore, there is bound to be tension between the two approaches to theology.

I, too, have reservations about the Orthodox phronema, although I believe a lot of their beliefs are correct. I can appreciate Augustine's use of reason, but I see that he was too detached from the Eastern Church Fathers and teaching, and so was easily distracted by his emotional issues and mental gymnastics.

WHAT A FOOL BELIEVES–AN INTRODUCTION TO THE TEACHINGS OF AUGUSTINE

It is difficult to separate much of Augustine's thoughts into different clear categories, as most of them lean on each other like a theological house of cards. However, one major issue that stands alone is his thinking on the Trinity, the "one-God-in-three-persons" concept. Before Augustine, the Church had formulated the Nicene-Constantinopolitan Creed, which states:

> We believe in one God, the Father Almighty, Maker of heaven and earth, and of all things visible and invisible.
>
> And in one Lord Jesus Christ, the Son of God, the only-begotten, begotten of the Father before all ages. Light of Light; true God of true God; begotten, not made; of one essence with the Father, by whom all things were made; who for us men and for our salvation came down from heaven, and was incarnate of the Holy Spirit and the Virgin Mary, and became man. And He was crucified for us under Pontius Pilate, and suffered, and was buried. And the third day He rose again, according to the Scriptures; and ascended into heaven, and sits at the right hand of the Father; and He shall come again with glory to judge the living and the dead; whose Kingdom shall have no end.
>
> And [we believe] in the Holy Spirit, the Lord, the Giver of Life, who proceeds from the Father; who with the Father and the Son together is worshipped and glorified; who spoke by the prophets.
>
> In one Holy, Catholic, and Apostolic Church. I acknowledge one baptism for the remission of sins. I look for the resurrection of the dead, and the life of the world to come. Amen.

This is as definite a description of God as the Church at that time had, and that was to defend against certain heresies about Jesus being a created being. The original creed of 325 did not include the wording about the Holy Spirit, as that was not in debate. The creed was amended in 381 to add that language and complete the statement of the Trinity.

Augustine, however, questioned, "If both Jesus and the Holy Spirit came from the Father, why aren't they both sons?" So, he reasoned that the Father and Jesus were co-equal and that the Holy Spirit (a lesser Person, apparently) proceeded from both the Father and the Son. As many of you are aware, the Western Churches all use amended language that says that the Holy Spirit "proceeds from the Father **and the Son.**" This change was done without the consideration of the Church as a whole and is still a big factor in the separation of the Eastern Orthodox Churches and those of the West. The Western Churches typically talk about this as a political issue, rather than a major difference in views of the nature of God.

My take on this is that I would vote with the Orthodox on this issue, but at the same time, I think that any attempt to describe something we don't understand is likely to produce error. So, we do the best we can now, and we'll find out eventually.

THE AUGUSTINIAN AMALGAM–GRACE, PREDESTINATION, AND ORIGINAL SIN, NOT NECESSARILY IN THAT ORDER

While some people try to deny it, I think it's pretty apparent that Augustine had a guilt issue, specifically relating to his sexual history. He talks about himself in the *Confessions* as if he had a sexual addiction, which could very well be the case. Being a thinker and having a history of wacko teachings, he had to try to figure some stuff out. Where did evil come from? Did God create evil? If so, then how could God be good? He had stopped believing in the Manichean concept of equally good and evil forces but was now left with this conundrum.

He concluded that God did not create evil, but it was Adam (and Eve) who allowed evil/sin into the world. He interpreted Paul to support his thinking in coming up with **original sin**:

> *Therefore, just as sin came into the world through one man, and death through sin, and so death spread to all men because all sinned. (Romans 5:12 ESV)*

Note that Paul says nothing here about sin being transmitted to others, much less guilt. He clearly states that death spread to all men *because all sinned*. Part of the problem was that apparently, the Latin Bible mistranslated this verse. So, Augustine believed that all humanity is therefore born sinful, which caused additional problems. Because of his Neo-Platonism, he believed that the soul was spiritual as opposed to the body. If the soul is born sinful, then the soul has to somehow be transmitted from Adam to his descendants, because God wouldn't create sinful souls. Follow so far?

He answered that the human body came from the mother and the soul came from the father, so therefore sin is inherited from the father (this is how Jesus could be born sinless). This is **original sin**, which became part of the human genetic makeup ever since Adam. Humanity is evil, therefore, because of this inherited sin, and so we all deserve death (contrary to Paul's statement). Furthermore, we are not just sinful, but we also inherit Adam's guilt.

This may sound a little bit (or a lot) crazy, but this is what most Western Churches believe. And it's incredibly destructive.

> More than any other idea, the doctrine of original sin has slowly eroded our understanding of our relationship with God. Rather than seeing our lives as naturally and deeply connected with God, original sin has convinced us that human nature stands not only at a distance from God but also in some inborn, natural way as contrary to God.[112]

Now, because evil is transmitted sexually, Augustine taught that sex is evil, even in marriage. (Here we see Augustine's sense of guilt coming through.) But, because that's the only way to have kids, God allows it for that purpose only. The problem with this system is that the blessing of children means that evil is also being propagated. What to do?

The remedy for this problem is grace, which for Augustine meant "a divine but created force, whereby God compels the will of man from evil to good and negates the consequences of 'original sin' in those who are baptized."[113] Furthermore, "The grace of the Sacrament of Baptism is given to 'many' while on the 'few' is imposed irresistibly 'the grace of perseverance' which denies apostasy to the elect. Saving grace is compulsory, because, if freely given, the wicked nature of man would reject it."[114]

Got that? There is no free will. God forces grace on people and erases original sin from those who are baptized, but that doesn't mean you are necessarily "saved." For that, you need more grace, which is also compulsory. This moves us on to the concept of *predestination*.

Because humanity is evil, we cannot choose to follow God on our own, requiring grace from God. So for whatever reason, God predestines some to be saved, while others are chosen to be damned, based on God's own decision. If you are destined to be damned, you're damned if you do and damned if you don't. This concept has been called "double predestination."

So, these are all Augustinian inventions, previously unheard of in the Church, and still not accepted for a few centuries in the West and rejected in the East. They became official Roman Catholic doctrines and served as the foundation for Reformed theology and modern evangelicalism.

BUT WAIT–THERE'S MORE: JUSTICE AND WRATH

Two of the favorite words for Calvinists, fundamentalists, and many evangelicals are justice and wrath. The concept is that God is, first and foremost, just. This is not simply a matter of being fair, which I do not doubt God is, but his being just is his primary, irresistible, essential nature. God is not totally free but is bound by his being just. Evangelicals would likely cringe at that, but that is essentially what they believe, rather than God being just because he chooses to.

God's wrath is another essential element of his nature. While wrath was originally more in the vein of justice, it became warped over time to refer to intense anger. As Jonathan Edwards preached,

> *The bow of God's wrath is bent, and the arrow made ready on the string, and justice bends the arrow at your heart, and strains the bow, and it is nothing but the mere pleasure of God, and that of an angry God,*

without any promise or obligation at all, that keeps the arrow one moment from being made drunk with your blood.

The God that holds you over the pit of hell, much as one holds a spider, or some loathsome insect over the fire, abhors you, and is dreadfully provoked: his wrath towards you burns like fire . . .[115]

Augustine discusses God's wrath in his work *The Trinity*. Shawn White writes,

To begin his explanation, Augustine argues that it is by "divine justice" that the human race was handed over to the power of Satan on account of the first sin of Adam. This original sin is subsequently passed down to all who are born "of the intercourse of the two sexes." Augustine claims that all humans are, by origin, "under the prince of the power of the air who works in the sons of unbelief." (Eph 2:2) Subsequently, it is on account of original sin that all are citizens of the kingdom of Satan . . . So Augustine concludes that it is through original sin that man is subjected to the devil, "through the just wrath of God."[116]

So here we have another two concepts invented by Augustine that have redirected Christianity to a belief in what I consider to be a different God. Thus, we have two general categories of heresy: First is a shift in the view of man from being made in the image of God, destined to be reunited with God, into a sinful, evil being destined for the pit of hell. Second (and undoubtedly worse), there is a change in how we view God from a loving Creator to a terrifying, vengeful being.

So yes, I have no problem calling Augustine a heretic.

THE SLIPPERY SLOPE CONTINUES–ANSELM

Anselm, another Western/Roman Catholic theological hero, lived in the eleventh century, was a monk, theologian, and philosopher, and served as the Archbishop of Canterbury. Anselm is credited with developing the Substitution Theory of the Atonement, a precursor to the Penal Substitution Theory as popularized by Calvin. Anselm, like Augustine, leaned toward Neo-Platonism and rationalism, and was interested in further defining the mechanics of how Christ's death saved us.

For Anselm, sin was an affront to God's honor and resulted in a debt that mankind was unable to satisfy. He did not see the death of Christ as punishment, but rather, it satisfied that debt. So, Anselm's theory did not suggest that God required Jesus to die. He wrote:

> God did not, therefore, compel Christ to die; but he suffered death of his own will, not yielding up his life as an act of obedience, but on account of his obedience in maintaining holiness; for he held out so firmly in this obedience that he met death on account of it.[117]

It was all about God's honor for Anselm (a concept that grew under Calvin).

> Anselm relies on the feudal images of honor and debt to express this disharmony. Human disobedience offends the honor of God, which cannot happen without consequences. Therefore, in order for God to protect God's honor, human beings must be punished (that is, suffering life without blessed happiness), or they must make recompense for the honor they have taken from God.[118]

Erdman goes on to explain that for Anselm, God's honor was the key to holding the whole universal order together. And, for God's justice to mean anything, human sin must be dealt with. Also key to Anselm's thinking is that "satisfaction" is not "punishment." The sin debt, then, can be either *satisfied* or the sinner punished. So, we have Substitutionary Atonement, but not *Penal* (punishment) Substitutionary Atonement.

OUR NEXT CONTESTANT–THOMAS AQUINAS

Aquinas, coming a couple of hundred years after Anselm, is perhaps the first Modern thinker. While another fan of Augustine (and Anselm), he was also into Aristotle's logic. He adopted, for the most part, Anselm's thoughts on the atonement, but with some key differences.

> *Unlike Anselm, who insists that it was necessary that God demand satisfaction, Aquinas argues that God could just as easily forgive our sins without it . . . God chose this scheme of atonement because it best fulfilled both God's justice and God's mercy.*[119]

Aquinas thought out a whole scheme having to do with man's rational ability to know he was obliged to worship God, and that failure to do so created our sin debt, and our separation from God. His thinking is that atonement is not about punishment, but about restoration of our relationship with God.

> *Natural reason tells man that he is subject to a higher being, on account of the defects which he perceives in himself, and in which he needs help and direction from someone above him: and whatever this superior*

being may be, it is known to all under the name of God. Now just as in natural things the lower are naturally subject to the higher, so too it is a dictate of natural reason in accordance with man's natural inclination that he should tender submission and honor, according to his mode, to that which is above man.[120]

While Aquinas was a great thinker and had some good thoughts, especially that Jesus was not punished by God on our behalf, he is still a problem, as his thinking is founded on faulty presumptions provided by Augustine and Anselm. It is possible to have a perfect argument, but still be wrong, if one's assumptions are wrong. An example of a basic logical syllogism (argument):

If A = B

And A = C

Then B = C

This is the simplest valid logical argument, a starting point for learning logic. The conclusion is undeniably true if (and only if) your first two statements are true. However, if A does not equal C, your conclusion is not true, even if the form of the argument is proper.

This is commonly referred to as GIGO, or, garbage in, garbage out. Faulty assumptions result in flawed conclusions. This is why I don't think either Anselm's or Aquinas's conclusions are worth thinking about (other than as a fascinating exercise) because regardless of how logical they are, it's all rearranging and modifying heresy about the natures of God and humanity. Much, if not most, of Western theology is built on Augustine's flawed theology and anthropology (theories about the nature of God and theories about the nature of man), so to argue about, say, Calvinism versus Arminianism is a waste of time. It's like trying to put a puzzle together when you are given the wrong pieces.

But, it's important to look at because this is how Western Christianity got so messed up.

FROM BAD TO WORSE

Which brings us to John Calvin. Calvin was not the only Reformation theologian who spent his time building on Augustine's flawed foundation, but he was the one who turned his amp up to eleven (*This Is Spinal Tap* reference). John Calvin was French, and twenty-six years younger than Martin Luther. By the time he entered the university in Paris, the Reformation had spread, and he became "evangelized" away from the Roman Catholic Church. A group known as the Huguenots formed under Calvin's teaching, and fleeing persecution, Calvin ended up in Geneva. For whatever reason, Calvin's theology spread like wildfire throughout France, Switzerland, Scotland, England, and the Netherlands, inspiring denominations like the Presbyterians, Congregationalists, and the Dutch Reformed.

Why it spread like wildfire is beyond me, except for the fact that it provided a theology that allowed you to condemn people who disagreed with you, much like it is today. It has spread so widely that many of you are likely Calvinists without realizing it.

Calvin's doctrine of penal substitution is the understanding of the atonement most evangelicals

were raised on, whether they consider themselves
Calvinist or not, and for many this doctrine is so
central to their faith that . . . they would claim that
to relinquish this doctrine is to abandon Christianity.
But the reality is that the doctrine is not the teaching
of the New Testament nor of the early Church but the
conscious invention of John Calvin.[121]

If you believe that Jesus was executed in your place to pay for your sins, you, my friend, are a Calvinist. Congratulations.

I will get more into atonement (essentially answering the question, "How are we saved?" or more accurately, "How do we become one with God?") theories in the next chapter. For now, we will just look at Calvin's many heretical teachings. It's probably best to start with the doctrines that Calvinists are most proud of, summarized as the five points, and also known by the acronym TULIP.

Total depravity
Unconditional election
Limited Atonement
Irresistible grace
Perseverance of the saints (elect)

While some Calvinists will try to soft-peddle some of these doctrines to make them sound more reasonable, my commentary will tend to be more caustic.

TOTAL DEPRAVITY

Based on the Augustinian doctrine of original sin, all of mankind is both sinful and guilty of the sin of Adam, as we were all "in Adam" when he sinned. In other words, it's genetics. We are genetically guilty because of something an ancestor did. (It bears mentioning that many people who believe this argue against our being guilty of the sins of our early American ancestors for slavery and evils done to Native Americans.) Because of original sin and guilt, we are 100 percent totally evil. There is absolutely nothing good in us. We were originally created in God's image, but apparently, that image is now nowhere to be found. We are like insects to God, only worth being crushed. We are so bad we can't even choose to follow God. As the saying goes, we are SOL.

UNCONDITIONAL ELECTION

Continuing that thought, there is nothing we can do to choose God or attempt to save ourselves. Don't bother responding to altar calls, and please don't bother sending money to any TV preachers, because you're wasting your time. However, before we were born, God decided that he would save some of us, and let the rest of us burn. It doesn't matter if we go to church, send money to TV preachers, or pray. If we're chosen ("elect"), we're chosen, and if we're not, we're not. (But wait—irresistible grace is coming!) So theoretically, one could repent, think they were following Jesus, and find out down the road that they're not chosen. Bummer.

LIMITED ATONEMENT

"Atonement" is an English word invented to try to express the concept of mankind being reconnected to God. Literally, "at-one-ment." The meaning has been changed through misunderstanding, as with many meanings. In theology, it refers to how Jesus saved us. For Calvin, Jesus only died for those who will be chosen (no use dying for the rest). Never mind Jesus dying *"for the sins of the world"* (1 John 2:2) or *"desiring that all men be saved"* (1 Timothy 2:4). And, as we'll see, Calvin's whole concept of atonement is perverted.

IRRESISTIBLE GRACE

Once again, because we're totally depraved, we couldn't follow God if we wanted to. However, God chooses the elect and gives them grace to be able to believe, which is like an irresistible "tractor beam" that "draws some men" to Jesus (John 12:32). Now, the concept of irresistible grace or irresistible love is an interesting discussion that can't be resolved from the Bible. Can we turn away from God's love, or does Romans 8 say otherwise? As interesting as this question is, I don't believe one can parse God's love between the sheep and the goats, although you could perhaps argue that grace operates differently than love. But, while I can (and probably do) accept the concept of irresistible grace, I think it goes hand in hand with God's love, which is universal. If we are drawn by God's love, we are assured that "he gives more grace." (James 4:6)

PERSEVERANCE OF THE SAINTS

To me, this one takes the cake. According to Calvin, if one is "elect," it doesn't matter if down the road they sacrifice babies to Satan. (My words, not Calvin's.) Elect is elect. Now I don't have a problem with the concept of eternal security, as Jesus has promised, *"I give them eternal life, and they will never perish. No one will snatch them out of my hand. My Father, in regard to what he has given me, is greater than all, and no one can snatch them out of the Father's hand."* (John 10:28-29) So why do I have a problem with Perseverance? It's for this reason: Perseverance is supposed to be comforting, as we will be saved no matter what happens, *if we are elect.* However, we can't know that we're elect for sure until we have persevered to death, which to me is more like "eternal *in–*security." And it is just too tied up in the whole Calvinist system.

BUT WAIT, THERE'S MORE . . .

The TULIP doesn't begin to cover Calvin's heterodox teachings, which are based on both a misrepresentation of the nature of God and a misrepresentation of the nature of man. We'll start with the nature of humanity and work up. The historic church's view on humanity is as the Bible says, God created us in his image, male and female. I believe it's fair to expand this to include intersex folks, trans folks, etc. Humans—again, *all* humans—are created in God's image, and though sin was in the world, nowhere does it say we stopped being in God's image. We are all created in God's image, with the goal of being reconciled to God. This was, again, the original Christian view of humanity, and it still is in the Eastern Churches. In Romans, Paul states, *"Yet death reigned from Adam to Moses, even over those whose sinning was not like the transgression of Adam . . ."* (Romans 5:14) Here Paul draws a distinction between the sin of Adam and the sin that followed.

Calvin's worst offense, in my opinion, is his teaching of the nature of God. For Calvin, God's sovereignty is above all, and God needs to protect that at all costs. Along with his sovereignty, God is also just and must punish sin, which of course is an affront to his sovereignty and honor. God is bound by his justice, which is why God is full of wrath and anger at humanity's sin. It is for this reason that Christ had to die and be punished for humanity's sin. As Calvin himself wrote:

> In order to interpose between us and God's anger, and satisfy his righteous judgement, **it was necessary that he should feel the weight of divine vengeance.** Whence also it was necessary that he should engage, as it were, at close quarters with the powers of hell and the horrors of eternal death.
>
> We lately quoted from the Prophet, that the "chastisement of our peace was laid upon him" that he "was bruised for our iniquities" that he "bore our infirmities;" expressions which intimate, that, like a sponsor and surety for the guilty, and, as it were, subjected to condemnation, he undertook and paid all the penalties which must have been exacted from them, the only exception being, that the pains of death could not hold him. Hence there is nothing strange in its being said that he descended to hell, **seeing he endured the death which is inflicted on the wicked by an angry God** (emphasis mine).[122]

In contrast to this evil nonsense, we have this from the Apostle John:

> Whoever does not love does not know God, for God is love. God's love was revealed among us in this way: God sent his only Son into the world so that we might live through him. In this is love, not that we loved

God but that he loved us and sent his Son to be the
atoning sacrifice for our sins. (1 John 4:8-10)

CALVIN'S LEGACY

Paul Axton asks whether Calvin created a new religion,
as his teachings divert so much from the understanding
of the early Church. He writes:

> *By changing the meaning of the death of Christ,*
> *making punishment of an innocent man the payment*
> *for the guilty and calling this justice, tying it to future*
> *eternal suffering or eternal death and making this*
> *suffering a legal requirement of God, and by then*
> *equating this with mercy, forgiveness and salvation,*
> *there is almost nothing left of New Testament*
> *salvation.*[123]

I would have to answer in the affirmative. With a
different God, a different humanity, a different concept
of the sin problem, and a different manner of salvation,
there is almost nothing in common between Calvinism
and pre-Augustinian Christianity. Of course, Calvin is not
solely to blame, as he relied heavily on Augustine, Anselm,
Aquinas, and his legal background. But Calvin brought
Augustinian heresy out of the Roman Catholic Church
and spread it like manure over the Protestant Churches.
Only Lutheranism seemed to have avoided Calvin's nonsense (although they also had Augustinian issues).

Damon Linker has this to say about Calvin's
influence:

> *Once an idea is unleashed upon the world, there's*
> *no telling where it will lead. That is one lesson to be*
> *drawn from studying the astonishing influence of*

John Calvin's theology on the subsequent history of the world. Born five hundred years ago today, Calvin deepened the Protestant Reformation by building on Martin Luther's break from Rome, formulating a sternly ascetic version of Christian piety that, as Max Weber powerfully argued more than a century ago, inadvertently laid the psychological groundwork for the development of capitalism.[124]

He also goes on in the same article to blame Calvinism for the concept of American Exceptionalism and Manifest Destiny, saying:

Early modern Christians in the Calvinist tradition strongly emphasized the absolute sovereignty of God, insisting that God ultimately controls all events in the natural world and human history.

The Puritans and other Reformed (Calvinist) immigrants often compared America with Israel, seeing America as the successor to Israel, carrying with it God's sovereign blessing and direction. It's not hard to see this mentality still at work in modern evangelicalism.

Adding to the spread of Calvinism in the US was the Great Awakening of the 1700s. As odd as it may seem, considering that Reformed theology teaches that it is God in his sovereignty who chooses who lives or fries, the great revivals were led by Calvinists. The reasoning is because then God's spirit can call out the elect, and also so that those who are to be damned cannot claim they had not heard the gospel. I still can't quite get my head around that one. Regardless, folks like Jonathan Edwards, who I have quoted earlier in this chapter ("Sinners in the Hands of an Angry God"), and George

Whitefield preached the Reformed gospel which spread throughout the country.

AND SO IT GOES

From Augustine to Calvin, to the Puritans and Congregationalists, to the revivalists, Calvinism has become embedded in evangelical Christianity (and in American conservative politics). If their teaching about God is wrong, and their teaching about why Jesus died is wrong, it seems to me they've got a whole 'nother religion.

And so, we in the West are left holding the bag, so to speak, of a crazy, mixed-up religion that differs significantly from that in the East.

CHAPTER 9

UNBOXING THE ATONEMENT

"So," you ask, "is 'atonement' just a made-up word?"

"Of course," I answer. *"All words are made-up words, when you think about it."*

"But I mean, it didn't exist before the Bible was translated into English?"

"That's what I understand. Christianity itself is not an 'English' religion, so everything about Christianity is translated, or even sometimes paraphrased, from older languages. The best translations likely come from the earliest documents we have, some written in Hebrew, Aramaic, and Greek. Although updated Bible versions are sometimes made from earlier translations as well. So William Tyndale came up with 'atonement' and everyone since him has accepted that word to mean 'one with God.'"

Then you say, "Well, that explains a lot about Christianity."

And you're right.

PART 1–ATONEMENT THEORIES UNBOXED

Atonement is one of the few theological words of purely English origin, that unfortunately has had its meaning changed over the years to serve a certain theological agenda. Consequently, its secular meaning has changed as well. Its root, *atone,* is commonly understood to mean to pay or work off a wrong, such as serving prison time, doing public service, or "making amends." This is a very convenient definition, as it fits in with the post-Calvin teaching about Jesus's death on the cross. Likely we all have heard how Jesus was punished on our behalf, paying our debts—*atoning* for our sins, often to make us feel guilty. As pastors and evangelists have discovered, guilt is a great motivator.

But this is not what the word originally meant, and this changes Christianity in a quite dramatic manner. In this chapter, we will explore both the meaning of *atonement* and the concept behind it in a more focused approach. There will undoubtedly be some repetition from earlier chapters because repetition is essential to learning (and because I tend to repeat myself). As Martin Luther reportedly said, "We need the gospel every day because we forget the gospel every day."

A MAN NAMED WILLIAM TYNDALE

Tyndale, an Englishman born eleven years after Martin Luther, was also a reformer who began to translate the Bible into English from the original Greek and Hebrew texts. While he was imprisoned and executed by the Roman Church before he could complete his work, much of his original translation became part of the King James Bible, and many of his words and phrases are still in use, such as "the powers that be" and "the salt of the earth" as well as the English words "Jehovah" and "Passover."

While translating the Old Testament, he came across the Hebrew c-p-r, or *Kippur*, as in the Day of Atonement, *Yom Kippur*, talked about in Leviticus 16. According to one source I found, Tyndale found the Septuagint and Latin Vulgate translation not fitting the context and thought a closer meaning would be to be "at one" with God, and so merged the words as *atone*, or *atonement*.[125] It has been suggested in the above source that perhaps a better translation would be "to cover," as there is some element of protection suggested, which is also an interesting possibility. However, I don't see any reason to redefine the word "atone" as a payment or sacrifice to compensate for sin, other than to justify a Calvinist understanding of Jesus's death.

While most sources will credit Tyndale with coining the word atonement, the "facts" behind its creation vary significantly. It's either that no one knows, or that certain stories have been developed to justify the definition of atonement that they want. Just read a half dozen different sources on the origin of atonement, and you'll understand why you can't believe everything (or perhaps anything) you read on the internet. For the time being, I'm sticking with the Yom Kippur origin. Most people will at least agree with the "at one" meaning, although they build different constructs behind it. Does Jesus make us one with God simply by being incarnated, or did he have to be brutally punished before he and we could be reunited with God? This is what we will be looking at in this chapter.

As we discuss the theology of atonement, we should keep in mind the different understandings of what the word means, and that some who talk about theories of atonement may mean something quite different than "at-one-ment." From here on out, keep in mind that atonement refers to us uniting with God, not paying off a debt.

ATONEMENT "THEORIES" VERSUS METAPHORS

Because we're all children of the Enlightenment, we have a natural tendency to try to figure out how everything works, put it in a box, label it, and patent it. (The natural progression then is to market it, which explains some denominations and megachurches.) It's no wonder, therefore, that we have several competing theories as to how the atonement works. And with these competing theories we have alternative facts (to borrow a recent political phrase) and alternative histories. I was shocked at how some rather spurious atonement theories have claimed to be the "original" beliefs of the early church. I guess it's pretty easy to make claims like that when you know that most people do not know anything of early church theology. I am therefore not surprised that one or more atonement theories have become merged with the gospel itself.

It should be emphasized that, as Bradley Jersak wrote, *"Let's be clear: atonement theories are not the gospel, nor are they to be confused with the biblical metaphors they claim to interpret."*[126] Many people don't understand that Jesus, Paul, and other NT writers used many different metaphors, or illustrations, to help explain difficult (or even unexplainable) concepts. For example, we find in 1 Timothy 2:5,6: *"For there is one God, and there is one mediator between God and men, the man Christ Jesus, who gave himself as a ransom for all . . ."* (ESV) Paul was not suggesting that God was holding us hostage and that Jesus was paid as ransom. Jesus himself said that he came *"to give his life as a ransom for many"* (Mark 10:45). Other metaphors include the Passover Lamb that was sacrificed (1 Corinthians 5:7-8), justification, the victor, healing, adoption, reconciliation, and so on.

None of these presents a complete picture, nor were they meant to. Each metaphor is an example used for a specific purpose that emphasizes one aspect of Christ's mission. From these metaphors, however, have grown a few atonement theories, attempting to provide a more specific technical explanation, or to put atonement in a box. Enlightenment people like boxes. As I've said, trying to be too specific and dogmatic to fit large concepts into small, modernist categories always results in heresy. We can't stick God, or theology, in a box. God is bigger than any theory or metaphor.

On the other hand, most evangelical Christians today would be shocked to know that there is more than one atonement theory, as all they've heard is the Calvinist/evangelical version which they accept as fact. This evangelical theory is known as "Penal Substitution," in which God who was bound by his own code of justice had to punish someone for our sins, so he took his wrath out on Jesus on our behalf. If this isn't obvious to you, this theory pits God *against* Jesus, essentially splitting up the Trinity for a time.

This of course supports the thinking that the God of the Old Testament is the harsh, judgmental God and Jesus is the nice, loving God. If this is your understanding (still), Stop it! Jesus is the full representation of God and is in perfect unity with the Father and the Holy Spirit. Full unity. No difference or division. If you've seen Jesus, you've seen the Father. Memorize this, if you haven't.

A PSA (PUBLIC SERVICE ANNOUNCEMENT) ABOUT PSA (PENAL SUBSTITUTIONARY ATONEMENT)

Start explaining to someone why penal substitutionary atonement is a sham, and you are likely to get a response like, "Then why did Jesus die?" This is because much of the Western Church since the Reformation has accepted PSA as the gospel because we are taught that we're all sinful so Jesus had to be punished for our sins. It has never occurred to them that Jesus would have died for us if he wasn't forced into it, that Paul and others used more than one metaphor to describe what happened at the cross, or that Jesus accomplished more than your individual salvation. (What?) We'll get into more of this in a moment.

It's been my thinking that Paul never meant to provide a technical analysis of the atonement—assuming he even had a technical understanding of the atonement. (Think about it.) If Jesus ever explained it in detail, it's not written down anywhere. Obviously, if all of the Apostles were taught the same thing by Jesus, there wouldn't be the arguments that there were over the gospel (read through Acts and Galatians).

But people will overlay their own relevant metaphors on top of biblical metaphors. Anselm lived in a feudal culture, and so used feudal language. Luther and Calvin, both trained in law, came along and used legal metaphors. However, that does not mean that this was Paul's intention; how could he use concepts that were foreign to him?

Just like many of us do not explain something the same way to every person or every time we talk about something, it seems that Paul came up with examples as he was writing. In effect, he was saying, "It's kind of like this . . . ", rather than, "This is exactly the way salvation works." Then when someone like Anselm reads Paul's example, he goes, "That's it!" and stops thinking. Dogmas are easy. Putting metaphors into perspective takes some thinking. Metaphors are essential to understanding concepts beyond our ken, but they only go so far. Brian Zahnd has this to say about biblical metaphors:

We cannot talk about God without using metaphor; it's the only option we have when speaking of the supremely transcendent. But to literalize a metaphor is to create an idol and formulate an error.[127]

However, from Anselm on, people have been trying to reverse-engineer the atonement from metaphors rather than accepting that a large part of what God does is a mystery. As Paul writes in Romans 11,

O the depth of the riches and wisdom and knowledge of God! How unsearchable are his judgments and how inscrutable his ways! "For who has known the mind of the Lord? Or who has been his counselor?" "Or who has given a gift to him, to receive a gift in return?" (Romans 11:33-35)

Do we know the mechanics of creation? No. Do we know how God came to Earth as Jesus? No. Do we know how Jesus rose from the dead or floated away into the sky? No. If you're someone who can't stand a mystery, in the words of the Dread Pirate Roberts (*The Princess*

Bride), "Get used to disappointment." How "it works" has never been the issue. *That* it worked is more to the point.

The basics of penal substitution (the worst offender of the atonement theories) are all dependent upon presumptions that are not specifically found in the Bible but are the creations of men—for example, original sin. Not in the Bible. Total depravity, not in the Bible. God's need to defend his honor—not in the Bible. PSA is also based on a misunderstanding of the Jewish system of sacrifices, thinking of killing an animal as punishment on our behalf. In a nutshell, the concept of penal substitutionary atonement is a house of cards built on a foundation of misunderstanding the nature of humanity and the nature of God. It's workable if you stop thinking.

PENAL ATONEMENT DISMANTLED

So, let us start to unpack this, piece by piece.

1. *There is no such thing as original sin. Original sin, the concept that man is born sinful and inherits sin and guilt from Adam, was an invention of Augustine. We are created in God's image—we aren't born with either the sin or the guilt of Adam.*

2. *Sin, rather than being an evil nature we are born with, is an affliction, a disease that humanity is plagued by, something external to humanity, that Jesus came to heal and free us from.*

3. *God does not hate us, his wrath is not directed toward us, and he has no intention of torturing us forever because we're afflicted by sin. More on this in a later chapter.*

4. *Whether we're talking about the Passover Lamb, the Lamb sacrificed on the Day of Atonement, or any other slain lamb, the lambs weren't killed to punish*

them. They weren't killed because they were sinful or defective; in fact, it was the opposite. On the Day of Atonement, the scapegoat carrying the sins of the people (which Jesus did for us) was let go. It was the perfect lamb who was sacrificed with no malice. Wrath had no part of it, and it wasn't a substitutionary sacrifice.

5. There is no metaphorical basis to believe that God poured out his wrath on Jesus instead of us. (It doesn't make any sense, at all, if you understand the nature of Jewish Sacrifice. That would have created a division between Jesus and the Father, which is a theological no-no, even though many will insist that God the Father turned away from Jesus on the cross, which is another glaring heresy.)

6. This is not about justice. "Do not call God just, for His justice is not manifest in the things concerning you." (St Isaac the Syrian)[128] If this was about justice, there would be no forgiveness. This is not justice, this is love and mercy.

7. This whole concept depends on believing that punishment is about retribution, not rehabilitation or restoration. Retributive punishment was the understanding centuries ago, but that is not necessarily our understanding now. Hebrews quotes Proverbs as, "My child, do not regard lightly the discipline of the Lord, or lose heart when you are punished by him; for the Lord disciplines those whom he loves, and chastises every child whom he accepts." (12:5-6)

8. So, ignore and forget everything you've been taught about the wrathful, vengeful God and the evil of humanity. We are all created in the image of a good and loving God. We are blessed, and we are being saved and perfected. The goal of the atonement was not to kill someone on our behalf but to make us one with God, which he accomplished through the

incarnation (and by this I mean Jesus' birth, life, death, and resurrection).

The atonement is good news. Penal substitutionary atonement isn't (especially if God intends to torture people even after Jesus was crucified). Like I always say, more on this later.

FORENSIC METAPHORS AND THEORIES

Forensic is a cool word that merely means "legal" or having to do with courts and lawsuits. Related to the Penal Atonement Theory, another forensic theory is simply that the law required a death penalty as a result of sin. Not that God was wrathful, but he had set up the rules and he now was bound to play by them. It's a conundrum in the same order as, "Can God create a rock so big that he can't lift it?" "Can God bind himself to his own laws?" This thinking is a trap that many theologians have found themselves in over the years. It places God's "law" over and above God himself, in effect making the law God. And again, forensic theories all come down to punishment for crimes committed. In one scenario, God is angry; in the other scenario, he's bound by his own law. These are sometimes referred to as "violence theories," for obvious reasons.

Paul used a variety of metaphors (sometimes more than one at a time), but again, just one example taken out of context or reinterpreted through current thinking can be misleading. Whereas the metaphor of a healer was the primary metaphor used in the early church, the criminal courts eventually became the primary way of viewing the atonement.

As the doctrine of original sin developed, the Western church began to move away from healing language and instead describe sin and salvation in legal terms.[129]

In some versions of these legal theories, people have cast Satan in the role of prosecuting attorney, holding up the law to explain why we are condemned. Then, as it was explained to me in Sunday School, after we are condemned to death Jesus stands up and volunteers to be killed for us. Except that's not what happened. As Paul writes,

And you, who were dead in your trespasses and the uncircumcision of your flesh, God made alive together with him, having forgiven us all our trespasses, by canceling the record of debt that stood against us with its legal demands. This he set aside, nailing it to the cross. He disarmed the rulers and authorities and put them to open shame, by triumphing over them in him. (Colossians 2:13-15 ESV)

Jesus didn't pay off the debt (to Satan or anyone else), he canceled it. It's called forgiveness. It's not payment, it's a gift. The law no longer applies to us. Jesus didn't decide at the last minute to hold on to the law for a bit more—no, he canceled the whole thing (because he had already fulfilled all of it).

. . . since all have sinned and fall short of the glory of God; they are now justified by his grace as a gift, through the redemption that is in Christ Jesus (Romans 3:23-24)

THE RANSOM THEORY/METAPHOR

Jesus uses a ransom metaphor in Mark 10:45, *"For even the Son of Man came not to be served but to serve, and to give his life as a ransom for many."* Here, the word in Greek is the word used to free someone from slavery, sometimes translated as "redeem" or simply "save." Paul also uses this metaphor when he writes, *"For there is one God, and there is one mediator between God and men, the man Christ Jesus, who gave himself as a ransom for all . . ."* (1 Timothy 2:5-6 ESV)

So, this seems pretty cut-and-dried, doesn't it? Jesus said it, Paul said it, so this must be the proper atonement theory, right? Before I begin to answer this question, I'd like to refer you to Chapter 12 in Brad Jersak's wonderful book, *A More Christlike God: A More Beautiful Gospel,* which I have and will continue to quote from. He does a marvelous job of discussing these metaphors.

So yes, it's a great metaphor for Jesus rescuing, saving, and redeeming mankind. Modern minds will typically go to kidnap situations, where payment is demanded to release someone or something. But ask yourself, "To whom is Jesus paying this ransom?" Aligning with penal substitutionary atonement, one option might be to God, but we know that doesn't work. Why would God have to ransom mankind from himself? Plus we can look back to the Old Testament,

> *Why should I fear in times of trouble,*
> *when the iniquity of those who cheat me surrounds me,*
> *those who trust in their wealth*
> *and boast of the abundance of their riches?*
> *Truly no man can ransom another,*
> *or give to God the price of his life,*
> *for the ransom of their life is costly*

and can never suffice,
that he should live on forever
and never see the pit. (Psalm 49:5-9 ESV)

Paying off God for a life is not an option for several reasons.

The next obvious suggestion is Satan again, which is what I've heard much of my life. Ever since the fall, we've been in bondage to Satan, and finally, Jesus has purchased us back. But where does it say that Satan ever owned mankind? Satan was something to be defeated, not to play "Let's Make A Deal" with. As Bradley Jersak wrote, *"There's no deal-making going on here."*[130] Satan is simply not that important.

Many Christians today have this thought that Satan is somehow a rival to Jesus, like they were equals. But no, Satan is not an equal. According to Jewish and Christian lore (and interpretations of some obscure Bible passages), Satan is a created being, possibly an angel. He's not omniscient, omnipresent, or omni-anything. He's clearly shown as having been defeated. Jesus told his disciples, *"He said to them, 'I watched Satan fall from heaven like a flash of lightning'"* (Luke 10:18). And of course, his final defeat was on the Cross. It's all over, baby.

So, who's left? My personal belief is that our "release" from sin and death was not negotiated with anyone but was won by destroying sin and death. In resurrecting, Jesus defeated sin and death, thereby freeing us from them. We were slaves of no one except our sin-plagued nature. He didn't pay off anyone, he just set us free from the bondage of our affliction. It's a great metaphor, which ties in nicely to what has been called the "Christus Victor" atonement theory.

CHRISTUS VICTOR

Another atonement theory has become known as the Christus Victor (or Victorious Christ) theory, in which Jesus did not die to take our punishment, but rather he chose to die and be resurrected to defeat sin and death, restoring humanity to its Edenic state. As Paul states in Galatians 1:4, Jesus *"gave himself for our sins to set us free from the present evil age."* This has become more popular in recent years and is quite close to the teaching of the early church. I believe the standard Orthodox answer to the question, "Why did Jesus die?" is "To defeat sin, death, and the devil," which are basically the same thing. I tend to avoid talking about the devil specifically because I have no clue about the devil, or Satan, or Lucifer. I believe evil is a thing, and if the devil is a personification of that, fine. Whatever falls in that basket is defeated, so I tend not to worry about it. He can "get thee behind me" too.

Saying that Jesus came to defeat sin, death, and the devil does not mean that the metaphors are not useful, because Paul thought they were for his purposes. The thing about the "victory" metaphor is that this is the gospel: Jesus died to save us from sin and death, and also so that we can become one with him.

ONE FINAL THEORY: LAST AND PROBABLY LEAST

A final theory I will mention, just so I can say that I did, is the "moral example" theory, in which Jesus simply came to teach and to set a good example. Which he did, obviously, but this excludes, in my opinion, the concept of atonement—that is, making us one with God.

Just keep this in mind: **An atonement theory is a modern, almost technical explanation of how salvation works. The gospel is not a theory and can't be broken down and diagrammed.** That is why in the Bible you will find various metaphors (examples) to help understand an aspect of salvation. The modern error is in choosing one metaphor and using it like it's a scientific theory.

PART 2-A CLOSER LOOK AT THE ATONEMENT
WHAT WAS ACHIEVED: THE PERCEPTION OF THE PROBLEM

The question of what the atonement achieved first needs to answer the question of **what needed to be achieved by Jesus.** Here is where the first big divide occurred, and of course, we go back to Augustine who dropped that fork in the road. (When you come to that fork in the road, listen to my GPS when it says, "Keep left to stay on the Eastern Way.")

This fork occurred when Augustine created the idea of original guilt and total depravity. The Eastern Way says that we're created in God's image and that the problem (as stated in Genesis) is death, from which we need saving. Sin is a plague on humanity, God loves and empathizes with us, and he promises to fix things for us. Augustine Avenue, which veers off into the wilderness and winds through Calvin Canyon into Evangelical Land, loses that concept and says that the problem is that we are all guilty of Adam's (and Eve's) sin, God hates us, and that we need to be punished more than by work, childbirth, eviction, and death. We need an everlasting, painful death. As the saying used to go, "It's all going to burn."

Now, you see the problem of the perception of the problem which created that fork in the road. Augustine and his friends needed to develop some kind of system in which there is punishment to satisfy God's terrible wrath, yet provide a loving salvation for some of us. Most of the Eastern/Orthodox Church (that is, the entire Church aside from those rascals in the West) did not need this kind of rescue. Rather, they understood that God planned that death, the devil, and sin had to be defeated once and for all, which would solve all our problems so that we could be united with Christ—theosis. Jesus became man so that we might become God. Changed from glory to glory, and all that.

BUT WAIT . . . WHAT IS SIN ANYWAY?

For many of us, the answer to the question, "What is sin?" is obvious. We've learned at an early age that sin is "missing the mark," or, in practical terms, doing bad things, or simply not being perfect. Bad things run the gamut from telling a lie to mass murder. Some sins are worse than others, but even the smallest, most minor sin will get you sent to hell. For that matter, Adam's sin, which you didn't even know about, will get you sent to hell, according to Augustinian thinking.

However, this might not be the case.

Several years back my wife and I taught a youth Sunday School class. It was very educational, and I hope the kids learned something as well. One of the things that struck me was that Jesus consistently treated sin not as something he had to punish people for, but rather that sin was a plague on humanity that we needed to be healed from. He didn't condemn, he forgave, and he healed, sometimes equating the two. At the time this seemed so radical to me that I questioned my insights, but have come to learn that this was the original church's (and still is the Eastern Church's) view of sin. Let's take a look.

> *When he returned to Capernaum after some days, it was reported that he was at home. So many gathered around that there was no longer room for them, not even in front of the door, and he was speaking the word to them. Then some people came, bringing to him a paralyzed man, carried by four of them. And when they could not bring him to Jesus because of the crowd, they removed the roof above him, and after having dug through it, they let down the mat on which the paralytic lay. When Jesus saw their faith, he said to the paralytic,* **"Child, your sins are forgiven."** *Now some of the scribes were sitting there questioning in their hearts, "Why does this fellow speak in this way? It is blasphemy! Who can forgive sins but God alone?" At once Jesus perceived in his spirit that they were discussing these questions among themselves, and he said to them, "Why do you raise such questions in your hearts?* **Which is easier: to say to the paralytic, 'Your sins are forgiven,' or to say, 'Stand up and take your mat and walk'? But so that you may know that the Son of Man has authority on earth to forgive sins"**—*he said to the paralytic*—**"I say to you, stand up, take your mat, and go to your home."** *And he stood up and immediately took the mat and went out before all of them, so that they were all amazed and glorified God, saying, "We have never seen anything like this!" (Mark 2:1-12, emphasis mine)*

And a few verses later:

> When the scribes of the Pharisees saw that he was
> eating with sinners and tax collectors, they said to
> his disciples, "Why does he eat with tax collectors
> and sinners?" When Jesus heard this, he said to them,
> "Those who are well have no need of a physician
> but those who are sick; I have not come to call the
> righteous but sinners." (Mark 2:16-17)

Despite Jesus equating sin and sickness in this passage, most will interpret this as sin *being the cause of
sickness,* because in their minds sin is us doing bad stuff
because we're bad people, not because we have a condition called sin. Do you condemn someone for being
blind, or for having a withered hand, or being dead? Of
course not! But we in the West are so programmed to
condemn, so that's all we can think about.

But does Jesus really equate sin to sickness (or infir-
mity)? In the second passage from Mark above, he uses
the analogy of "those who are sick" with "sinners," but
that *could* just be an analogy—the Bible is full of them.
Going back a few verses to the story of the paralytic,
we see something a little more direct, although it might
not seem that way. How does "your sins are forgiven"
(5) equate to healing paralysis? And what does it mean
to forgive sins?

There could have been many causes for the man's
paralysis—he could have been injured, it could have
been a neurological disease, etc. Even if his paralysis was caused by the man's sin, perhaps in the act of
stealing a camel, forgiving that sin wouldn't fix the
man's paralysis. Paralysis is a physical problem; sin is
a spiritual problem (there's that dualism again). Jesus,
however, doesn't ever draw that distinction. As he said,

"What's the difference?" It's all caused by an affliction. Jesus said, *"'But that you may know that the Son of Man has authority on earth to forgive sins'—he said to the paralytic—'I say to you, rise, pick up your bed, and go home.'"* (Matthew 9:6)

The obvious takeaway here is that Jesus can forgive it all and heal it all. This has me thinking about what Jesus meant when he said, "Forgive sins." I don't think he's talking about forgiving individual sins. Many people believe you have to ask forgiveness for every little thing, and woe is me should I miss something, but this is not how Jesus acts. I think Jesus is making the point here that he can heal the cause of paralysis as well as heal the cause of those individual sins. He came to heal the cause of sin (for everyone), and this was just a small demonstration.

As I just mentioned, the Orthodox have always looked at sin in this way, which changes everything.

> *Because they knew themselves so well and therefore had a deep knowledge of human nature, our holy Fathers and Mothers speak of sin, festering within us, as an illness. So we aren't guilty, but sick and we need to seek a cure . . .*[131]

Brad Jersak, a theologian who is an Orthodox convert, writes:

> *In [the Orthodox] version, sin is not merely law-breaking behavior but, rather, a fatal disease. The sin condition is a suffering of the soul that is rooted much deeper than our thoughts and deeds. This disease— this condition—makes us subject to futility and death. In this analogy, more of a hospital or hospice than a courtroom, God comes not as a punishing*

judge, but as the Great physician who would heal our brokenness and rescue us from the curse of death.[132]

German (and Lutheran) theologian Helmut Thielicke wrote,

Jesus did not identify the person with his sin, but rather saw in this sin something alien, something that really did not belong to him, something that merely chained and mastered him and from which he could free him and bring him back to his real self.[133]

THIS CHANGES EVERYTHING

Viewing sin as a plague, an infection of the human race should change everything for us. Do you need to repent because you have a hereditary condition? Of course not! You need to repent (to turn around) from actively participating in the condition (such as eating too much sugar for a diabetic or drinking if you're an alcoholic). These things are bad, *because they're bad for you.* Sin hurts us (and sometimes others). So when Jesus told people "Stop it!" it was good advice, not a warning that they'd be punished if they didn't (more on this in a bit).

In Genesis 4:7, God warns Cain, " . . . *sin is crouching at the door waiting to devour you, but you must subdue it.*"[134] Different translations use different phrases, but in all of them it's clear that sin is something external to Cain, and this was after Adam's sin—if sin was inherited, then why would God warn that sin was waiting at the door?

Understanding sin as an affliction, a disease, should also change how we see ourselves. As long as we think we're evil because we have this sin-sickness, we'll be burdened and often controlled by guilt, which doesn't help anything. You are not perfect—so get over it. We all have a "genetic" tendency to be *afflicted* by sin (though not inheriting Adam's sin and guilt as Augustine thought), and we should oppose this tendency because sin harms us and others. Regardless, you will do stupid and sometimes bad things, which should make you feel bad. However, you never have to feel condemned, because Jesus doesn't condemn you. He simply wants to heal and free you.

> ***Therefore there is now no condemnation*** *for those who are in Christ Jesus. For the law of the Spirit of life in Christ Jesus has set you free from the law of sin and of death. For God has done what the law, weakened by the flesh, could not do: by sending his own Son in the likeness of sinful flesh and to deal with sin,* ***he condemned sin*** *in the flesh, so that the just requirement of the law might be fulfilled in us, who walk not according to the flesh but according to the Spirit. (Romans 8:1-4, emphasis mine)*

We are not condemned—it is *sin* that is condemned, "setting us free from the law of sin and death."

To recap, the original understanding of sin (and still the correct understanding) is that sin is a curse (to use one more metaphor) upon humanity and that Jesus came to free us from this curse, defeating sin and death. It's as simple as that. After the detour down Augustine Alley, etc., we are told that we are full of sin and evil from birth and that God would like to burn us all up. We deserve eternal punishment. But, because he has this good side, he kills Jesus instead so now some of us are forgiven (the rest will still burn forever—bummer for them).

264 • ALDEN SWAN

If you have some sick desire to see others suffer, pick option B. If you want the good news, pick option A.

SO WHAT ABOUT GOD'S WRATH?

"Wrath" is another funny English word that we easily misunderstand. For us speaking the English language, wrath has a very dark, angry connotation. It's like hellfire. The wrath of God supposedly declares to those not fortunate enough to make the list, "Sorry, it's eternal punishment for you." Then, after everyone is suffering, God sits back and says, "Oh, I feel so much better."

No.

To see God as this angry, vengeful god who looks forward to sending folks to hell, you'd have to be very, very, screwed up. But yes, I know you're out there.

J.D. Myers quotes Walter Wink on this shift in the Church:

> The God whom Jesus revealed as no longer vengeful, but unconditionally loving, who needed no satisfaction by blood—this God of mercy was changed by the church into a wrathful God whose demand for blood atonement leads to God's requiring his own Son's death on behalf of us all. The nonviolent God of Jesus becomes a God of unequaled violence . . .[135]

Myers also says:

> We often make the mistake in Scripture of thinking that God's warnings are threats. That is, we think God is threatening people with punishment when in reality He is simply warning them about the natural consequences of sin.[136]

WRATH IS LIKE GRAVITY

This is how I've come to view God's wrath: It's like gravity. I have a very uncomfortable relationship with heights, especially if I can see the drop-off. I don't like it one bit. Others are different, but the reality is the same—should you step off the edge of the cliff, you'll fall and likely get hurt and possibly die. Is that punishment? No, that's simply gravity. There's no judgment there, aside from determining that you left your point of safety and found yourself like Wile E. Coyote, treading air. Falling is the only option.

If there was a sign at the edge of the cliff saying "Stop or you'll likely fall and die" would you take that as a threat? Some legalistic park ranger threatening you with death for disobeying the sign? No, a reasonably prudent person would understand that this is a warning for your good. Falling and being injured, perhaps fatally, is not punishment, it is the direct result of your actions. Think of it as the "wrath of gravity."

In John's gospel, we see a couple of examples of this. In this first instance, Jesus heals a man who has been paralyzed for many years:

> Later Jesus found him in the temple and said to him, "See, you have been made well! Do not sin anymore, so that nothing worse happens to you." (John 5:14)

Now was this a threat (I hear the Wicked Witch of the West saying, "I'll get you, my pretty!")? Or was Jesus giving an informed warning not to live a lifestyle that would cause more misery? Now look at the famous story of Jesus and the woman caught in adultery:

> *Jesus straightened up and said to her, "Woman,*
> *where are they? Has no one condemned you?" She*
> *said, "No one, sir." And Jesus said, "**Neither do I***
> ***condemn you.** Go your way, and from now on do not*
> *sin again." (John 8:10-11, emphasis mine)*

"Neither do I condemn you." Jesus, of course, knows the details of the woman's life, but he does not condemn her. So when he says "From now on sin no more," is there any condemnation in that warning? It doesn't seem that there could be. "There is therefore now no condemnation . . ." Past, present, or future.

One of the favorite hellfire verses is Romans 6:23, *"For the wages of sin is death, but the free gift of God is eternal life in Christ Jesus our Lord."* To paraphrase a bit, "The consequence of sin is death." The consequence of stepping off a cliff is also death. The correct understanding of the wrath of God is not God's anger directed to someone who fails, or even consciously disobeys, but the natural consequence of making bad choices.

As Brian Zahnd writes,

> *The wrath of God is a biblical metaphor we use to*
> *describe the very real consequences we suffer from*
> *trying to go through life against the grain of love.*[137]

Brad Jersak echoes this thought:

> *If God operates in the world by consent, then we see*
> *wrath, not as the retribution of a willful God, but as*
> *a metaphor for the consequences of God's consent to*
> *our non-consent.*[138]

Wrath is like gravity. God's mercy does not stop gravity from operating, nor does it stop the natural effects of sin. What God's mercy does is promise that things will be restored. Death is defeated and sin will no longer have any power.

WHY IS IT CALLED "THE WRATH OF GOD?"

Let's look at the curious case of Romans 5:9:

> *Much more surely, therefore, since we have now been justified by his blood, will we be saved through him from the wrath of God.*

What's interesting is that the phrase "of God" does not appear in Greek—it's an addition because ending the sentence with "from the wrath" doesn't sound complete, so the presumption that it is God's wrath led to this addition to the Bible. It happens. At least in the New American Standard Version, they put "of God" in italics to draw attention to that fact. Not all translations do.

> *What Paul actually says is that God through Christ was saving us from the wrath. Period.*[139]

Now Paul does use the phrase "wrath of God" in Romans 1, and Brad Jersak writes, *"He defines 'wrath' three times as the 'giving over' (God's consent) of rebellious people to their own self-destructive trajectories . . ."*[140]

God is not seething with anger at our stupidity and evilness, but he does give us over to the natural consequences of our actions (most of the time—miracles do still happen). As a wise genie once said, "Be careful what you wish for." Once again, this reveals that God is not the angry judge just waiting to toss us in the lake of fire. Rather, God is exactly like Jesus (for obvious reasons), showing love and compassion to those caught in sin.

ORIGINAL BLESSING, NOT ORIGINAL SIN

We've already seen the problem with the concept of original sin:

> *More than any other idea, the doctrine of original sin has slowly eroded our understanding of our relationship with God. Rather than seeing our lives as naturally and deeply connected with God, original sin has convinced us that human nature stands not only at a distance from God but also in some inborn, natural way as contrary to God.[141]*

It's a dangerous myth. It doesn't exist. There's no such thing as original sin. It's a guilt-induced fantasy of Augustine's. Millions of people believe it does not make it true. The Bible doesn't say it, the early church didn't say it, and wise people today don't say it.

Danielle Shroyer suggests that what we have instead is an **original blessing**. The doctrine of original sin defines humanity by its sin—sin is the start of evangelical theology, and the core of it, right up until the end. Under the theory of original blessing, we are created in God's image and God declared us "good." Sin did not destroy our relationship with God, it just changed some things. We are still loved and in a relationship with God, and our goal in life is to become more good. Gooder. Whatever.

> *Original blessing means realizing your sin is not the most important thing about you, even if the world— or the church—makes you feel like it is. . . . Original blessing is the stubborn assertion not that we are perfect, but that we are loved. And this love has the power to transform even our shadows into light.[142]*

Again, this changes everything. It changes our view of ourselves, and it should change our view of God. He is not on the opposite side of the sin chasm, he is on our side, working beside us to help us along. This is the core of my theology: God loves us, he's for us, and he won't desert us. All of us.

Seeing people as inherently sinful allows for all kinds of evil. As Shroyer states,

> I'm also wary of the idea of a sin nature because it devalues humanity. I don't mean that we ought to put humanity on a pedestal, but there's a direct correlation between how we value something and how we treat it. If we see someone doing something wrong, original sin gives us an easy way to categorize him as evil. And if we feel justified in calling someone evil, or even bad, we tend to use very different criteria in the way we treat them. We lose our Christian conviction in that moment, because we no longer seek to serve the other, much less love the other. Seeing people as inherently flawed is a terribly convenient way to devalue each other, even if that isn't what the doctrine intended.[143]

In Matthew 5:22, we see Jesus saying:

> But I say to you that if you are angry with a brother or sister, you will be liable to judgment, and if you insult a brother or sister, you will be liable to the council, and if you say, 'You fool,' you will be liable to the hell of fire.

I pondered this verse for years and finally came to understand that what Jesus was getting at was the act of dehumanizing someone else. It's not the specific language that's at issue, it's categorizing someone as somehow less than equal, or less than fully human. The notion of original sin allows us to categorize some as suitable for massacre (like the heathen American Indians), for slavery, for needless incarceration, for lives of poverty, or to simply have fewer human rights than us. If we saw all humans as falling under God's Original Blessing, how could we continue to allow such behavior?

> *Especially in a world that seems more and more prone to religious extremism, I believe it's both healthy and necessary to be resistant to any religion or belief that requires someone to deny her personhood.*[144]

All of humanity is created in the image of God. Everyone is a person, and everyone falls under God's blessing and has the potential for godliness. Got it?

WHY, THEN, DID JESUS HAVE TO DIE?

This is the key question, isn't it? If sin hasn't separated us from God and he doesn't need to kill us or anyone to forgive us, why the need for a human/God sacrifice?

The problem in providing a concise, complete, and accurate answer to this question is likely impossible. If you search for answers online, you will find dozens upon dozens of essays which never really provide this kind of an answer. It's like asking, "What was the cause of the American Civil War?" You could answer slavery and be partially correct, but how many books have been written trying to answer that question? So in answer to our question, we could simply answer "to defeat sin and death" and be correct, but it still doesn't fully answer the question.

Let's back up for a moment: We have already discussed that sin is a sickness, a plague on humanity. And Paul tells us in Romans 6:23 that sin is a terminal disease—the end result of sin is death. Looking back at the incarnation, we know that Jesus was fully human, except he was without sin; he did not have that disease that would result in death. He became human so that he could become joined forever with humanity.

Fr Stephen Freeman has probably the most concise answer to our question that I have found:

And this goes to the heart of the answer to the question posed: why did Christ die? Christ died because we were dead. We were trapped in the lifeless death of sin (which yields corruption and physical death as well). Christ is God who has come to rescue us from our prison of sin and death. He became what we are that we might have a share in what He is. We were created in the image and likeness of God—but our sin had marred us.

We did not inherit guilt and a legal penalty from Adam and Eve. We inherited a world dominated by death. In such a world we behaved as the slaves of sin and sought to live our lives apart from God Who alone is Life. God alone could rescue us from the place where we had confined ourselves. Christ enters death. Christ enters Hades and makes a way for us to follow Him into true life.[145]

Further, Paul writes in Romans 6:

For if we have been united with him in a death like his, we will certainly be united with him in a resurrection like his. We know that our old self was crucified with him so that the body of sin might be destroyed, so we might no longer be enslaved to sin. For whoever has died is freed from sin. But if we died with Christ, we believe that we will also live with him. We know that Christ, being raised from the dead, will never die again; death no longer has dominion over him. The death he died, he died to sin once for all, but the life he lives, he lives to God. So you also must consider yourselves dead to sin and alive to God in Christ Jesus. (Romans 6:5-11)

Here again are metaphors. Died with Christ. Dead to sin. Keep reading Paul and you'll find metaphor after metaphor, to draw word pictures of inexplicable truths. Just don't take every metaphor too literally, or you'll end up really confused. And we wouldn't want that.

The two main truths I would like you all to walk away with are:

1. Jesus came to defeat sin and death. And,

2. Jesus became one of us so that we could become like God.

That's the atonement in a nutshell.

CHAPTER 10

GRACE AND SALVATION

"So," you say at this point, "I think I understand why Jesus died. But do I need to do the 'born again' thing? Isn't it enough to just believe? Do I need to 'get saved?' And what do I have to do to get saved?"

"To your first question, yes," I answer. *"Or, no—it depends on your definitions. 'Born again' and 'get saved' are more metaphors that need to be understood in the context of the bigger picture of salvation. And as far as what you need to do, the answer is 'absolutely nothing.' You are saved by the grace of God alone. You only need to believe to make it real to you."*

"Say what?" you respond.

"It's true," I answer. *"Just read on."*

BAD EVANGELISM

By purely modern evangelical standards, Jesus probably fails miserably as an evangelist. He chased the rich young ruler away, healed people, and told them not to tell anyone, he would draw large crowds and then chase them away with his teaching, and he never asked even one person to let him into their heart. Not one! And never an altar call. It doesn't even seem like he was interested in people getting saved. And finally, he tells the thief on the cross next to him that he is being saved, and we don't even know if the thief knew who Jesus was.

This is not what I would expect from the Jesus of evangelical Christianity. Jesus's style of evangelism has always struck me as markedly different than that promoted by contemporary Western Christianity. Maybe he knew something that we don't know? Perhaps "getting saved" is more than just purchasing a "get out of hell free" card?

For much of my life, I remained a Lutheran at heart while living among evangelicals, sort of a Lutheran expatriate. While I tried to be evangelistic, I just couldn't do the evangelism stuff that was popular at the time. It just didn't "gel" with me. I was involved in an evangelistic ministry; I promoted Christian concerts and speakers and performed in Christian coffeehouses. However, I always questioned the motivation behind it. What do we do with these people who got saved? Don't we have a responsibility to develop relationships with them, instead of just praying with them and hoping they find a church? And what did simply praying a prayer do, anyway? Were they saved for life, or just for the moment? It seemed so many were only "momentary" Christians or "repeat repenters."

THE PROBLEM WITH "GETTING SAVED"

Western Christianity has turned "getting saved" into a goal for us to attain, as if it's all our responsibility, both to get saved and to save others. Even when we're told that salvation is by grace and not by works (Ephesians 2:8, 9) we are then told that we must do something first, like bow your head, raise your hand, come forward, repent (and mean it), join the Church, or simply believe enough. After we do our part, grace kicks in, but only if we're serious enough or it won't stick. Did you repent enough? Did you really mean it? Are you sinning too much? What if you haven't been baptized? Can you lose your salvation? A lot of Christians live their lives in a state of "eternal insecurity" because that's the way a lot of Christian traditions have been developed. This can result in multiple salvation experiences and/or a continual state of guilt for not trying hard enough. Plus, it keeps people dependent on abusive, controlling churches. Too much faith in grace, and you're completely impossible to control.

We also tend to think of being saved as if it's like flipping on a light switch: Off, unsaved. On, saved. Off, not saved. On, saved again. A lot of people will accept that the switch is locked in the "on" position (but they must keep working to earn other rewards). For others, it's a life of saved, not saved, saved, not saved. Eventually, the switch wears out, and then what? What if you die in the "off" position? And what if you die while sinning and don't get a chance to repent? I heard of a pastor who claimed you would go to hell if you died in a movie theater. Again, this is a great way to control people, but not a great way to build faith. What kind of God is this? What is salvation about, anyway? Is it a constant high-wire act, or is it as Jesus said, a place of rest? (Matthew 11:28)

What they've done is put both God and salvation in more boxes. Again, the curse of modernism. We must take things apart, analyze them, and categorize them so we can control them. It's the only way to create a life of certainty. But where's the adventure? Where's the wonder? Where's the awesomeness of God if you can put him in your back pocket?

However, salvation is a timeless event (that's an oxymoron, isn't it?). Revelation 13:8 says that our names have been written in the Book of Life from the foundation of the world. Paul says in Ephesians 2 that we have been saved, again past tense. In 1 Corinthians 1:18 he writes, *"to us who are being saved,"* using present continuous tense. Then, in Romans 5:9 we read, *"we will be saved,"* which is future perfect tense (okay, so I had to look these up). So, salvation is past (long past), present, and future. It's not a binary situation, it's not off or on, it's a continuum, something that happens throughout all time, or perhaps even outside of time. It's an unending conveyor belt of salvation.

SET THEORY

I've always loved set theory and Venn diagrams, possibly because they brought a little philosophy into mathematics. If you need a bit of a reminder, the universe of all things is represented by a rectangle, in which circles are placed depicting a "set" of like things. For example, the set of blue things would be filled with blue things, and all red, green, and yellow things would be outside of the circle. These are known as "bounded sets" because they have hard boundaries. Sets could intersect. For example, the blue circle could intersect the yellow circle, and things in the common area would be green. It's pretty fun.

Much later, I learned about the "centered set" theory, in which the circle was not defined by the circle boundary but by the center point, without any defining circle at all. In a centered set of blue things, pure blue things would be closest to the center, and the further away you got, you'd get lighter blues, perhaps turning to purple or greenish blues, etc.

Many Christian groups have always seen Christianity (and everything else) as bounded sets—either you're in, or you're out. And, it should be mentioned, that every group has its criteria for establishing who is in or out. However, I see salvation—the process of being saved, deified or made holy—as a centered set, with Jesus at the center. You can be varying distances from Jesus, either moving away or moving inwards, or perhaps orbiting (you can think of your own analogies here, it's a metaphor). The question remains whether there exists a boundary at some point. Some believe there is a boundary, perhaps one of your own making. Others, like me, tend to think there are no circle boundaries, just a center point, which is Jesus. This, of course, invites the question, "What if there are no circles? How can we tell if we're saved?"

THE PROBLEM OF FREE WILL

I'd like us to forget for a time about the whole issue of free will, which is way more important to us than it should be. It gets silly wondering if we are discussing free will because we're programmed to talk about free will. Honestly, we'll never know. The only reason we ask questions like that is because we have too much time on our hands. We've reached the pinnacle of Maslow's Hierarchy, so we worry about nonsense questions.[146] My response to this issue is that as long as we appear to have the ability to make choices, try to make good ones, and don't blame God for the outcome. Take credit and responsibility for your decisions like an adult. It won't change the outcomes, but it will be good for your character. As therapy groups say, "The first step to recovery is admitting you have a problem." The proper response to making a bad choice is to say, "Well, that didn't work." That's what free will is all about.

When it comes to salvation, many people have strong objections to the notion that we may not have a say in our destiny and so will argue for free will on moral grounds. If it's good to take responsibility for our choices, it must be good to take responsibility for our salvation, right? But let's take a step back and look at our lives so far. Did we have a say in when we were born? Were we asked which parents we wanted, or what color skin we wanted? Did we choose the culture we were born into? Were we asked what color hair we wanted or what talents we would have? The answer is obviously that these were all chosen for us, even as to whether we were raised Christian or not. So there goes total free will right out the window. Let's just start there and see where we go.

THE PROBLEM OF GOD'S WILL

On the opposite side of free will, there's the issue of God's will. One position is that everything that happens is God's will. Death and sickness is God's will. Who we marry is God's will—*Is he/she the one?* Being abused is God's will. If tragedy strikes, we say, "It must have been God's will." I think that's a lot of baloney (another theological term). The God who is love would not cause terrible things to happen to you. Don't assume that God is behind any of the misery in your life.

Remember the line, "Everything happens for a reason," and my favorite version, ". . . and sometimes the reason is that you're stupid and make bad choices?" I think this is the case more often than not. Why did God even give you the ability to think if he was going to make all your choices for you?

Another aspect of the God's will issue is believing that we have free will but thinking that God wants to mandate every little detail of our life—and if we don't guess what God wants, we could screw up our lives. We even ask dumb questions like, "Does God want me to buy this car?" It's ridiculous. People have even invented categories of God's will, his "perfect" will, and his "permissive" will, which is kind of like "do this at your own risk." The goal is, therefore, to try to stay in God's perfect will, which creates a lot of anxiety as we try to determine what that is rather than rely on the good sense God gave us.

Peter writes,

His divine power has given us everything needed for life and godliness, through the knowledge of him who called us by his own glory and excellence. Thus he has given us, through these things, his precious and very great promises, so that through them you may escape from the corruption that is in the world because of lust and may become participants of the divine nature. *For this very reason, you must make every effort to support your faith with excellence, and excellence with knowledge, and knowledge with self-control, and self-control with endurance, and endurance with godliness, and godliness with mutual affection, and mutual affection with love.* For if these things are yours and are increasing

among you, they keep you from being ineffective and
unfruitful in the knowledge of our Lord Jesus Christ.
For anyone who lacks these things is blind, suffering
from eye disease, forgetful of the cleansing of past
sins. Therefore, brothers and sisters, be all the more
eager to confirm your call and election, for if you do
this, you will never stumble. For in this way, entry
into the eternal kingdom of our Lord and Savior
Jesus Christ will be richly provided for you. (2 Peter
1:3-11, emphasis mine)

Does this sound as if we should stop thinking and
making our own decisions? Obviously not. What is
God's will? *"So that you may become participants of the*
divine nature." Once again, Jesus became human so that
we could become like God, aka "participants of the divine nature." Whether or not we get a tattoo or take that
new job doesn't change the big plan. God wants us to
"grow in the knowledge of our Lord Jesus Christ." I think
that can happen regardless of who we marry, what job
we have, or what country we live in. Stop focusing on
the small stuff and start looking at the big picture (you
know, all that stuff that Jesus talked about). As Martin
Luther famously said, "Love God and do as you please."
Christianity is not following rules or having to do everything right. We don't become holy by not dancing or not
going to movies (or even by tithing). These rules have
nothing to do with God's will, which is focused on you
becoming more like Christ, through his grace.

THE SEGUE TO GRACE

Speaking of grace (see what I did there?), the standard
definition for "grace" has been "God's unmerited favor,"

which I think is a poor definition. If you replace "grace" with that phrase in the Bible, you'll see that it doesn't make sense much of the time. A better definition is, "God's empowering presence" (which I heard first in a sermon by my then pastor Ken Blue). It is by God's power working in our lives that we have been saved, and it is by that grace that we continue living. Being saved is by grace and becoming like Christ is by grace. Neither is by our effort.

This is why Paul wrote to the Galatians, *"I am astonished that you are so quickly deserting the one who called you in the grace of Christ and are turning to a different gospel—."* (1:6) The Galatian Church was believing the teaching from some Jewish Christians who still taught that what was important was keeping the Jewish law, including following dietary laws and being circumcised. Paul drew a sharp contrast between human effort and the transformative grace from God, even leading Paul to suggest that anyone who gets circumcised should go all the way and cut their whole penis off. (He was not very concerned about offending anyone when it came to the gospel.) The point is, it's grace all the way, from start to finish. As an old pastor used to say, "The way in (grace) is the way on (grace)." We don't earn our salvation, and we don't earn godliness. They're simply gifts.

We are justified freely, for Christ's sake, without the exertion of our strength, gaining of merit, or doing of works. To the age old question, "What shall I do to be saved?" the confessional answer is shocking: "Nothing! Just be still; shut up and listen for once in your life to what God Almighty, creator and redeemer, is saying to his world and to you in the death and resurrection of his Son!"[147]

Our "free will" does not defeat grace—regardless of our decisions, grace follows us around, as does God's love. As Paul writes in Romans 8:38-39, *"For I am convinced that neither death, nor life, nor angels, nor rulers, nor things present, nor things to come, nor powers, nor height, nor depth, nor anything else in all creation will be able to separate us from the love of God in Christ Jesus our Lord."* However, it does seem that we can throw a wrench in the works, at least for a time. As Paul asks, *"What shall we say then? Are we to continue in sin that grace may abound?"* (Romans 6:1) The answer of course is an emphatic, No. Grace will abound, but due to the harmful effects of sin, we should choose and live wisely. To put it another way, you're destined for heaven, but there's no need to rush it by making stupid choices. However, as we will see shortly as we look at my favorite parable, God's grace abounds despite our bad choices.

To recap just a bit, it seems to me that while God created us and has decided to save us from sin and death (good news), he does not seem to want to control every little area of our lives, having granted us *"all things that pertain to life and godliness."* God may certainly choose to act in our lives and he certainly has emphasized that he keeps his eye on the sparrow. (Matthew 6:25-27)

DEFECTIVE CONCEPTS OF GRACE

Should you be daring enough to do an online search of the meaning of grace (which I, of course, did), you will find that it is a lot like disturbing a hornet's nest. With grace, as with a lot of things, everyone seems to have their own angle which they believe to be definitive and/ or obvious. And, as with many subjects I've discussed, trying to define something too narrowly tends toward error. Western Christianity in all its forms, as we have also explored over and over, seems to like things as defined as possible. This leads to sub-categories of grace, including irresistible grace, common grace, special grace, prevenient grace, justifying grace, and sanctifying grace. (Just what is "common" grace, anyway? Is any grace common?)

None of these terms are found in the Bible. They are just names of the various boxes people have created to control God. The first three terms are typical in Reformed theologies, with special grace only given to those whom God has chosen to save. Common grace is apparently for everyone, including those who don't make the cut. Basically, God will help everyone out until you die, and then you find out if you have saving grace or not. All grace is irresistible grace because you can't resist God.

Prevenient grace, justifying grace, and sanctifying grace are found in Methodist/Armenian-style theology, referring to grace given before salvation, grace for salvation, and continuing grace to become holy. It's all the same grace, but for whatever reason it's important to distinguish timing. Methodist grace is resistible. Free will rules.

The worst definition of grace I know of is the Calvinist idea that "special grace" is given to the elect. That is, before the elect were even born, they were chosen to receive saving grace, which they cannot resist. If you're a *Star Trek* fan, it's like a tractor beam that sucks you into eternal life. The fact that they teach that God gives a lesser grace to the damned bothers me (along with the belief that God "damns" anyone). I should probably stop here because discussing Calvinism makes me so mad I want to spit purple.

It seems from hearing a lot of folks talk about grace that they see grace as sort of a dam that holds God's wrath back from us. Like we're doomed under the threat of wrath until God dams the river of wrath so we can be saved. Consider how different this is from viewing God's wrath as his loving power at work in our lives.

"CHEAP" GRACE

There are those legalists who claim that those of us who teach a radical, no-works kind of grace are preaching a "cheap" grace, somehow cheating Christians out of a life of guilt and hard work. The response is, "If we're not accused of preaching cheap grace, we're not preaching the gospel." Another truth is that if we never get to the point of Paul in Galatians 6 where Paul asks rhetorically, "So, should we sin more?" then we haven't grasped the truth of grace.

There are those in the evangelical world who want to post the Ten Commandments in schools. Why? How are they relevant? If you're a Christian, they have no meaning or relevance. Grace frees us to love, and so frees us from being bound by religious or moral legalism. As Augustine wrote, *"love, and do what you will."*[148] Love fulfills the law. It would be far better to post this than the Ten Commandments. As writer Kurt Vonnegut put it,

> *For some reason, the most vocal Christians among us never mention the Beatitudes. (Matthew 5) But, often with tears in their eyes, they demand that the Ten Commandments be posted in public buildings. And of course, that's Moses, not Jesus. I haven't*

heard one of them demand that the Sermon on the Mount, the Beatitudes, be posted anywhere. 'Blessed are the merciful' in a courtroom? 'Blessed are the peacemakers' in the Pentagon? Give me a break![149]

THE GREATEST STORY EVER TOLD

To me, the best story ever told is commonly known as that of the Prodigal Son, although there is so much more to the story than that. It could better be called "The Father's Love." Found in Luke 15:11-32, it deals with sin, grace, free will, legalism, and more grace. It's short, but it's brilliant.

"There was a man who had two sons." The older son was mature and responsible. The younger son was a bit of a problem child who had very little regard for his father or the family business. He asks for his share of his future inheritance (quite a bit of nerve) and takes off. He uses his free will badly, spending his money on drinking, drugs, sex, and partying. He had a good time but ended up homeless, friendless, broke, and took to eating pig slop to stay alive.

So, this is the set-up. The prodigal can represent a huge gamut of people. He could represent an atheist, taking the gifts God has given him but denying God's existence, choosing to live life on his terms. We can call this radical free will. Or, he could be someone who has grown up in the Church but found that a life away from God was more enticing. He could have been abused by the Church or by an untrustworthy adult, he could have been selfish and felt misunderstood, or any number of situations that caused him to want to sever relationships with his family. We will rule out any mistreatment by his father, who remains blameless in the story.

Now, the son has reached the end of his rope, to the point that he considers going back and begging his father to work for room and board, knowing that his dad's lowest employee is treated better than the prodigal's current situation. This is his positively last resort. He is not asking, or even hoping, to be welcomed back into the family—He knows that he has screwed up royally and is just looking for a smidgeon of mercy.

Off he trudges home, practicing his apology, "Dad, don't hate me, I know I've been a jerk. I'm not asking for anything except a menial job." He is now at the lowest, most humiliating place in his life. He hopes he doesn't run into his brother, who will no doubt never let him hear the end of it. You know how older brothers are.

The father has been watching, hoping that his son would return home, and finally sees him. He takes off running and hugs his son before his son even gets a chance to apologize. The son starts on his apology, but his dad ignores him, instead dressing him in his fanciest robe, putting the family ring on his finger, and instructing the servants to throw a party, saying, "For my son was dead, and is alive again; he was lost, and is found."

At this point, you could conclude that the Father saw that his son was truly sorry and decided to forgive him, which would be a grand, noteworthy gesture. But according to the story, the father embraced the prodigal without even listening to his apology. He was welcomed as a son before the son was able to ask for a job. And rather than offering a paycheck, he was given a family ring, which likely was the equivalent of signing authority on the family bank account and a huge celebration. No embarrassment there, the father is ecstatic and wants to show off that his son is back home.

ETERNAL SONSHIP

There are many things we could talk about here. One of the most important is that even though the prodigal had severed ties, from the father's point of view he had never stopped being his son. It was not, "I'll adopt you again" or "You can come back with conditions." No, this was a full-on, "You're here, it's like you never left. All the privileges of being my son are still in effect because you've never stopped being my son." Of course, we can understand that his father never stopped loving him, but this goes further than that. You can love people that you don't trust or won't name in your will. This is the father saying, "From my point of view, nothing has changed in the least."

What this means is that all the time the prodigal is out doing whatever he wanted, whether in sin or feeding pigs (pigs were unclean animals for Jews, and a good Jewish boy wouldn't have been caught dead feeding a pig), the prodigal never stopped being a son to his father. There was no difference from the point of view of the father, the difference was from the point of view of the son.

And now here's the real interesting part that I missed for many years—the prodigal had already been given his share of the family fortune. But now, coming back after blowing his share, he gets full access to what's left. The first takeaway from this is that the father can do whatever he wants. The second takeaway is that the father isn't fair. That's right, the father doesn't even consider what's fair. He gives the son one-half and then opens up the bank to him again. And we get the idea that the father would do the same thing all over again.

THE "GOOD" SON

The older, more dutiful son picked up on this inequity straight off:

> "Now his elder son was in the field, and as he came and approached the house, he heard music and dancing. He called one of the slaves and asked what was going on. He replied, 'Your brother has come, and your father has killed the fatted calf because he has got him back safe and sound.' Then he became angry and refused to go in. His father came out and began to plead with him. But he answered his father, 'Listen! For all these years I have been working like a slave for you, and I have never disobeyed your command, yet you have never given me even a young goat so that I might celebrate with my friends. But when this son of yours came back, who has devoured your assets with prostitutes, you killed the fatted calf for him!'" (Luke 15:25-30)

The older son is right, of course. It's not fair. But on the other hand, neither is his father playing favorites. He responds by explaining that the older son has had everything of the Father's his whole life. The third take-away from this story is that the father's fortune is not a scarce resource, it is infinite, and like the prodigal, the older son will continue to have infinite resources. The father will never run out of love for either the legalistic older son or the unrepentant younger son. God's love is not a scarce resource—there are no limits to God's love.

Who shall separate us from the love of Christ? Shall tribulation, or distress, or persecution, or famine, or nakedness, or danger, or sword? . . . No, in all these things we are more than conquerors through him who loved us. For I am sure that neither death nor life, nor angels nor rulers, nor things present nor things to come, nor powers, nor height nor depth, nor anything else in all creation, will be able to separate us from the love of God in Christ Jesus our Lord. (Romans 8:35, 37-79 ESV)

The elder son is what we could call a legalist, or a fundamentalist. He thinks he knows his father very well—and he should, having spent all his life working for his father. He thinks he understands the rules of the family business; he knows what his father expects from their employees, and he sees how hard his father works. He's lived his whole life showing his father what a good and faithful son he is. And, he has developed certain judgments about the younger prodigal son, who in his eyes does not deserve to be welcomed back, much less given access to the elder son's inheritance.

However, he doesn't understand just how big his father is. The elder son has created a box—a framework—in which to view his father, and he operates within that framework. He's put his father in a box, just as the prodigal son has. They both saw their father as someone who followed rules, who had certain expectations, and they saw his love as being limited by that box. Neither son knew just how big their father was, and just how great his love for them was.

THE FATHER

We know, obviously, that the father represents God in this story, the point of which is that neither son—no one—grasps just how big the Father is. We don't know how big the father's love for us is, or how rich the father is. With God, there are no scarce resources, there's just more grace.

Notice how the father reacts to the prodigal returning home. He takes off running, which is not easy to do in a robe and sandals. Notice that the father has forgiven the son long before he embraces him. In response to the prodigal's small "Father Box," the father demonstrates that he has never stopped being a son and that his inheritance is still waiting for him. The son thought he'd taken his share, but there is no such thing as a "share." Everything that is the father's is the son's.

Likewise, to the elder son, the father demonstrates the extent of his riches and grace and love, showing that the elder son's work hadn't gained him anything; the elder son has always possessed everything, regardless of his work. It's enough to drive a legalist crazy.

NO RULES, NO BOXES

Regardless of how theologically educated we might be, or how many times we've read the Bible, we have no right to decide who will and who won't be saved. We might think we know, but if we're really smart, we won't rely too heavily on our opinions. For God has never been one (or three . . . a little Trinity joke) to follow man's rules. Just read the story of Jonah in, you guessed it, the Old Testament book of Jonah.

We all know about the whole whale thing, but we're going to move past that. Once Jonah went to Nineveh and threatened them with destruction (Jonah 3), they repented, and God forgave them. Now Jonah, in true elder son fashion, became very angry with God because the city wasn't wiped out. (Jonah Chapter 4) Jesus refers to himself in the context of Jonah, saying that he is even greater than Jonah:

> But he answered them, "An evil and adulterous generation asks for a sign, but no sign will be given to it except the sign of the prophet Jonah. For just as Jonah was three days and three nights in the belly of the sea monster, so for three days and three nights the Son of Man will be in the heart of the earth. The people of Nineveh will rise up at the judgment with this generation and condemn it, because they repented at the proclamation of Jonah, and indeed something greater than Jonah is here!" (Matthew 12:39-41)

The implication here is that Jesus, being greater than Jonah, brings a bigger message of salvation. The judgment is there, but the capacity for forgiveness is there as well. To quote a wise man,

> Seek the LORD while he may be found;
> call upon him while he is near;
> let the wicked forsake their way
> and the unrighteous their thoughts;
> **let them return to the LORD, that he may have mercy on them,
> and to our God, for he will abundantly pardon.
> For my thoughts are not your thoughts,
> nor are your ways my ways, says the LORD.**
> For as the heavens are higher than the earth,

so are my ways higher than your ways
and my thoughts than your thoughts. (Isaiah 55:6-9,
emphasis mine)

Jesus directly warns against placing our boxes on God and others when he said, *"Judge not, that you be not judged. For with the judgment you pronounce you will be judged, and with the measure you use it will be measured to you."* (Matthew 7:1-2 ESV) Of course, ultimately there is forgiveness for that as well.

Of course, this raises all kinds of questions about judging behavior. The way I look at is that we do have some basic standards—like loving everyone—that no one can keep, but there are general behaviors that are loving and others that are not. Bullying is not loving, stealing is not loving, etc. Can we judge these behaviors? I believe we are called to, to be a prophetic voice against the forces of hate and evil in the world. And, yes, if we judge these things in others, we also judge them in ourselves. Such is life.

However, judging motives is another thing altogether. Are they acting out of hate, or hurt? We have to be careful when we start believing evil about someone who could be acting out of completely different motives. As the saying goes, don't judge a man until you've walked in his shoes.

We all fail at this; I know I do. The good news is that we're always forgiven, which leads us to another issue. Remember when Jesus taught us to pray "forgive us as we forgive others?" This is another type of box-building. When we fail to forgive, we build a set of standards that just so happen to be standards for us, too. Oops. Building boxes, you see, always end up imprisoning us. Again, the good news is that when we fail at this, we're forgiven for that, too. Tear down your boxes—smash those suckers flat. We don't need theological boxes or frameworks, we just need God, whose thoughts are higher than our thoughts and whose ways are higher than our ways.

Anthropomorphosis is placing human traits on non-human entities. We normally think of this about pets, for example, but we also do this to God. We treat pets like they have human emotions and intent, and we also constrain God according to our own inadequate emotions and fallen character. God's anger isn't like ours, and his love isn't imperfect and limited like ours is, either.

SALVATION AND GRACE, AGAIN

This is what we're talking about, being saved from all the inadequacies that drive us insane. Those who believe salvation is a one-time thing often struggle with these ongoing sins that we encounter daily, which is why Paul talks about *"those of us who are being saved."* (1 Corinthians 1:18) It's history, it's future, and it's a present process. That's what grace is for. Grace is the ongoing involvement of God in our lives that is bringing us from darkness into light, saving us, and renewing us, making us into the likeness of Christ. In one sense we have been saved by the defeat of death and sin, in another, we will be saved with the final restoration of all of creation, and in yet another we are being saved day by day, all through the work of God in our lives.

As Paul wrote,

For by grace you have been saved through faith, and this is not your own doing; it is the gift of God—not the result of works, so that no one may boast. For we are what he has made us, created in Christ Jesus for good works, which God prepared beforehand so that we may walk in them. (Ephesians 2:8-10)

According to Paul, our work does nothing to get us saved, we are saved completely by the gift of God. Works, rather, are the result of grace working in our lives. As John put it, *"We love because he first loved us"* (1 John 4:19). And, to blow a few minds, I will add that I believe this holds for non-Christians as well. We know that love operates in many non-Christians—where does it originate except from God? *". . . Because love is from God; everyone who loves is born of God and knows God."* (1 John 4:7)

God, through the prophet Joel and echoed later by Peter in Acts 2:17, said, *"I will pour out my spirit upon all flesh."* (Joel 2:28) I tend to believe that when God said "all," he meant "all." The grace of God is in operation wherever you look—if only we look. So how does this apply to salvation? Stay tuned.

UH . . . WHAT ARE WE SAVED FROM, ANYWAY?

Raise your hands if the thought has crossed your mind, "So exactly what are we saved from?" Okay, you can put them down. The rest of you should stop and try to answer that question. What is salvation anyway?

Most people from Western traditions will answer something about going to heaven forever when you die, even if you're not a Christian. Just listen to Norman Greenbaum's classic song "Spirit in the Sky." Salvation is a combination of a golden ticket to heaven and a "get out of hell free" card. That's the common concept of the afterlife—so what's the new earth for?

Hopefully, if you've made it this far in the book you will understand that being saved is not about "going to heaven when you die." It's about being saved from sin and death and becoming like Christ. It's a constant process of being freed from the sickness and torment that is sin. So, it's not getting a golden ticket to heaven, it's about being transformed into godliness. With sin defeated along with death, who knows what kind of miraculous existence awaits?

There are those (many of those, actually), who believe the afterlife is a kind of purgatory, a slow, painful, purifying process. But I'm thinking, if you're cured of a sickness—I mean really cured, like having sight restored—aren't you completely well? Can't you see again? If not, you're still suffering from the sickness. Well, if sin is anything like that, with sin defeated along with death and the devil (whoever he is), why should we still be "defective?" I don't know, it's just something to ponder. Remember, not all those who *wonder* are lost . . .

This is why the whole process of salvation—of healing—is due solely to grace. We're completely unable to rid ourselves of sin; our medicine is imperfect, so our healing skills also are lacking. It's basic logic. It's solely the power of God that heals us, restores us, and makes us whole and "saved," from start to finish. Grace—the power of God—is the only cure. All grace is saving grace.

IT'S A COMMUNITY THING

Now try this one on: The gospel has never been about individual salvation.

I will just let this sit here for a moment.

Most of us have been raised with a very individualistic concept of Christianity. "It's about me and Jesus." "I have a personal relationship with Jesus." "Jesus lives in my heart." This is more than likely due to Descartes, whom we discussed a few chapters ago. For him, reality came down to his own individual existence. However, the whole world up until that time (as far as I know) viewed their existence as a member of a group. Everyone had an identity that was essentially related to their family, their tribe, etc. Rugged individualism, which we're so proud of in the USA, didn't exist—it would have been seen as more or less traitorous to set yourself apart from the community.

Let's look at a few examples of OT history. First, there's Noah. God called Noah, but he also included Noah's family. God called Abram, which included his entourage, and the calling extended to his future family. When God called a few Israelites out of Egypt, he didn't pick and choose the best—he called them all, complainers included. Were all of the Israelites saved? I believe so. "And in this way all Israel will be saved" (Romans 11:26). This is corporate, not individual, salvation.

Now consider this from Paul:

> For the unbelieving husband is made holy through his wife, and the unbelieving wife is made holy through the husband. Otherwise, your children would be unclean, but as it is, they are holy. (1 Corinthians 7:14)

Say what? Once again, we have this family-community belonging thing happening. Noah saves his family, Abraham saves his, Moses saves the whole community, and so on. In Acts, we see what happens when Paul's Roman jailer gets converted:

> Then he brought them outside and said, "Sirs, what must I do to be saved?" They answered, "Believe in the Lord Jesus, and you will be saved, you and your household." They spoke the word of the Lord to him and to all who were in his house. At the same hour of the night he took them and washed their wounds; then he and his entire family were baptized without delay. He brought them up into the house and set food before them, and he and his entire household rejoiced that he had become a believer in God. (Acts 16:30-34)

ONCE AGAIN, MEMBERSHIP HAS ITS PRIVILEGES.

But then the Western world gets "enlightened" and suddenly everything is about me and my individual salvation, even when Jesus teaches "for God so loved the world . . ." (John 3:16). Is there an individual component to salvation? Certainly. Noah's wife and family were personally saved from the flood. If you had lived in Noah's day and snuck aboard the Ark, you would have been saved, too. Think about it: God chose Noah, and you get saved, just because you're on the boat. And if you're a servant in the above Jailer's household, you get saved, too. It's great to be included among the saved.

THE ROMAN ROAD TO . . . ?

I think I was in college, thrown in among the evangelicals before I first heard of the "Roman Road," which was a series of verses torn out of Romans that laid out a case for individual conversion and salvation. It's a nice, boxed, and gift-wrapped version of the evangelical gospel that makes the speaker feel like they've done their evangelical duty. It goes like this:

1. *3:23—All have sinned and fallen short of the glory of God.*

2. *5:12—Therefore, just as sin came into the world through one man, and death through sin, and so death spread to all men because all sinned.*

3. *6:23—For the wages of sin is death, but the free gift of God is eternal life in Christ Jesus our Lord.*

4. *5:8—but God shows his love for us in that while we were still sinners, Christ died for us.*

5. *10:9—because, if you confess with your mouth that Jesus is Lord and believe in your heart that God raised him from the dead, you will be saved.*

6. *10:13—For "everyone who calls on the name of the Lord will be saved."*

The only catch is that Romans is not really talking about individual salvation. Let's take a look.

Paul's letter to the Romans was written specifically to the Roman Church, which is believed to be comprised of mainly Jews who had converted to Christianity. By the time Paul wrote this letter, there were thousands of Jews in Rome, including many Christian converts who met in small house groups. There was a bit of discrimination going on, with the Jewish Christians judging the Gentiles. Paul's rhetoric beginning in Romans 1:18 is likely a standard condemnation of non-Jews, similar to that found in the Book Wisdom of Solomon, chapters

13 and 14. Here Paul sets an obvious trap for the Jewish hearer (the letter would have been read out loud, probably with much agreement from the Jews present), as we move into Chapter 2 verse 1: *"Therefore you have no excuse, O man, every one of you who judges. For in passing judgment on another you condemn yourself, because you, the judge, practice the very same things."*

It is obvious at this point that Paul is not writing to individuals, but to the entire community of Jewish believers; certainly not every single Jewish Christian who judges Gentiles practices idolatry or keeps slaves for sexual purposes. However, as people groups, Jews have the same sinful urges and sins as non-Jews, as Paul goes on to explain.

> *There will be affliction and distress for everyone who does evil, both the Jew first and the Greek, but glory and honor and peace for everyone who does good, both the Jew first and the Greek. For God shows no partiality. (Romans 2:9-11)*

This letter is not geared toward individual issues of salvation, but about how both Jews and non-Jews have the same need for salvation, and that all people groups can be saved. Is there an individual component to this? Certainly, as they are part of the communities in question. But salvation here is offered to the community, not to specific individuals.

Let's jump forward to the second step on the Roman Road in Chapter 5:12: *"Therefore, just as sin came into the world through one man, and death through sin, and so death spread to all men because all sinned . . ."* However, in verse 18 we read: *"Therefore, as one trespass led to condemnation for all men, so one act of righteousness leads to justification and life for all men."* In other words, Jesus was the anti-Adam. Adam introduced sin to the whole world—Jew and non-Jew, every single individual—and Jesus brought salvation to the whole world, all people groups, and every single individual.

There are a couple of different ways to read this. One is that if all individuals became sinners through Adam, all individuals will be saved through Jesus. I like this interpretation, but I don't think that's what Paul is aiming at here. Rather, it seems that in context, Paul is talking about "all" in reference to all people groups, specifically both Jews and Gentiles. Throughout Romans, this is what is being discussed. In fact, in Chapter 1 Paul makes the introductory statement: *"For I am not ashamed of the gospel; it is the power of God for salvation to everyone who has faith, to the Jew first and also the Greek."* (16) This is his point: The gospel applies equally to both Jews and non-Jews. So "all" can be read as "all people groups."

Of course, it's possible, and likely, that both readings are correct, and that Paul is talking about all Jews and Gentiles, not just some chosen people from all people groups. There are some later sections in Romans that seem to point to this interpretation, and I've heard the Greek words used in Chapter Five lend themselves to refer to all individuals. The bottom line is that if Paul is saying that all individuals became sinners in Adam, then all will also be saved in Jesus. To say that "all" doesn't mean that all are saved, you'd have to consider that also means that not all were made sinners.

Paul goes on to say, *"For there is no distinction between Jew and Greek, for the same Lord is Lord of all, bestowing his riches on all who call on him."* (10:12) Here, we note again the equality of Jews and non-Jews, but also the possibility that he is talking about individuals within these groups, which is the standard reading. But then in Chapter 11 Paul starts talking about how the Jews "stumbled" (fallen into disbelief) so that the Gentiles would be led to salvation:

> So I ask, have they stumbled so as to fall? By no means! But through their stumbling salvation has come to the gentiles, so as to make Israel jealous. Now if their stumbling means riches for the world and if their loss means riches for gentiles, how much more will their full inclusion mean! Now I am speaking to you gentiles. Inasmuch as I am an apostle to the gentiles, I celebrate my ministry in order to make my own people jealous and thus save some of them. For if their rejection is the reconciliation of the world, what will their acceptance be but life from the dead? (Romans 11:11-15)

Here we come back to hints of universal salvation, although that will be argued against by most evangelicals, including verses 26-29:

And in this way all Israel will be saved, as it is written,

> "Out of Zion will come the Deliverer;
> he will banish ungodliness from Jacob."
> "And this is my covenant with them,
> when I take away their sins."

> As regards the gospel they are enemies for your sake, but as regards election, they are beloved for the sake of their ancestors,
> **for the gifts and the calling of God are irrevocable.** (emphasis mine)

Here, many try to separate the individual from the group, reading this as referring to the elect among the group. But is this what it says? I suspect that when Paul says, "all Israel will be saved," he means just that it extends to non-Jews. While I embrace a theology of universal salvation, I always leave room for the possibility that I am wrong. But I'm putting my money on this one.

Regardless of the universal interpretation, it's clear in reading the entire letter of Romans that Paul's goal is to convince the Jewish Christians to mellow out and embrace the Gentile believers. The Roman Road could go like this:

1. Jews and Gentiles alike have broken God's law (either the given law or the natural law).

2. Mankind sinned, so death entered the world for all mankind.

3. Even though the result of sin is death, but God gives grace to all humanity.

4. Christ's death showed God's love for all humanity.

5. If either Jews or Gentiles believe that salvation is through Jesus, they will experience salvation.

6. God's salvation is for all men—both Jew and non-Jew.

GALATIANS—PAUL'S ANGRY LETTER

I love Galatians. You gotta love Paul when he gets riled up. Once again, this letter is about the relationship between two groups, the Jews and the non-Jews. In

Romans, Paul identified himself as the apostle to the Gentiles (basically anyone who is not a Jew), and he invested himself in these people. However, some Jewish big-shot Christians have come and tried to convince them that they needed to be circumcised (in essence, becoming Jews) to be saved. Paul suggests that these Jews should emasculate themselves or go even to hell.

In Chapter 2, Paul addresses an encounter he had with Peter in Antioch, where apparently the Jews would sit at different tables than the Gentiles, because of Jewish dietary laws. Peter had been somewhat two-faced, separating himself from the Gentiles with Jewish bigwigs were around. Paul's concern here is the rift between these two groups of Christians, and his focus is once again on showing that no one is saved by keeping Jewish rules, it's all through grace. In Chapter 3, he explains:

> . . . so, you see, those who believe are the descendants of Abraham. And the scripture, foreseeing that God would reckon as righteous the gentiles by faith, declared the gospel beforehand to Abraham, saying, "All the gentiles shall be blessed in you." For this reason, those who believe are blessed with Abraham who believed. (Galatians 3:7-9)

Paul is making a new claim here, that the covenant made with Abraham to bless his descendants also applies to Gentiles—"and so shall all nations be blessed." His focus here is not on individual salvation, but on the eligibility of Gentiles and Jews to get in on the Abrahamic blessing without keeping the law (which was a curse, not a blessing).

. . . for in Christ Jesus you are all children of God through faith. As many of you as were baptized into Christ have clothed yourselves with Christ. There is no longer Jew or Greek; there is no longer slave or free; there is no longer male and female, for all of you are one in Christ Jesus. And if you belong to Christ, then you are Abraham's offspring, heirs according to the promise. (Galatians 3:26-29)

Cultural equality is of the utmost importance to Paul; no longer a Jew nor Greek (Gentile), but all one people, all heirs to the Covenant. Here again, we see Paul's emphasis on people groups and the blessings that then filter down to individuals. The gospel was never just about "me and Jesus," it was about community, about Jews, Samaritans, Romans, Greeks, etc., loving your foreign neighbor, forgiving your enemies, and so on. We treat Jesus as we treat others. We are forgiven in the same way that we forgive. It was never about just you. It's about time that we got over that notion.

I haven't done an exhaustive study on all of the passages relating to people groups as opposed to individuals here, but I think you get the idea. Unity among all of God's created peoples is a big deal, and the door is open to all. This is not to say that there isn't an individual component here—there is. However, salvation, as we will see in the next chapter, is bigger than just you and Jesus. It's about you, your family, your tribe, that person over there, that other person over there . . .

ANOTHER GOSPEL

The other thing that is clear about Galatians is that teaching salvation by doing anything—even eating kosher—is following another gospel, and Paul won't have any of it. You are saved by grace alone; that is the gospel that Paul preached, and he's very serious about it. Yes, he's mad about the cultural issues, but he's also incensed by any teaching that adds anything to grace. You see, salvation is by grace plus nothing. If you try to preach grace plus following rules, you haven't added to the gospel, you've destroyed it completely.

So, the moral is this: Don't add anything to grace. Salvation is free.

CHAPTER 11

UNBOXING SALVATION

> *"Before you ask any more questions—not that you should ever stop asking questions—let me just say that here is where things get really big. We're un-boxing everything, looking at how everything fits together, and imagining just what that could mean regarding salvation and God's plan for creation. If you're afraid to follow things to their logical conclusions, then perhaps this chapter isn't for you."*
>
> "Ah, it can't be that big," you respond.
>
> *"Well,"* I propose, *"take a chance, and let's see."*

THE EVANGELICAL GOSPEL

First, let's look at the gospel the way most people in the West see Christianity, whether they're Christians or atheists. We start with everyone being sinful. If we die before we ask Jesus into our hearts, we will go directly to hell, do not collect $200. Death is the presumed cutoff point for getting saved. For the millions of people who aren't Christians at the time of their death, they can look forward to an eternity of suffering in a lake of fire.

On the other hand, if we have accepted Christ as our personal savior (not saved by association or membership, but made a personal commitment to Christ), we will go to heaven when we die. For some, this is a guaranteed deal, regardless of our backsliding or "falling." For others, a poorly- timed backsliding moment could get us barred from heaven and sent to the bad place instead.

The choice here is between "Sinners in the hands of an angry God,"[150] or dancing on streets of gold while your unsaved friends and family attend a roast. For most Western Christians and casual observers, this is the dichotomy, with no third option. Now, I know a lot of you would dearly love for me to tell you that none of this is true, so I will. This is NOT the situation that the Bible lays out.

WHAT WE'VE LEARNED

We've (or at least I have) seen that Jesus died and rose again to defeat sin, death, and the devil, which are all related concepts. We could simply say "evil," but it's worth emphasizing these three things individually, especially as Paul states in 1 Corinthians 15:26, *"The last enemy to be destroyed is death."* So, theoretically, sin and the devil are defeated first. There are many metaphors used to explain the hows and whys, but I think we can all agree that the bottom line is that Jesus died to defeat sin and death and the devil (the source of evil in the world).

We know that Jesus defeated all three with his birth, death, and resurrection, however, the victory is not fully realized in this age; we still suffer the effects of all three, some more than most. However, the time will come when the defeat is final, and sin, the devil, and death will all be a thing of the past. This means, presumably, that the defeat is total—that is, there won't be any sin or evil hanging around anywhere to be a problem for anyone. Logically, at this point, all humanity will be sinless. With me so far?

We've also seen that all of humanity did not inherit sin and guilt from Adam, and we're not totally depraved. We are all created in God's image (all of us), but all are plagued by the disease of sin, which came into the world through Adam (interestingly, the word "Adam" can also refer to mankind in general). So, sin is a disease leading to death that plagues all of mankind and has also plagued all of creation. There is a difference between viewing sinful people as the source of evil, as opposed to good creatures plagued by evil. Sin makes us sinful, in the same way that sickness makes us sick. God, speaking of the results of being plagued with sin (instead of issuing a punishment, as many think) way back in Genesis 3:15, said that he had a plan of redemption.

And, we have seen that our salvation, redemption, atonement, etc., is a gift from God, not something that we can earn by doing good or avoiding evil (good luck with that). God, through Jesus (who is also God) saves us from sin, death, and the devil solely by his own power (which we call "grace") and his love. Because we all know *"for God so loved the world He gave His only son."* (John 3:16)

So how does this knowledge impact our understanding of the evangelical gospel?

LET'S TALK PUNISHMENT

The traditional concept of spending an eternity in hell is based on a **retributive** theory of punishment. *"This theory holds that the punishment of a criminal is justified, not on the basis of its rehabilitative effect, nor on the basis of its crime-deterring impact, but on the grounds that the criminal deserves it . . . God punishes the sinners in hell because they deserve it, because justice is served in this way."*[151] Of course, thinking in terms of fairness (justice?), we would expect that the judgment should equal the crime. Our old friend Anselm suggested that God is so holy that any transgression is worthy of eternal torture, and in essence, every sin is the same.[152] I've heard this argument my whole life, and chances are you have as well.

However, there is another concept of punishment that is backed up by the Bible, and that is that punishment is for rehabilitation, restoration, and healing. As an example, let's look at how Paul treats the adulterer in the Corinthian church. He says,

> *. . . you are to hand this man over to Satan for the destruction of the flesh, so that his spirit may be saved in the day of the Lord. (1 Corinthians 5:5)*

Is this because he deserved this punishment? Paul had a restorative purpose in mind. The Middle Ages retributive concept of punishment doesn't appear to hold water here. One of the early Church Fathers, Clement of Alexandria, had this to say:

> *Now God does not exact vengeance (for vengeance is retribution for evil), but rather he punishes for the good, both public and private, of those who are being punished.*

As we've seen before, sometimes our English translations get in the way of understanding. Consider these two verses from Matthew 25, which you're likely familiar with:

> "Then he will say to those at his left hand, 'You who are accursed, depart from me into the eternal fire prepared for the devil and his angels' . . . And these will go away into eternal punishment but the righteous into eternal life." (25:41, 46)

Here we have what seems to be a clear statement from Jesus that the "accursed" spend an eternity being punished by fire. However, as Brad Jersak explains,

> Had penal retribution been intended, Matthew could have used the applicable Greek word, timōreō/timōria. (Acts 22:5; 26:11; Heb 10:29) Instead, he chose the restorative term kolasis, usually [over]translated as punishment, but which carries a connotation of corrective discipline or chastisement.[153]

Furthermore, the word translated as "eternal" can simply mean "in the next age;" it does not imply that there is no end to the discipline. When we remove our prejudicial translations, what we have is a picture of something other than eternal torment, but rather a future (the next life) time of correction. If you're thinking that this sounds a lot like purgatory, you're kind of right; the Bible speaks of things like a refiner's fire, a purging or cleansing process that occurs after this life.

> But who can endure the day of his coming, and who can stand when he appears?

*For he is like a refiner's fire and like washers' soap; he will sit as a refiner and purifier of silver, and he will purify the descendants of Levi and refine them like gold and silver, **until they present offerings to the** LORD **in righteousness.** Then the offering of Judah and Jerusalem will be pleasing to the LORD, as in the days of old and as in former years. (Malachi 3:2-4, emphasis mine)*

So we see that God's judgment is restorative, and not an eternal tortuous punishment. While the Roman Catholic version of purgatory turned punitive, this was not the case for the Eastern church, which sees God's love as that refiner's fire. As the Orthodox see it, we are all going to be in the presence of God; the pure will experience God's love as a state of joy, and others will experience God's love as fire. As Brad Jersak puts it, *"Consequently, paradise and hell are not a reward or a punishment (condemnation), but the way that we individually experience the sight of Christ, depending on the condition of our heart . . . "*[154]

Paul writes in 1 Corinthians,

*Now if anyone builds on the foundation with gold, silver, precious stones, wood, hay, straw—the work of each builder will become visible, for the day will disclose it, because it will be revealed with fire, and the fire will test what sort of work each has done. If the work that someone has built on the foundation survives, the builder will receive a wage. If the work is burned up, the builder will suffer loss; **the builder will be saved, but only as through fire.** (1 Corinthians 3:12-15, emphasis mine)*

For some of you (like me), this verse has never made sense until now.

HELL, NO!

One thing that I've given up is the concept that Jesus died so that we can go to heaven or escape hell, whichever is the bigger attraction for you. Hell, as we tend to think of it, is not a biblical idea. Once again, we've been boxed in by the way the Bible has been translated. The English word "hell" is used to replace a few Greek words that have different contexts and meanings. The Greek word typically translated as "hell" refers to a valley outside of Jerusalem which was the site of historic death and destruction, including at one time, the sacrifice of children to Molech (a rather harsh, vengeful god).[155] And, its use always refers to a possible reality in this world, not a punishment in the next. Here is a discussion on a passage in Mark that seems to expressly warn of a potential eternity in hell:

> In Mark 9:42-50, we read one of Jesus' stern warnings about avoiding the fires of Gehenna. It climaxes with the words, ". . . to be cast into the hell, where 'their worm does not die, and the fire is not quenched.' For (gar) everyone will be salted with fire."

> The words "for everyone will be salted with fire" are offered as an explication of the comments about Gehenna. The verse has long perplexed commentators, but it seems to indicate that the fires of Gehenna function as a place of purification. Presumably, if everyone must pass through eschatological fire to enter the Kingdom (compare Matt 3:11), then Gehenna is only one mode of such purification and, clearly, the mode to avoid at all costs.[156]

Our modern concept of hell, rather than being Biblical, is likely based more on mythology (Hades) and literature such as Dante's *Inferno*. It certainly wasn't the concept of hell found in the first century. Gregory MacDonald writes, *"There was no single concept of hell in Second Temple Judaism but a cluster of images and concepts that held in common the claim that God would bring the wicked to account and punish them."*[157]

And also,

> *"When we find Jesus drawing on the idea of Gehenna, we must remember that it was not a clearly worked out concept. Beyond its being a place of fiery punishment for the wicked, the details, if anyone wanted to fill them in, were up for grabs."*[158]

I could simply quote a whole chapter of MacDonald's book as well as present lengthy quotes from other sources, but I will just summarize and suggest that you read the books that I am quoting from to flesh out what I am saying here. The bottom line, and as I have said earlier, hell as we have been taught is not a biblical concept. Looking at the actual meanings of the words translated as "hell," "eternal," and so forth, we find that nothing indicates that eternal punishment lasts forever. Hell typically refers to a "this world" context—ask people suffering around the world if they are experiencing hell. There is real-world suffering of biblical proportions.

That is not to say that there will not be a refiner's fire; we have already seen that this is the case, but there's no indication that this process is an eternal one or a literal one.[158] What can be said about the experience of hell's refining, even if it's not a literal lake of fire, is that it's best to avoid it if you can. There are still benefits to believing in the gospel.

GOD'S BIG PLAN

Jesus died to defeat sin, death, and the devil. However, we then come to something of a dilemma in evangelical theology— does God defeat all of sin and death, or does he just partially defeat them? If most of humanity is not saved, which it wouldn't be if you look at the number of Christians and Jews (I'll include them) compared to the total unsaved population, how is that winning? Did Jesus just defeat sin for the elect? What does defeating death mean for the unsaved dead? And when Paul says that Jesus canceled the written code, did he cancel it just for the chosen few? Did God so love the world that he only saved a handful (John 6), leaving most of them to suffer eternally? Let's look at a few things the Bible says.

> For the creation waits with eager longing for the revealing of the children of God, for the creation was subjected to futility, not of its own will, but by the will of the one who subjected it, in hope that the **creation itself will be set free from its enslavement to decay and will obtain the freedom of the glory of the children of God.** (Romans 8:19-21, emphasis mine)

> He is the image of the invisible God, the firstborn of all creation, for in him all things in heaven and on earth were created, things visible and invisible, whether thrones or dominions or rulers or powers— **all things have been created through him and for him.** He himself is before all things, and in him all things hold together. He is the head of the body, the church; he is the beginning, the firstborn from the dead, so that he might come to have first place in everything. For in him all the fullness of God was pleased to dwell, **and through him God was pleased to reconcile to himself all things, whether on earth**

or in heaven, by making peace through the blood of his cross. (Colossians 1:15-20, emphasis mine)

Are you starting to see the big picture now? Jesus defeats sin, death, and the devil to redeem and reconcile to himself all of creation. The whole shootin' match, as they used to say. So not only is God redeeming the select few, but all of creation, on Earth and in heaven, physical and spiritual. Back to my earlier Venn diagram discussion, we're talking about entire rectangle, the universe of all things, visible and invisible. Just let that sit a bit because it's huge.

We're so used to thinking about salvation in terms of our individual states and free will and so on that we fail to grasp the big picture. We are, by nature, creatures with very small minds, rarely thinking globally, much less universally. So many of us are so concerned with individual salvation (and the alternative) that we've missed the real good news—salvation is now, the Kingdom of God is now, and the future is going to be huge, for all of creation. New heavens, new earth—God wants to save it all, to set everything to rights (which is a phrase N.T. Wright uses). The real gospel message is this: Life's short, start now, and the Kingdom is here for everyone. Remember the old ads? "Be the first on your block to—."

By spending our lives in small theological boxes, we've missed the beauty of reality. We're like the poor saps in Plato's Cave, fighting over shadows when reality is just outside. Going back to John 3:16, *"For God so loved the world that he gave his only son, that whoever believes in him will have everlasting life."* Again, life is short, start now. You've likely noticed that "whoever believes" caveat; well, we'll get to that shortly.

UNIVERSAL SALVATION

You've probably gathered that I'm talking about universal salvation, where everyone who ever lived ends up in the same place. And that's true, this is what I'm talking about because that's what I believe the Bible teaches once the blinders come off. I have a couple of arguments that seem to make sense to me. Let's see if they make sense to you.

The first is that Colossians 1 (quoted above) states that all things were created for Jesus and that Jesus reconciled all things (in heaven and earth) to himself. This verse seems to echo Jesus' words in John 6:

> *Everything that the Father gives me will come to me, and anyone who comes to me I will never drive away, for I have come down from heaven not to do my own will but the will of him who sent me. And this is the will of him who sent me, that I should lose nothing of all that he has given me but raise it up on the last day. (6:37-39)*

And in John 10:

> *"My sheep hear my voice. I know them, and they follow me. I give them eternal life, and they will never perish. No one will snatch them out of my hand. My Father, in regard to what he has given me, is greater than all, and no one can snatch them out of the Father's hand. The Father and I are one." (10:27-30)*

There are some implications here. The first is that everything the Father gives Jesus will come to him. That is, all things on heaven and earth, and Jesus won't lose anything. In John 10, he repeats that nothing will be snatched out of the Father's or Jesus's hands. But again, we see the caveat of *"my sheep hear my voice . . . I give them eternal life."* I am not forgetting that. But let's look at a few more verses. (I have added the bold print.)

. . . he has made known to us the mystery of his will, according to his good pleasure that he outlined in Christ, **as a plan for the fullness of time, to gather up all things in him, things in heaven and things on earth.** *(Ephesians 1:9-10)*

Once again, a statement about the reconciliation of all things. The following passage from Romans starts off talking about the salvation of all of Israel, but then extends the thought to "all."

And in this way **all Israel will be saved,** *as it is written,*

"Out of Zion will come the Deliverer; he will banish ungodliness from Jacob."

"And this is my covenant with them when I take away their sins."

As regards the gospel they are enemies for your sake, but as regards election, they are beloved for the sake of their ancestors, for the gifts and the calling of God are irrevocable. Just as you were once disobedient to God but have now received mercy because of their disobedience, so also, they have now been disobedient in order that, **by the mercy shown to you, they also may now receive mercy. For God has imprisoned all in disobedience so that he may be merciful to all.** *(Romans 11:26-32)*

The following verse we all know but have assumed that it refers to all people in heaven and hell, the latter who acknowledge Jesus as their captor and punisher, to the glory of God. I suggest we rethink that whole scenario, especially since confessing Jesus as Lord is a key to being saved. (Romans 10:9) It should be noted that there is nothing in the Bible indicating that one cannot be saved post-death; we've seen that the opposite is the case.

> *Therefore, God exalted him even more highly and gave him the name that is above every other name, so that at the name given to Jesus every knee should bend, in heaven and on earth and under the earth, and **every tongue should confess that Jesus Christ is Lord**, to the glory of God the Father. (Philippians 2:9-11)*

Another verse that we typically overlook:

> *Now is the time for judgment on this world; now the ruler of this world will be driven out. But I, when I am lifted up from the earth, **will draw all people to myself**. (John 12:31-32)*

Now we're getting a bit more direct:

> *. . . and he is the atoning sacrifice for our sins, **and not for ours only but also for the sins of the whole world**. (1 John 2:2)*

> *The saying is sure and worthy of full acceptance. For to this end we toil and suffer reproach, because we have our hope set on the living God, **who is the Savior of all people, especially of those who believe**. (1 Timothy 4:9-10)*

See ". . . *all people, especially those who believe.*" How can you take this any other way than Jesus being the savior of "all people?"

Now we come to a great verse, that deserves to be unpacked a bit. Here Paul is comparing the sin of Adam (even though the word for Adam can refer to humankind in general, Paul gives him individual status) to the work of Jesus.

> *Therefore just as one man's trespass led to condemnation for all, so one man's act of righteousness **leads to justification and life for all. For just as through the one man's disobedience the many were made sinners, so through the one man's obedience the many will be made righteous.*** (Romans 5:18-19)

If Adam is the cause of the sinfulness of every single person who ever lived, why shouldn't Jesus save every single person who ever lived? How is Jesus's death not as powerful as Adam's sin? Think about that for a bit.

ARGUMENT #2

If you're like me, you'll have often thought of how someone uninterested or even opposed to being saved by God (I know many) would even consent to being saved after they die. Does God compel them to be saved? That's unlikely given human history. We will assume that they retain free will; if God didn't populate his world with robots, why change course now?

First of all, remember that we're not talking about individual salvation so much as the salvation of the whole shebang. It's like the Earth is about to be destroyed by a giant asteroid and God reaches down and flicks it away. Did you individually consent to being saved? No, and you might not have known you needed saving. Were you saved just the same? Yes. You might even be grateful, or you could remain clueless. You might have even been somewhat suicidal and are upset that you're still alive. But you're on Earth, so you're saved regardless.

But what about the individual nature of salvation? To get to the "every knee shall bow" stage, we need to reconcile with everyone individually. Now in general, we have three types of people: those who already follow Jesus, those who are anti-Christian, and those who are simply non-Christian. We can see how the already believers and the unreached would react positively to being saved, but what about the atheist or anti-Christian? This troubled me for some time until I had something of a revelation.

I think we could conclude with reasonable certainty that the cause of someone being an atheist or anti-Christian is the effect of sin. Regardless of how you perceive the post-death purgatorial state, we've seen in 1 Corinthians 3:12-15 that the metaphorical refiner's fire will do its work, so that *the builder will be saved, but only as through fire.* The inference here is that the refiner's fire is not an eternal process, but that at some point the person is purified and saved.

A few years ago, I discussed this with an old friend who had converted to Orthodoxy. He was explaining to me the Orthodox concept of God's presence being experienced as heaven by believers, and as hell by those who did not want to be there. My friend did not accept universal salvation because God would not override someone's free will, so they could spend eternity in their self-chosen misery. The issue in this scenario is whether someone can resist God's love for eternity.

However, I don't see this as a reasonable scenario. We've already talked about what Jesus accomplished by his death and resurrection, namely the complete and total defeat of sin, death, and the devil. Now, if the victory is complete, sin will be destroyed. This means that the refiner's fire cannot be a never-ending process, or there would never be victory. If sin is what keeps us from embracing God, and sin is eradicated, there would be nothing keeping anyone from confessing that Jesus Christ is lord. The picture is then complete. No more sin, everyone changed (1 Corinthians 15:51), and everyone saved from sin and death.

So what about Hitler? He is often used to represent the evilest of humanity. I don't think he was the most evil person who ever lived, but he'll do for an example. What made Hitler evil? Sin, obviously. Without sin, he undoubtedly would have been just a nice guy with a funny mustache. So what about Hitler after sin has been eradicated? With the plague of sin gone, we're left with a man whose entire life has gone up in flames, so to speak. Saved, as though through fire. Would he even be the same man as the Hitler we know? I would say not; I don't think any of us would be the same without the plague of sin in our lives. This is how we shall all be changed, all of us. Even Mother Theresa might be unrecognizable. Who knows? With sin defeated, even the worst people in history become people who have suffered great loss and are deserving of mercy. As Jesus said, *"Blessed are the poor in spirit, for theirs is the kingdom of heaven."* (Matthew 5:3) And if death is not the cutoff point for mercy, I would think this would apply.

MERCY...

Mercy triumphs over judgment. (James 2:13) Those
enamored with Calvinist or Reformed theology will
always point out that God's justice demands judgment
and punishment. They, of course, will follow Anselm
and treat all sins equally, so all deserve eternal torment.
(I've always wondered what would make someone want
to believe in eternal torment?) But what is justice? Isn't
it following God's Old Testament command of an eye
for an eye? The whole sentence reads, *"If anyone in-
jures his neighbor, as he has done it shall be done to him,
fracture for fracture, eye for eye, tooth for tooth; whatever
injury he has given a person shall be given to him."* (Leviticus 24:19-20 ESV) The point here is that the punishment
should not exceed the crime. That's justice. So why
should someone like Gandhi deserve the same punishment as Stalin (I hate to overuse Hitler)? Why would
God choose a different standard than he gave to Israel?

But God is not controlled by the rules of justice,
because we're told that God's mercy triumphs over
judgment. And, as it says in Lamentations 3:22, *"The
steadfast love of the LORD never ceases, his mercies never
come to an end;"* Mercy triumphs over judgment, and
never ends. And then we have 2 Peter 3:9, which reads,
*"The Lord is not slow about his promise, as some think of
slowness, but is patient with you, not wanting any to perish but all to come to repentance."* Patience, love, mercy.
This is how God is described.

But what about judgment? We know that we will all
be judged. Here's my understanding of judgment, once
again quoting 1 Corinthians:

> *Now if anyone builds on the foundation with gold,
> silver, precious stones, wood, hay, straw—the work*

of each builder will become visible, for the Day will disclose it, because it will be revealed with fire, and the fire will test what sort of work each has done. If what has been built on the foundation survives, the builder will receive a reward. If the work is burned up, the builder will suffer loss; the builder will be saved, but only as through fire. (1 Corinthians 3:12-15)

Isn't this God's judgment, to determine what stays and what goes through the fire? Does that mean eternal fire, or am I correct in understanding that this will not kill the "builder," but will only destroy what has been built of sin? I don't know exactly how it will work; I consider (and hope) that voluntary repentance will avoid some of the fire, but we'll just have to see. Regardless, I expect all will be purified and saved, either by grace or through fire.

THE PROBLEM OF FREE WILL

As I touched on above, one of the questions that often comes up when discussing universal salvation – that is, the predestination of everyone for salvation—is that of free will: Does being saved without your permission, or even against your will, overrule the individual's free will? The quick and obvious answer would appear to be, "Of course it does." But does it really? Or could predestination actually be compatible with free will?

The whole concept of free will seems a bit overblown in my opinion, as I have said previously. First, we have to accept the reality of the universe in which we live and the reality of our existence. Did anyone have a choice as to where or when they would be born? Are you proud to be an American (or anything else) because you chose to be born where you were, or are you simply proud of an accident of birth? Personally, I don't recall being asked when I wanted to be born, or to which parents. Considering that I'm diabetic, I think I would have chosen better genes.

And what about life? How much of our lives are due to things outside of our control? Would it be your free will to be injured in a car accident that was not your fault, or any number of other calamities that have befallen you due to things outside of your control? Where is the free will in that? Then, of course, there's the problem of death. Most of us won't have any say whatsoever about when or how we'll die. Our whole lives are subject to the wills of others, or to seemingly random acts of life.

Certainly, we have a certain amount of free will within the above constraints. Most of us can choose various paths for our lives, including education, what kind of jobs we get, who we marry, what kind of car we drive, whether we're Democrat or Republican, and so on. I don't believe any of these things are predestined for us (even who we'll marry). We are free to make any number of decisions, good or bad, and hopefully we learn from the past and improve our lives as we go on. But at some point, our ability to make decisions comes to an end, and we're faced with the possibility of eternal salvation. Do we have a say in that?

PREDESTINATION

If we were discussing Calvinist-style predestination, where God chooses individuals to save (and chooses those who don't get saved), then we may have an argument that predestination takes away free will of the individual. But you could always argue that God only predestines those for salvation who would make the right choice anyway. It gets a bit stretched, I think. Fortunately, we are not talking about this sort of predestination.

Let's look at predestination from more of a cosmic viewpoint: God chooses to save the whole of creation. In other words, creation itself is predestined to be saved. We make whatever free will choices we make, but Jesus comes to defeat sin and death, and as a result the whole universe is redeemed. The universe was always predestined to be restored and reconciled to God, and we were born into this flawed system that is destined to be fixed. We were born into a fallen universe and will just happen to benefit from its salvation as residents of this universe.

HOWEVER . . .

I can still hear people questioning whether God would save someone against their will, or raising the question of whether one is free to resist God's love. C. S. Lewis in *The Great Divorce* suggests that one can resist God's love. But this raises another issue: What would be the cause of someone wanting to resist God's love?

The answer is undoubtedly sin, which is the underlying cause of selfishness, bitterness, and so on. If, as I have said, sin is totally defeated along with death (the final enemy to be defeated), then it suggests that all become totally sinless, removing any reason for rejecting God's love. This would not be quashing free will but removing the root cause for choosing evil (which would no longer exist). Bottom line, I can't see where universal reconciliation in any way removes free will, to the extent that we have free will. There are obviously limitations to our free will—for example, we cannot choose to live forever. But within these limitations our free will is alive and well.

FINALLY

There are, as we have seen, some Bible passages that seem to disagree with what I have said here. This is the case with many topics in the Bible, and that's what God has given us to work with. We must carefully evaluate and weigh certain passages against others. For those who insist on believing in hell and eternal damnation, they also have to deal with these verses that I have quoted (and others) that support universal salvation. **It's a matter of starting with who we know God to be as revealed in Jesus, and then weighing the writings we have.** If we don't start with knowing who God is, then we're in trouble and likely to end up with doctrines like penal substitutionary atonement (I couldn't resist).

CHAPTER 12

FINAL THOUGHTS

"So," you wonder, "what happens when we die?"

I respond, *"Don't know, don't care."*

"I'm being serious!" you protest.

"I'm not joking," I reply. *"I've heard a lot of theories about the afterlife, have discarded some of them, and am open to the rest. I don't have a say in the matter anyway, so I figure I'll be fine with what everyone else is doing."*

"But the end of life and the end of the world are big deals, aren't they? Can we talk about them?"

"Certainly," I answer. *"And,"* I add, *"maybe I care a bit after all."*

SO, WHAT HAPPENS WHEN WE DIE?

I love a song by the Avett Brothers called "No Hard Feelings" that asks these questions, concluding that whatever happens the writer will die with no hard feelings. I share the sentiment.

So it's like, whatever. I used to have this terrible fear of dying. Actually—it wasn't fear of the dying part but of the unknown afterward. However, as I've aged, that's changed, although anxiety about the unknown tends to creep back at times. A couple of years ago I almost died. Literally. I knew I was having a risky surgery, and for the first time in my life I wasn't afraid of the outcome (other than that I might survive but be drastically impaired). As it turned out, there were complications, and I spent the next few days on a respirator with internal bleeding that they couldn't track down. But, I was not stressed (except for the hallucinations that nearly drove me crazy). I was okay with whatever happened; I was ready to go.

I also realized that if there's absolutely nothing after death, I'm okay with that. I have nothing more that I need. Like the Avett Brothers song, I have no hard feelings. I have no remorse, no regrets, nothing more that I need to do or have. I've lived a good life, have a happy family, and am happier than I deserve to be. And if there's something better, as we're assured there is, then I'm okay with that, too. It would be nice to not have to worry about my blood pressure, glucose levels, or my sodium intake, but I'm in no hurry to go anywhere. I am just a happy, satisfied guy. (But I'd like there to be dark chocolate.)

BEFORE WE GET THERE . . .

It is perhaps a good thing to talk about what the point of life is, regardless of what comes after. When I was in high school, I wore this pin on my jacket that said, "Is There Life After Birth?" It's humorous, but more profound than you first think. If the point of life is not to get to heaven (which I don't think it is), then what is it? Many people think in terms of some kind of merit system, like in my favorite comedy series *The Good Place*, in which your score when you die determines whether you go to the Good Place or the Bad Place. (It turns out that it's often hard to tell which is which.) God becomes Santa Claus, keeping his list of who's naughty and who's nice. I remember this terrible old song we used to sing in Sunday School that went, "Be careful, little eyes, what you see," because God was watching everything we did. I do believe that God sees us, but not to keep score.

If there's no point system, no reward, and no karma, then what's the point? For that matter, what's our motivation to be "good" if we don't benefit from it? I think we could get some great input from atheists on this, as many out there are neither living full of despair nor living a life of narcissism (narcissists are narcissists regardless of their belief system) I happen to know that there are some very great atheists out there, people who are kind, generous, loving, and who don't do these good things for a payout in any kind of afterlife. If you don't have any friends who are atheists, you should get at least one. Atheists, in my opinion, are gifts from God. Besides just being great friends, they will challenge you to ask the kinds of questions that you should be asking yourself about what you believe and why.

Phil Zuckerman Ph.D. writes in *Psychology Today*,

> . . . *many highly secular societies in the world today with the lowest rates of belief in God—such as Sweden, Japan, and the Netherlands—are among the safest, most well-functioning, and most humane societies on earth, with the lowest murder rates, violent crime rates, infant mortality rates, child abuse fatality rates, incarceration rates, etc. Conversely, those nations with the highest rates of corruption, murder,*

inequality, political repression, and violence—such as Colombia, El Salvador, and Jamaica—are among the most religious.[160]

He points out that this is only a correlation, not proof of causation, but it gets one thinking about the basis for morality. This same correlation is also found in states within the US, comparing the most religious populations to those states that are more secular.

On the other hand, some atheists will agree that without the existence of God, there is likely no objective basis for morality, which is kind of circular. If there were to be an absolute morality, where would it come from? A Platonist would argue that it exists in the world of ideals, similar to a theist's belief in a god-source. One could argue that the human brain has evolved to possess certain beneficial moral standards, or that this has evolved within functioning societies.

Tomas Ståhl, of the University of Chicago, recently conducted surveys to study how theists differ from atheists in how they view morality. In a review of his paper in *Science Daily*, the author writes,

> *Analysis of the results suggests that theists are more inclined than atheists to endorse moral values that promote group cohesion. Meanwhile, atheists are more likely to judge the morality of an action based on its consequences. However, atheists and theists appear to align on moral values related to protecting vulnerable individuals, liberty versus oppression, and being epistemically rational, i.e.: believing in claims when they are evidence-based and being skeptical about claims not backed by evidence.*[161]

Ståhl himself writes,

The most general take-home message from these studies is that people who do not believe in God do have a moral compass. In fact, they share many of the same moral concerns that religious believers have, such as concerns about fairness, and about protecting vulnerable individuals from harm.[162]

The point of all of this is to support a couple of my ideas concerning the meaning of life and all that.

1. Morality is not based on religion, but it does come from God as evidenced through nature and evolutionary development. *My thinking comes directly from Paul, in the first chapter of Romans:*

For what can be known about God is plain to them, because God has made it plain to them. Ever since the creation of the world God's eternal power and divine nature, invisible though they are, have been seen and understood through the things God has made. (Romans 1:19, 20)

I know that atheists will object to this claim, but I think it's just as valid as a belief that universally shared moral beliefs evolved on their own. (I could argue that in many areas, such as gun violence and human rights, the US appears to be devolving.) But whether you insert God into the equation or not, it seems pretty clear that there is a universal human morality, and that atheists can be, and often are, more moral than religious fundamentalists.

2. The point of life is relationship. *From a secular/ atheist perspective, relationship is high on the list* *of values. Richard Dawkins, one of the so-called "New Atheists," proposed his version of the Ten Commandments:*[163]

• *Do not do to others what you would not want them to do to you.*

• *In all things, strive to cause no harm.*

• *Treat your fellow human beings, your fellow living things, and the world in general with love, honesty, faithfulness, and respect.*

• *Do not overlook evil or shrink from administering justice, but always be ready to forgive wrongdoing freely admitted and honestly regretted. Live life with a sense of joy and wonder.*

• *Always seek to learn something new.*

• *Test all things; always check your ideas against the facts and be ready to discard even a cherished belief if it does not conform to them.*

• *Never seek to censor or cut yourself off from dissent; always respect the right of others to disagree with you.*

• *Form independent opinions based on your own reason and experience; do not allow yourself to be led blindly by others.*

• *Question everything.*

His list is similar to others I found, as well as those found in the Ståhl study mentioned above. Taking care of others, including the less fortunate, and often including nature, are shared values.

From a Christian standpoint, we universally (I use that word cautiously) accept that we were created to be in a relationship with God and that Eve was created for a relationship with Adam. They were to people the Earth, presumably for more relationships. A primary focus of Paul's writing is *reconciliation,* or restoring relationships to that Edenic state. So, relationship.

It is interesting to note that a major difference between the values of theists and atheists is the application of these values. Theists are more likely to value group adherence to principles, whereas atheists see the values are important regardless of the group context. I think we have all seen how this group adherence principle leads religions, especially the more fundamentalist ones, to have an us-versus-them mentality and so would apply moral rules differently inside and outside the group. This is clearly against any teachings of Christianity, by the way, although extremely pervasive in American evangelicalism. This is why those who study such things see extreme atheists as more moral than extreme theists.

To conclude this section, I would repeat that the point of life on Earth is a relationship—with family, friends, community, the world, and all of creation. And God, of course, when we choose to acknowledge him. There is no longer slave or free, male or female, or Jew or Gentile. The Spirit has been poured out on all flesh, God so loved the whole world, and he who does not love does not know God. Love each other, love your enemies, and forgive no matter what. Live in humility, and serve others, especially those who are not worthy. (Because we're not worthy, either.) This all works whether there's an afterlife or not.

PURPOSE

One of the things about being in a relationship with people is that you tend to do many of the things the other(s) are doing. Likewise, being in a relationship with Creator God means participating in whatever in the world he is doing. Many Christians, especially in the West, seem to believe that they have to be destined for greatness, despite the servant example Jesus showed us. They want to be special; they want to be famous, they want to be rich, they want to be powerful, they want to be a great leader, you name it. Being in a relationship with God and moving toward *theosis*, will likely result in the opposite of these goals. Someone once told me that anyone who wants to be a leader should not be one. I have found that to be true. Just look at our leaders. Few, if any, just want to serve.

God's present purpose is to, as N.T. Wright puts it, "put the world to rights."[164] Only Jesus could have defeated death, so that part is taken care of. But, we find that evil and chaos still run rampant throughout the Earth, as it's still inhabited by people living under the old system.

> *For the creation waits with eager longing for the revealing of the children of God, for the creation was subjected to futility, not of its own will, but by the will of the one who subjected it, in hope* **that the creation itself will be set free from its enslavement to decay and will obtain the freedom of the glory of the children of God. We know that the whole creation has been groaning together as it suffers together the pains of labor,** *and not only the creation, but we ourselves, who have the first fruits of the Spirit, groan inwardly while we wait for adoption, the redemption*

of our bodies. For in hope we were saved . . . (Romans 8:19-24, emphasis mine)

How do we participate in whatever God is doing, without getting a text from heaven saying, "Do this?" I have come to look at things in terms of **entropy**, which is a sciency word talking about the loss of thermodynamic energy, and how this loss increases over time. However, it has also become philosophically understood in a general sense as "chaos" or "disorder," and the same principle applies. Entropy/chaos is here at work and increases over time. Things fall apart. Things and people get old. A phone charger cord left in a drawer will tie itself in knots (well, it seems that way). Evil brings chaos. Mass murders, war, tornados and earthquakes, abuse, hunger, the list goes on.

I have made it my goal (or at least a plan) to oppose entropy, to fight against chaos and disorder however I can. This is what God's goal is for creation, and it just so happens that atheists often like to fight chaos as well. We work to combat climate change, the effects of water and air pollution, crime, war, and suffering, regardless of whether we believe in God or not.

One caveat here—those Christians who believe in the false narrative that "it's all going to burn" or that they will be "Raptured" up out of the mess often wash their hands of any responsibility to those around them. They've become "so heavenly-minded that they're no earthly good," as the old saying goes. Their relationship growth has been stunted, and they're of little use to anyone around them. It is the opposite of our goal of undoing chaos. As long as we're working to put things in proper order, I believe we're on point.

SO, BACK TO THE ORIGINAL QUESTION: WHAT HAPPENS WHEN WE DIE?

Once again, my answer is, "Don't know, don't care (much)." But humans keep asking, so let's take this a little deeper.

The honest answer is that we do not know. We do know that the common depiction of heaven has no basis in reality (and I don't believe any of the stories about people going to heaven have any basis in reality either) as well as no biblical basis (if you pay attention to what it says).

Jesus told the thief on the cross next to him, *"Today you will be with me in paradise."* (Luke 23:43) However, our understanding is that Jesus went to preach to those who were in the place of the dead. (I Peter 3:18-20; 1 Peter 4:6; Ephesians 4:9-10) Traditional translations say "hell," but that hardly sounds like paradise. We do know that at some point we end up in the place that Jesus has prepared for us.

> *My Father's house has many rooms; if that were not so, would I have told you that I am going there to prepare a place for you? And if I go and prepare a place for you, I will come back and take you to be with me that you also may be where I am. You know the way to the place where I am going." (John 14:2-4)*

This, of course, started a discussion among the disciples, who didn't get it either. All we know is that at some point we'll end up in the Father's house, which no doubt is another metaphor for being in God's presence. So when Jesus told the thief "today," was he meaning that what we've understood to be hell is paradise, or was he referring to the "Father's house?" These are good questions, and I don't have the answers. I just believe that it's all good.

SO WHAT ABOUT THE RAPTURE?

Not gonna happen. Referencing Colossians 1, N.T. Wright has this to say:

> Redemption is not simply making creation a bit better . . . Nor is it rescuing spirits and souls from an evil material world . . . It is the remaking of creation, having dealt with the evil that is defacing and distorting it.[165]

The whole concept of the "Rapture," when Christians supposedly disappear up in the clouds, is a relatively recent invention. Legend has it that a Scottish woman named Margaret MacDonald had a vision in 1830 in which the Rapture and other "left behind" elements were revealed to her. Another story is that the Rapture was developed by a rather poor scholar and preacher named John Darby, also in 1930. Darby's ideas were then incorporated into the Scofield Study Bible, which further popularized the teachings.[166] Because, after all, it wouldn't be in the Bible if it weren't true, right?

While largely incoherent and dependent upon taking various Bible passages out of context, the concept of the Rapture is still defended by many today. But, in my opinion, it's largely nonsense and avoids the plain reading of Scripture. For a more detailed explanation than I care to include here, I suggest reading N. T. Wright's book, *Surprised by Hope*. The bottom line, no Rapture will happen and no one will be left behind. The world is not "all gonna burn," as the saying used to go. Rather, the Kingdom of Heaven will finally appear as all of creation is reconciled to God. As Wright writes,

> What has happened in the death and resurrection of Jesus Christ, in other words, is by no means limited to its effects on those human beings who believe the gospel and thereby find new life here and hereafter. It resonates out, in ways that we can't fully see or understand, into the vast recesses of the universe.[167]

> . . . the gospel of Jesus Christ announces that what God did for Jesus at Easter he will do not only for all those who are "in Christ" but also for the entire cosmos. It will be an act of new creation, parallel to and derived from the act of new creation when God raised Jesus from the dead.[168]

> . . . So when Paul says, "We are citizens of heaven," he doesn't at all mean that when we're done with this life we'll be going off to live in heaven. What he means is that the savior, the Lord, Jesus the King—all of those were of course imperial titles—will come from heaven to earth, to change the present situation and state of his people.[169]

Wright also explains that the concept of raising up in the clouds is not to be taken literally, and is used elsewhere:

> Then there is the story of Daniel 7, in which the persecuted people of God are vindicated over their pagan enemy by being raised up on the clouds to sit with God in glory. This "raising up on the clouds," which Jesus applies to himself in the gospels, is now applied by Paul to the Christians who are presently suffering persecution.[170]

Hopefully, the age of "don't be left behind" as an evangelism tool is over, but that's likely too much to hope for. What we know is, that when the end of this age happens, Christ will return—Paul twice refers to the sound of a trumpet—the dead will be raised, and we will all be changed. (1 Thessalonians 4:16, 1 Corinthians 15:52)

WHAT ABOUT THE JUDGMENT?

First, let's stop thinking of judgment in terms of condemnation—judgment is about making decisions. God's judgment doesn't mean he's going to destroy everything, it means he's going to decide what is worth keeping, and what needs to go. Not people, but people's characters:

> For no one can lay any foundation other than the one that has been laid; that foundation is Jesus Christ. Now if anyone builds on the foundation with gold, silver, precious stones, wood, hay, straw— the work of each builder will become visible, for the day will disclose it, because it will be revealed with fire, and the fire will test what sort of work each has done. If the work that someone has built on the foundation survives, the builder will receive a wage. If the work is burned up, the builder will suffer loss; the builder will be saved, but only as through fire. (1 Corinthians 3:11-15)

Once again, if a builder's work doesn't survive, he will still be saved, but only after the defects are burned away. This, I believe, is what God's judgment is about. If you want to talk about sheep and goats, or grain and weeds, fine—the result is the same. We will all be judged (2 Corinthians 5:10) by God's fire (aka God's love), and whatever remains will be good. Now obviously this is still a metaphor, but you get the idea.

Surviving the Day of Judgment (which I presume can also represent an extended time of judgment and purification) with our works intact depends upon how we've lived our lives. The key appears to be love; if we've lived a life of love, I have a feeling that we'll enjoy judgment day much better than those who lived self-focused lives. We look again at 1 John 4:7-8:

> Beloved, let us love one another, because love is from God; everyone who loves is born of God and knows God. Whoever does not love does not know God, for God is love.

As we discussed earlier in the book, Christianity is a religion of mystery and wonder—God is so much bigger than we can imagine that we fail if we try to grasp it. We can be doctrinally incorrect and biblically illiterate, but our love shows that we know God. As Martin Luther put it, the key to life is to "love God and do as you please." Love God, love your neighbor, love your enemy—against this, there is no law (Galatians 5:22).

REVELATION–AKA THE APOCALYPSE

You've likely heard about the Book of Revelation, with its Armageddon, horsemen, beasts, and of course, 666 and the Antichrist. And you probably wonder what it's all about, especially since I've shot down the Rapture already. To be honest, I wonder what it's all about, too. I'm leaning towards agreeing with those brave souls throughout history who don't think Revelation is all that inspired. But I could be wrong; it's entirely likely that it references first century Rome's control over Israel and the destruction of the temple, etc. One thing I am sure of is that you can't read it literally.

Revelation, or more accurately, the Revelation of John, is an example of apocalyptic literature, not uncommon at the time it was written. It tells of visions full of highly symbolic imagery that more than likely had to do with current first century happenings rather than futurist events. It was a way of writing social and political commentary without getting into trouble; think of it like an early form of Orwell's *Animal Farm*. However, in the final chapters there is a description of the *real* end times, while still full of imagery, presents some very interesting concepts that we should consider. Again, these chapters could have referred to first century life, however, we can find some potential future relevance.

For a deeper understanding of these final chapters of Revelation, I will point you to Bradley Jersak's book *Her Gates Will Never Be Shut: Hope, Hell, and the New Jerusalem*, which is my source for this section. Jersak points out that what we are reading is the retelling of a series of visions; John would have described them as best he could. And, as with our dreams, the imagery may not be consistent from vision to vision.

Revelation 21 starts us off with a vision of the New Jerusalem, and the announcement, *"See, I am making all things new."* (21:5) He continues that the conquerors will inherit the water of life, and to the *"cowardly, the faithless, the polluted . . ."* they will go to the lake of fire. Verse 26 states that nothing unclean will enter God's new city. Seems pretty clear so far, right?

Chapter 22 talks more about the city, and then we get to verses 14 and 15:

> Blessed are those who wash their robes, so that they will have the right to the tree of life and may enter the city by the gates. Outside are the dogs and sorcerers and sexually immoral and murderers and idolaters and everyone who loves and practices falsehood.

So, those who have washed their robes (aka the Bride) will enter the city, but the unclean (who were thrown into the lake of fire), are outside. We no longer see a lake of fire, so we assume this is a new image John is seeing. Now we come to the famous song in verse 17:

> The Spirit and the bride say, "Come." And let everyone who hears say, "Come." And let everyone who is thirsty come. Let anyone who wishes take the water of life as a gift.

So now we have God and the people of God offering admittance to all who are outside the city, presumably the sinners previously excluded and/or thrown into the lake of fire. What are we to make of this?

My thinking is that the lake of fire represents the purifying fire of God's love, which would be synonymous with washing their robes in the River of Life that flows from the throne. Those who have already "washed their robes" have admittance into the city, and then they welcome all the "unsaved" to be washed/saved. It is presumed that this will happen after this life is over and that these are visions of eternity. However, it is also possible to see this as a metaphor for our earthly life, illustrating once again the potential for universal salvation. As we see in verse 21:25, the city's gates will never be shut. In other words, it's never too late to "wash your robes." As with Mr. Jersak, I opt for the futurist interpretation because it seems a better fit. I appreciate Jersak's work examining these last two chapters; it helps make sense of what is to me an overwhelming collection of strange visions. Hopefully, it (and even my brief overview) will have the same impact on you.

I BELIEVE

Rather than being a religion of rules, and judgments, and having to get things right, I see Christianity as a religion of love, a few certainties, a lot of "I don't knows," and a whole lot of wonder. A difference between me and many who call themselves "progressives" is that while I don't believe in biblical inerrancy or a literal interpretation of creation, and I reject penal substitutionary atonement and believe in the possibility of universal salvation, I hold to the early belief of the Church as stated in the creeds such as the Apostles' Creed, perhaps the oldest of the creeds:

I believe in God, the Father almighty,

creator of heaven and earth.

I believe in Jesus Christ, God's only Son, our Lord,

who was conceived by the Holy Spirit,

born of the virgin Mary, suffered under Pontius Pilate,

was crucified, died, and was buried;

he descended to the dead.

On the third day he rose again;

he ascended into heaven,

he is seated at the right hand of the Father,

and he will come to judge the living and the dead.

I believe in the Holy Spirit, the holy catholic Church,

the communion of saints,

the forgiveness of sins,

the resurrection of the body, and the life everlasting.

Some of you might have questions about what this creed is saying. We should take a few moments to break it down and discuss it.

I Believe in God, the Father Almighty, Creator of Heaven and Earth.

I believe in the God of creation (however he chose to do it). He could have taken six days (and rested on the seventh), or he could have taken billions of Earth-years to get to the point of Adam, who may or may not have been an actual person; he could be a metaphorical representation of all humanity. Either way, I believe that we are God's creation, as is the rest of the cosmos. The Bible tells us this but does not tell us how; it's not a science or history textbook. The creed does not specify particulars.

I Believe in Jesus Christ, God's Only Son, Our Lord, Who Was Conceived By the Holy Spirit, Born of the Virgin Mary, Suffered Under Pontius Pilate, Was Crucified, Died, and Was Buried; He Descended to the Dead.

Do you remember our chapter on the incarnation? I believe that Jesus is the Son of God (that is, he *is fully God*). The Nicene Creed states it like this: *"We believe in one Lord, Jesus Christ, the only Son of God, eternally begotten of the Father, God from God, Light from Light, true God from true God, begotten, not made, of one Being with the Father; through him all things were made."* I believe that the Bible makes it clear that Jesus was God, and that it wasn't just a later development by some second or third century theologians. Jesus was God from the beginning, both at the beginning of creation and as a first century baby born to Mary. He died, and "descended to the dead." Earlier translations say "hell," but that's a presumptuous interpretation. More literally, he went to wherever the dead were staying and preached the good news to them.

On the Third Day He Rose Again; He Ascended into Heaven, He Is Seated at the Right Hand of the Father, and He Will Come to Judge the Living and the Dead.

I believe that Jesus bodily rose from the dead, and after forty days he "ascended into heaven." I understand that the words "descended" and "ascended" are not necessarily literal—that is, the dead are not necessarily living under the earth, or that heaven is somewhere directly overhead of Jerusalem. But we know he is back with the person of God the Father (who is not male nor female but was best represented by a male parent at that time). I also believe that Jesus will return to be with us, and he will judge us as I discussed earlier in this chapter.

I Believe in the Holy Spirit . . .

These last lines seem to be an attempt to toss in everything else, don't they? The Nicene Creed fills this out a bit more: *"We believe in the Holy Spirit, the Lord, the giver of life, who proceeds from the Father, who with the Father and the Son is worshiped and glorified, who has spoken through the prophets . . ."* In other words, the Holy Spirit is also fully God.

. . . The Holy Catholic Church, the Communion of Saints . . .

I understand the biggest problem people have with the closing of the Apostles' Creed is the line about the "holy Catholic Church." This is not referring to the Roman Catholic Church, which didn't even exist when the creed was written. "Catholic" merely means "universal." There are not thousands of churches, there is only one church, to which all believers belong. There are thousands of individual man-made church groups which don't matter all that much, as far as I'm concerned. One Church, universal. Here, I have to disagree with the Eastern Orthodox churches, who believe that they are the only true church. They obviously have the best historic claim, but as Jesus said to the Jewish believers, *"I have sheep not of this fold"* (John 10:16), which I think would also apply here in a metaphorical sense. Some Orthodox believers will agree with me, but many will not, which is their prerogative.

. . . The Forgiveness of Sins, the Resurrection of the Body, and the Life Everlasting.

I wholeheartedly believe in forgiveness, and forgiveness, and forgiveness. I also believe that we will be bodily resurrected, with a new, perfect body, even if we were dismembered or cremated. Don't ask me how it works, I just believe that it does and that we will all live forever and ever, amen, somewhere in God's presence.

WHY THE CREEDS?

The creeds of the Church are important to me because they are my anchor—I can wonder about a lot of things, but for me, I am anchored to the gospel through the basic teachings of the Church. This is a bit ironic because many evangelicals don't even hold to the creeds. The creeds are important because this is what the early church believed were essential beliefs, as basic as possible. There's no statement about how to baptize anyone, how to get saved, or any number of things some churches think are important. In the words of a famous humorless TV policeman, "Just the facts." No matter how much I wonder and wander—and I do both—I remain fully connected to the ancient, universal church through the creeds, and my belief that God loves me.

A QUICK RECAP

Now that we're coming to the end (this has been fun, hasn't it?), I thought I would try to summarize everything we've talked about in one final section, what they call an Executive Summary.

It seems to me that the modern church has tried to do whatever it can to take the wonder out of faith in God. There are too many rules, regulations, expectations, and hoops to jump through, when all you have to do to worship God is to lay in the grass, look up at the sky, and go "Wow!" So, I've tried to smash several popular boxes that have kept God and our faith from running wild and free, without losing the plot, because the plot is important. As G. K. Chesterton wrote,

> The more I considered Christianity, the more I found that while it had established a rule and order, the chief aim of that order was to give room for good things to run wild.[171]

We find the plot in the Bible, which is full of stories, poetry, musings, history, and a few hundred laws, written down over a couple thousand years by several mostly unknown people. The plot of the Old Testament is that God, who created the world in some remarkable way we don't understand, has a plan for all creation. The main characters in the story are the Israelites, through whom God chose to reveal himself to the rest of the world. The Jews failed and ended up in exile. Then Jesus came, taught us who God was, died, rose again, and set the plan in motion to defeat sin, death, and the devil, and by doing to redeem the whole world.

The New Testament is a collection of stories, letters, and one apocalyptic piece that explains why Jesus came through stories, metaphors, and teachings. Taking any small part out of context will lead you in weird directions. The whole Bible is inspired, but that doesn't mean that there are no contradictions or differences of opinion between writers. But I believe that the Bible that we have is the Bible we are meant to have, complete with disputing translations and all.

A few centuries down the road, Augustine started melding his prior philosophies into Christianity, taking small parts of the NT out of context and setting the Western Church off in a strange new direction, which has led to hundreds of different denominations of Christianity, each with their own little weirdnesses and errors. The Eastern Church remains, along with what I consider to be some cultural and traditional baggage. This will no doubt offend the Orthodox, but I'm just being honest about my own opinions. I owe a lot to the Eastern Church and don't mean to offend them in any way.

Despite this baggage, as I've called it, peeling back layers of Western misdirection led me to find that many of my ideas about God, man, salvation, and eternity were very similar to the thinking of the early (and the current Eastern) church. Their stability for over 2,000 years has preserved the thinking of the early church fathers, which I believe is important for us today. The Orthodox does not believe that the teaching can be separated from the traditions and attitudes of the Church, however, as a rebellious modernist, I have parsed out the teachings anyway. What I have come to believe is that God is not a god of wrath, but a God of love. We are created in God's image. Not evil creatures deserving death, instead humanity is plagued by sin and in need of rescue. We were created to exist in a relationship with God, and that is our destiny. As one of the Church Fathers put it, "Jesus became man so that we could become God(like)." Jesus became fully man while remaining fully God. He sacrificed himself to resurrect and defeat sin and death. He will come again to rescue the whole of creation, us included.

It is only through Jesus that we are saved, whether we believe in Jesus now or follow some other path. Not all paths lead to Jesus, but through death or Jesus reappearing I believe we will all be met by Jesus in the afterlife. There is nothing that says that our options for salvation end at death—believing in Buddha will not save you, but believing in Jesus when you see him will. Again, I believe all will meet Jesus eventually—as the Bible says,

> . . . at the name of Jesus every knee should bend, in heaven and on earth and under the earth, and every tongue should confess that Jesus Christ is Lord, to the glory of God the Father. (Philippians 2:10-11)

I do not believe that sinners will suffer in hell forever, separated from God. Rather, I believe that we will all exist in God's presence but may experience it differently. Some will experience God's overwhelming love; others will experience that love as a purifying fire, until all the works of sin are destroyed. As the final chapters of Revelation show, all are invited to enter the New Jerusalem. Details yet to be announced.

In my humble opinion, the Western Church deviated from the truth at Augustine and has continued in error, especially through the teachings of Calvin. These Western theologies have created theological boxes that have kept their god imprisoned. In truth, no box can hold God, who is bigger than we can imagine. He does not live in fear of liberalism, science, or doubt. If anything, he is the God of these things and they all exist to serve him. As someone once said, all we have to fear is fear.

ACKNOWLEDGEMENTS

Thank you, readers. I appreciate that you had my book in your hands, whether in paper or some digital format. It means a lot to me, and I hope that it has meant something to you.

ENDNOTES

1 G. K. (Gilbert Keith) Chesterton, *Orthodoxy* (Waking Lion Press, 2007).

2 Ken Blue and Alden Swan, *The Gospel Uncensored: How Only Grace Leads to Freedom* (Westbow Press, 2010).

3 Gore Vidal, *Reflections Upon a Sinking* Ship (1. Ed.) (Boston: Little, Brown, 1969).

4 Jack Jenkins, "'Nones' Now as Big as Evangelicals, Catholics in the US," (https://religionnews. com/2019/03/21/nones-now-as-big-as-evangelicals-catholics-in-the-us/, March 2019).

5 Ryan Burge, "The 2018 GSS Was Just Released and There's Some Big News. Those of "No Religion" (23.1%) Are Statistically the Same Size as Evangelicals (22.8%) There Was Also a Small Resurgence of Mainline Protestants, While Catholics Are down 3% in the Last Four Years. https://t.co/uiyDSe7M6f," Tweet, *Twitter*, March 2019.

6 Walter C. Smith. "Immortal, Invisible, God Only Wise," 1867.

7 Peter Enns, *The Sin of Certainty: Why God Desires Our Trust More Than Our "Correct" Beliefs* (Reprint edition),(HarperOne, 2016), 8.

8 Joel Osteen, *Your Best Life Now: 7 Steps to Living at Your Full Potential* (Special 10th Anniversary Edition) (FaithWords, 2014).

9 Peter Enns, *How the Bible Actually Works: In Which I Explain How an Ancient, Ambiguous, and Diverse Book Leads Us to Wisdom Rather Than Answers and Why That's Great News* (Reprint Edition), (HarperOne, 2019).

10 Augustine of Hippo, *The Literal Interpretation of Genesis (De Genesi Ad Litteram)*, vol. 1 Ch. 19, n.d.

11 Kelly James Clark, ed., "Mortimer J. Adler, A Philosopher's Religious Faith," in *Philosophers Who Believe: The Spiritual Journeys of 11 Leading Thinkers*, (IVP Academic, 1997), 207.

12 Russell Shorto, *Descartes' Bones: A Skeletal History of the Conflict Between Faith and Reason* (Reprint Edition), (Vintage, 2009).

13 Martin Luther, *Luther's Works. Volume 54, Table Talk* (Philadelphia (Pa.) : Fortress Press, 1967).

14 https://www.azquotes.com/quote/575002?ref= faith-and-reason

15 Shorto, *Descartes' Bones*, 2.

16 Richard A. Watson, *The Breakdown of Cartesian Metaphysics* (Indianapolis: Hackett Publishing Company, Inc., 1998).

17 Shorto, *Descartes' Bones*, 78–79.

18 Shorto, 83.

19 Francis Collins, "The Question of God. Other Voices. Francis Collins". PBS, 2004. https://www.pbs. org/wgbh/questionofgod/voices/collins.htm.

20 Immanuel Kant, *Critique of Pure Reason* (Cambridge University Press, 1999).

21 Richard Dawkins, *The God Delusion* (Houghton Mifflin Co., 2006).

22 Bertrand Russell, *The Problems of Philosophy: A 1912 Book by the Philosopher Bertrand Russell, in Which the Author Attempts to Create a Brief and Accessible Guide to . . . Focusing on Knowledge Rather Than Metaphysics* (Les Prairies Numeriques, 2020).

23 Enns, *The Sin of Certainty*, 17.

24 Carl Sagan, *Pale Blue Dot: A Vision of the Human Future in Space* (Reprint Edition), (New York: Ballantine Books, 1997).

25 Douglas A. Knight and Amy-Jill Levine, *The*

Meaning of the Bible: What the Jewish Scriptures and Christian Old Testament Can Teach Us (HarperOne, 2012).

26 Amy-Jill Levine and Marc Zvi Brettler, *The Bible With and Without Jesus: How Jews and Christians Read the Same Stories Differently* (Annotated Edition), (HarperOne, 2020), 2.

27 Knight and Levine, *The Meaning of the Bible.*

28 Bradley Jersak and Peter Enns, *A More Christlike Word: Reading Scripture the Emmaus Way* (Whitaker House, 2021).

29 Vance Morgan, "God Said It, I Believe It, That Settles It? Not so Much." *Freelance Christianity*, June 2021.

30 Morgan.

31 Enns, Peter and Meredith Riedel. "Episode 226: What Is Byzantine Christianity? (And Why Should We Care?)" The Bible For Normal People (Podcast). November 2022, https://thebiblefornormalpeople.com/episode-226.

32 Shorto, *Descartes' Bones*, 78–79.

33 Jared Yates Sexton, *American Rule: How a Nation Conquered the World but Failed Its People* (New York: Dutton, 2020).

34 Peter Enns and David Lambert, "Episode 232: Is the Bible 'Scripture?'" February 2023.

35 The Bible for Normal People, "A Technical Term That Will Change Your Life Forever," February 2019.

36 Peter Enns, *The Evolution of Adam: What the Bible Does and Doesn't Say about Human Origins* (Illustrated Edition), (Grand Rapids, MI: Brazos Press, 2012), 47–48.

37 Enns, 50.

38 Enns, *How the Bible Actually Works*, 2019, 108.

39 Richard Elliott Friedman, *Who Wrote the Bible?* (2nd Edition), (Simon & Schuster, 2019), 17.

40 Enns, *How the Bible Actually Works*, 2019, 84.

41 Adele Berlin and Marc Zvi Brettler, eds., *The Jewish Study Bible: Second Edition* (2nd Edition), (New York: Oxford University Press, 2014), 3.

42 Friedman, *Who Wrote the Bible?*, 22.

43 McGrath, James F. *The A to Z of the New Testament: Things Experts Know That Everyone Else Should Too* (Kindle Edition), Eerdmans, 23.

44 Enns, Peter. *The Bible Tells Me So: Why Defending Scripture Has Made Us Unable to Read It* (Reprint Edition), (HarperOne, 2014), 75-77.

45 McGrath, James F. *The A to Z of the New Testament*, 29.

46 Phillip Cary, *Good News for Anxious Christians: 10 Practical Things You Don't Have to Do* (Grand Rapids, MI: Brazos Press, 2010), 31.

47 Enns, 61.

48 George Cronk, *The Message of the Bible: An Orthodox Christian Perspective* (St Vladimirs Seminary Press, 2010), 21.

49 McGrath, James F. *The A to Z of the New Testament*, 216.

50 Levine and Brettler, *The Bible With and Without Jesus*, (HarperOne, 2020), 11.

51 Levine and Brettler, xiii.

52 The International Council on Biblical Inerrancy, "The Chicago Statement on Biblical Inerrancy," *Journal of the Evangelical Theological Society* 21, no. 4 (December 1978): 289–96.

53 Anthony Thomas, "Questioning Darwin" (HBO, August 2014).

54 Religion Prof: The Blog of James F. McGrath, "Unfalsifiable Inerrancy," *Religion Prof: The Blog of James F. McGrath*, February 2014.

55 The International Council on Biblical Inerrancy, "The Chicago Statement on Biblical Inerrancy," Article X.

56 Cronk, *The Message of the Bible*, 22.

57 N T Wright, "How Can The Bible Be Authoritative? (The Laing Lecture for 1989)," *Vox Evangelica* 21 (1991): 7–32.

58 Jersak and Enns, *A More Christlike Word.*

59 Enns, *How the Bible Actually Works*, 2019, 77.

60 Enns, 79.

61 Enns, 166–67.

62 Jersak and Enns, *A More Christlike Word.*

63 Jersak and Enns.

64 Jersak and Enns, l. 903.

65 Martin Luther and John Dillenberger, "Preface to the Epistles of St. James and St. Jude," *Martin Luther: Selections from His Writings*, (Garden City, N.Y.: Anchor, March 1958), 35–36.

66 Psalm 40:6-8

67 Wes Seeliger, *Western Theology* (Atlanta: Forum House, 1973).

68 Enns, *The Sin of Certainty*, 53.

69 A slapstick silent film comedy ensemble.

70 Jersak and Enns, *A More Christlike Word*, l. 345.

71 Cronk, *The Message of the Bible*, 55.

72 Levine and Brettler, *The Bible With and Without Jesus*, 3.

73 Levine and Brettler, 4.

74 Søren Kierkegaard (May 5, 1813 - November 11, 1855) was a Danish theologian and philosopher, considered to be the father of existentialism.

75 The multiverse theory is that there are an infinite number of universes, so the odds would be in favor of one being able to support life. Again, my incredible oversimplification.

76 Let the Quran Speak, "A Muslim Understanding of God's Perpetual Activity | Dr. Shabir Ally," December 2021.

77 Stephen De Young, *Religion of the Apostles: Orthodox Christianity in the First Century* (Ancient Faith Publishing, 2021), 35.

78 "Nicene Creed" (Evangelical Lutheran Worship, 2006).

79 "Incarnate," *Merriam-Webster.com*, https://www.bing.com/search?pglt=41&q=Incarnate.

80 Patrick Henry Reardon, *Reclaiming the Atonement: An Orthodox Theology of Redemption: Volume 1: The Incarnate Word* (Ancient Faith Publishing, 2015), 268–72.

81 Eugenia Scarvelis Constantinou, *Thinking Orthodox: Understanding and Acquiring the Orthodox Christian Mind* (Ancient Faith Publishing, 2020), 27. *Phronema* involves the mind, but while it can be described as "mentality" or "mindset," it is neither formed nor tested by rationalism nor is it proven by empirical methods. The most significant link is between mind and behavior.

82 Bradley Jersak, *A More Christlike God: A More Beautiful Gospel* (1st Edition), (CWR Press, 2015), 99.

83 De Young, *Religion of the Apostles*, 35.

84 De Young, 27.

85 De Young, 42.

86 Constantinou, *Thinking Orthodox*, 123–24.

87 Irenaeus, "Against Heresies (St. Irenaeus)," in *Ante-Nicene Fathers*, ed. Alexander Roberts, James Donaldson, and Cleveland Coxe, trans. Alexander Roberts and William Rambaut, vol. 1, Ante-Nicene Fathers (Buffalo, NY: Christian Literature Publishing Co, 1885).

88 Irenaeus.

89 Reardon, *Reclaiming the Atonement*, 1697–1700.

90 Reardon, 1560–62.

91 Peter Enns, *Inspiration and Incarnation: Evangelicals and the Problem of the Old Testament* (Annotated Edition), (Grand Rapids, Mich: Baker Academic, 2005), 6.

92 Reardon, *Reclaiming the Atonement*, 1482–87.

93 Reardon, 231—233.

94 Reardon, *Reclaiming the Atonement*, 1746—1748.

95 Reardon, 1788—1790.

96 Reardon, 983—986.

97 Jersak, *A More Christlike God*, 2015, 226.

98 Jersak, 227.

99 C. S. Lewis, *The Weight of Glory* (1st Edition), (San Francisco: HarperOne, 2001).

100 Dietrich Bonhoeffer, *The Cost of Discipleship* (New Edition), (SCM Press, 2015).

101 Michael Azkoul, *The Influence of Augustine of Hippo on the Orthodox Church* (Lewiston, NY: Edwin Mellen Pr, 1991).

102 Azkoul.

103 Stephen A. Cooper, *Augustine for Armchair Theologians* (Louisville: Westminster John Knox Press, 2002).

104 My earlier critique of Western authors and Augustine holds true for this book as well.

105 Neo-Platonism is a mishmash of Platonism and other philosophies that were originated by Plotinus in the 3rd Century.

106 A short explanation of East versus West: As centuries went by, greater and greater division occurred between the Church as a whole and the branch of the church that was centered in Rome. They eventually excommunicated each other in the 11th Century. We refer to the Roman church (and their descendants) as the "West" and everyone else as the Eastern Church, AKA the Orthodox.

107 Full text of "Fr. Michael Azkoul - The influence of Augustine of Hippo on the Orthodox Church"

108 Azkoul, *The Influence of Augustine of Hippo on the Orthodox Church*.

109 Constantinou, *Thinking Orthodox*, 43.

110 Essentially, "mindset" Constantinou, *Thinking Orthodox*, p. 34

111 Constantinou, 312.

112 Danielle Shroyer, *Original Blessing: Putting Sin in Its Rightful Place* (Minneapolis: Fortress Press, 2016).

113 Azkoul, *The Influence of Augustine of Hippo on the Orthodox Church*, 2401—2402.

114 Azkoul, 2402—2404.

115 Johnathan Edwards, "Sinners in the Hands of an Angry God" (Sermon, July 1741).

116 Jonathan Cleland, "Augustine's Doctrine of the Atonement as Presented in The Trinity," *Center for Ancient Christian Studies*, March 2021.

117 Anselm, "Chapter 9," in *Cur Deus Homo*, trans. Sidney Deane, vol. Book 1 (Chicago, IL: The Open Court Publishing Company, 1903).

118 Rachel Erdman, "Sacrifice as Satisfaction, Not Substitution: Atonement in the Summa Theologiae," *Anglican Theological Review* 96, no. 3 (2014): 461–80.

119 Erdman.

120 Thomas Aquinas, "Llallae. Question 85, Article 1, Response," in *The Summa Theologiae*, trans. Fathers of the English Dominican Province, Second and Revised, 1920.

121 Paul Axton, "Did John Calvin Invent Penal Substitution?" *Forging Ploughshares*, May 2021. https://forgingploughshares.org/2021/05/20/did-calvin-invent-penal-substitution/.

122 John Calvin, "Chapter 16, 10," in *Institutes of the Christian Religion (1581)*, trans. Henry Beveridge, vol. Book II (Edinburgh: The Edinburgh Printing Company, 1885).

123 Axton, "Did John Calvin Invent Penal Substitution?"

124 Damon Linker, "Calvin And American Exceptionalism," *The New Republic*, July 2009.

125 Harry Freedman, "Atonement- A Made Up Word with an Impossible Meaning," *The Times of Israel* (https://blogs.timesofisrael.com/atonement-a-made-up-word-with-an-impossible-meaning/, May 2019).

126 Jersak, *A More Christlike God*, 2015, 228.

127 Brian Zahnd, *Sinners in the Hands of a Loving God: The Scandalous Truth of the Very Good News* (Colorado Springs, Colorado: WaterBrook, 2017), 14.

128 Alvin F. Kimel, *Destined for Joy: The Gospel of Universal Salvation* (Independently published, 2022), 27.

129 Shroyer, *Original Blessing*.

130 Jersak, *A More Christlike God*, 2015, 245.

131 Fr. Andreas Agathokleous, "Sin as Sickness," *Orthodox Christian Network*, Pemptousia Partnership, February 2021. https://myocn.net/sin-as-sickness-2/.

132 Jersak, *A More Christlike God*, 2015, 268.

133 Helmut Thielicke, *Christ and the Meaning of Life* (Lutterworth Press, 1988).

134 My paraphrase

135 J. D. Myers, *The Atonement of God: Building Your Theology on a Crucivision of God* (Redeeming Press, 2016).

136 Myers.

137 Zahnd, *Sinners in the Hands of a Loving God*, 16.

138 Jersak, *A More Christlike God*, 2015, 189.

139 Jersak, 209.

140 Jersak, 207.

141 Shroyer, *Original Blessing*.

142 Shroyer.

143 Shroyer.

144 Shroyer.

145 Fr Stephen Freeman, "The Death of Christ on the Cross - the Life of Man," *Ancient Faith Ministries: Glory to God For All Things*, September 2013.

146 Maslow's Hierarchy of Needs proposes that basic needs like food, shelter, and safety must be met before we have time to worry about things like existence and free will.

147 Oswald Bayer, *Martin Luther's Theology: A Contemporary Interpretation*, trans. Thomas H. Trapp, Illustrated edition (Grand Rapids, Mich: Wm. B. Eerdmans Publishing Co., 2008), 43.

148 Augustine, Hom. on 1st John 7:8

149 Kurt Vonnegut, *A Man Without A Country*. (New York: The Dial Press, 2017).

150 Edwards, "Sinners in the Hands of an Angry God."

151 Gregory MacDonald, *The Evangelical Universalist: The Biblical Hope That God's Love Will Save Us All* (SPCK, 2008), 23.

152 MacDonald, 23.

153 Bradley Jersak, *Her Gates Will Never Be Shut: Hope, Hell, and the New Jerusalem* (Wipf & Stock: 2010), 30.

154 Jersak, 79.

155 MacDonald, *The Evangelical Universalist*, 199.

156 MacDonald, 208–9.

157 MacDonald, 196.

158 MacDonald, 202.

159 Jersak, *Her Gates Will Never Be Shut*, 2010, 116.

160 Phil Zuckerman, "Atheism, Morality, and Society," *Psychology Today*, August 2020.

161 PLOS, "Atheists and Believers Both Have Moral Compasses, but with Key Differences," *ScienceDaily*, February 2021. www.sciencedaily.com/ releases/2021/02/210224143306.htm.

162 Tomas Ståhl, "The Amoral Atheist? A Cross-National Examination of Cultural, Motivational, and Cognitive Antecedents of Disbelief, and Their Implications for Morality," *PLOS ONE* 16, no. 2 (February 2021): e0246593, https://doi.org/10.1371/ journal.pone.0246593.

163 Dawkins, *The God Delusion*.

164 N. T. Wright, *Surprised by Hope: Rethinking Heaven, the Resurrection, and the Mission of the Church* (Reprint Edition), (HarperOne, 2009), 139.

165 Wright, *Surprised by Hope*, 97.

166 Dave MacPherson, *Incredible Cover Up* (Omega Pubns, 1975).

167 Wright, *Surprised by Hope*, 97.

168 Wright, 99.

169 Wright, 100.

170 Wright, 132.

171 G. K. Chesterton, *Orthodoxy* (Waking Lion Press, 2007).

BIBLIOGRAPHY

Agathokleous, Fr. Andreas. "Sin as Sickness." Orthodox Christian Network, February 3, 2021. https://myocn.net/sin-as-sickness-2/.

Ally, Dr. Shabir. "A Muslim Understanding of God's Perpetual Activity." *Let the Quran Speak*, December 2021. https://www.youtube.com/watch?v=pvFcaqpIU3Q.

Anselm. *Cur Deus Homo*. Translated by Sidney Deane. Chapter 9, Book 1. Chicago, IL: The Open Court Publishing Company, 1903.

Aquinas, Thomas. "Llallae. Question 85, Article 1, Response." In *The Summa Theologiae*, translated by Fathers of the English Dominican Province, Second and Revised, 1920.

Augustine of Hippo. *The Literal Interpretation of Genesis (De Genesi Ad Litteram)*. Vol. 1 Ch. 19, n.d.

Axton, Paul. "Did John Calvin Invent Penal Substitution?" *Forging Ploughshares*, May 20, 2021. https://forgingploughshares.org/2021/05/20/did-calvin-invent-penal-substitution/.

Azkoul, Michael. *The Influence of Augustine of Hippo on the Orthodox Church*. Lewiston, NY: Edwin Mellen Pr, 1991.

Bayer, Oswald. *Martin Luther's Theology: A Contemporary Interpretation*. Translated by Thomas H. Trapp. Illustrated edition. Grand Rapids, Mich: Wm. B. Eerdmans Publishing Co., 2008.

Berlin, Adele, and Marc Zvi Brettler, eds. *The Jewish Study Bible: Second Edition*. New York: Oxford University Press, 2014.

Blue, Ken, and Alden Swan. *The Gospel Uncensored: How Only Grace Leads to Freedom.* Westbow Press, 2010.

Bonhoeffer, Dietrich. *The Cost of Discipleship.* New edition. SCM Press, 2015.

Browne, David. "Dolores O'Riordan: Cranberries' Noel Hogan Talks Singer's Life and Legacy." *Rolling Stone,* January 2018.

Burge, Ryan. "The 2018 GSS Was Just Released and There's Some Big News. Those of "No Religion" (23.1%) Are Statistically the Same Size as Evangelicals (22.8%). There Was Also a Small Resurgence of Mainline Protestants, While Catholics Are down 3% in the Last Four Years. https://t.co/uiyDSe7M6f." Tweet. *Twitter,* March 2019.

Calvin, John. *Institutes of the Christian Religion (1581),* translated by Henry Beveridge. "Chapter 16, 10." Vol. Book II. Edinburgh: The Edinburgh Printing Company, 1885.

Cary, Phillip. *Good News for Anxious Christians: 10 Practical Things You Don't Have to Do.* Grand Rapids, MI: Brazos Press, 2010.

Chesterton, G. K. (Gilbert Keith), *Orthodoxy,*1994 Reprint Edition. Waking Lion Press: 2007.

Clark, Kelly James, ed. "Mortimer J. Adler, A Philosopher's Religious Faith." In *Philosophers Who Believe: The Spiritual Journeys of 11 Leading Thinkers,* 207. IVP Academic, 1997.

Cleland, Jonathan. "Augustine's Doctrine of the Atonement as Presented in The Trinity." *Center for Ancient Christian Studies,* March 2021. https://www.ancientchristianstudies.com/blog/2021/3/4/augustines-doctrine-of-the-atonement-as-presented-in-the-trinity.

Collins, Francis. "The Question of God. Other Voices. Francis Collins | PBS." *PBS.* https://www.pbs.org/wgbh/questionofgod/voices/collins.html, 2004.

Constantinou, Eugenia Scarvelis. *Thinking Orthodox: Understanding and Acquiring the Orthodox Christian Mind.* Ancient Faith Publishing, 2020.

Cooper, Stephen A. *Augustine for Armchair Theologians.* Louisville: Westminster John Knox Press, 2002.

Cronk, George. *The Message of the Bible: An Orthodox Christian Perspective.* St Vladimirs Seminary Press, 2010.

Dawkins, Richard. *The God Delusion.* Black Swan, 2007.

De Young, Stephen. *Religion of the Apostles: Orthodox Christianity in the First Century.* Ancient Faith Publishing, 2021.

Edwards, Johnathan. "Sinners in the Hands of an Angry God." Sermon. Enfield, CT, July 1741.

Enns, Peter. *How the Bible Actually Works: In Which I Explain How an Ancient, Ambiguous, and Diverse Book Leads Us to Wisdom Rather Than Answers and Why That's Great News.* Reprint edition. HarperOne, 2019.

———. *Inspiration and Incarnation: Evangelicals and the Problem of the Old Testament.* Annotated edition. Grand Rapids, Mich: Baker Academic, 2005.

———. *The Bible Tells Me So: Why Defending Scripture Has Made Us Unable to Read It.* Reprint edition. HarperOne, 2014.

———. *The Evolution of Adam: What the Bible Does and Doesn't Say about Human Origins.* Illustrated edition. Grand Rapids, MI: Brazos Press, 2012.

———. *The Sin of Certainty: Why God Desires Our Trust More Than Our "Correct" Beliefs.* Reprint edition. HarperOne, 2016.

Enns, Peter and David Lambert. "Episode 232: Is the Bible 'Scripture'?" *The Bible For Normal People* (Podcast).

February 2023. https://thebiblefornormalpeople. com/episode-1.

Enns, Peter and Meredith Riedel. "Episode 226: What Is Byzantine Christianity? (And Why Should We Care?)" *The Bible For Normal People* (Podcast). November 2022. https://thebiblefornormalpeople.com/ episode-226.

Erdman, Rachel. "Sacrifice as Satisfaction, Not Substitution: Atonement in the Summa Theologiae." *Anglican Theological Review* 96, no. 3 (2014): 461–80.

Fearnow, Benjamin. "Pastor Rick Joyner Urges American Christians to Prepare for Civil War." *Newsweek.* https://www.newsweek.com/pastor-rick-joyner-urges-american-christians-prepare-civil-war-1576570, March 21AD.

Freedman, Harry. "Atonement- A Made Up Word with an Impossible Meaning." *The Times of Israel.* https:// blogs.timesofisrael.com/atonement-a-made-up-word-with-an-impossible-meaning/. May 2019.

Freeman, Fr Stephen. "The Death of Christ on the Cross - the Life of Man." *Ancient Faith Ministries: Glory to God For All Things*, September 2013.

Friedman, Richard Elliott. *Who Wrote the Bible?* Simon & Schuster, 2019.

"Incarnate." *Merriam-Webster.com.* https://www.merriam-webster.com/dictionary/incarnate.

Irenaeus. "Against Heresies (St. Irenaeus)." In *Ante-Nicene Fathers*, edited by Alexander Roberts, James Donaldson, and Cleveland Coxe. Translated by Alexander Roberts and William Rambaut. Vol. 1. Ante-Nicene Fathers. Buffalo, NY: Christian Literature Publishing Co, 1885.

Jenkins, Jack. "'Nones' Now as Big as Evangelicals, Catholics in the US." https://religionnews.com/2019/03/21/

nones-now-as-big-as-evangelicals-catholics-in-the-us/, March 2019.

Jersak, Bradley. *A More Christlike God: A More Beautiful Gospel.* 1st edition. CWR Press, 2015.

———. *Her Gates Will Never Be Shut: Hope, Hell, and the New Jerusalem.* Wipf & Stock, an Imprint of Wipf and Stock Publishers, 2010.

Jersak, Bradley, and Peter Enns. *A More Christlike Word: Reading Scripture the Emmaus Way.* Whitaker House, 2021.

Kimel, Alvin F. *Destined for Joy: The Gospel of Universal Salvation.* Independently published, 2022.

Knight, Douglas A., and Amy-Jill Levine. *The Meaning of the Bible: What the Jewish Scriptures and Christian Old Testament Can Teach Us.* July 22, 2012 edition. HarperOne, 2012.

Levine, Amy-Jill, and Marc Zvi Brettler. *The Bible With and Without Jesus: How Jews and Christians Read the Same Stories Differently.* Annotated edition. HarperOne, 2020.

Lewis, C. S. *The Weight of Glory.* 1st edition. San Francisco: HarperOne, 2001.

Linker, Damon. "Calvin And American Exceptionalism." *The New Republic*, July 2009. https://newrepublic.com/article/50754/calvin-and-american-exceptionalism.

Luther, Martin. *Luther's Works. Volume 54, Table Talk.* Philadelphia, PA: Fortress Press, 1967.

Luther, Martin, and John Dillenberger. "Preface to the Epistles of St. James and St. Jude." *Martin Luther: Selections From His Writings,* (Garden City: NY, Anchor) March 1958.

MacDonald, Gregory. *The Evangelical Universalist: The Biblical Hope That God's Love Will Save Us All.* SPCK, 2008.

MacPherson, Dave. *Incredible Cover Up.* Omega Pubns, 1975.

McGrath, James F. *The A to Z of the New Testament: Things Experts Know That Everyone Else Should Too*. Eerdmans, 2023.

McGrath, Religion Prof: The Blog of James F. "Unfalsifiable Inerrancy." *Religion Prof: The Blog of James F. McGrath*, February 2014.

Morgan, Vance. "God Said It, I Believe It, That Settles It? Not so Much." *Freelance Christianity*. Patheos, June 2021. https://www.patheos.com/blogs/freelancechristianity/god-said-it-i-believe-it-that-settles-it-not-so-much/

Myers, J. D. *The Atonement of God: Building Your Theology on a Crucivision of God*. Redeeming Press, 2016.

"Nicene Creed." *Evangelical Lutheran Worship*, 2006.

"No One Is Alone." Rilting Music Inc., 1991.

Osteen, Joel. *Your Best Life Now (Special 10th Anniversary Edition): 7 Steps to Living at Your Full Potential*. FaithWords, 2014.

PLOS. "Atheists and believers both have moral compasses, but with key differences." ScienceDaily. www.sciencedaily.com/releases/2021/02/210224143306.htm.

Reardon, Patrick Henry. *Reclaiming the Atonement: An Orthodox Theology of Redemption: Volume 1: The Incarnate Word*. Ancient Faith Publishing, 2015.

Russell, Bertrand. *The Problems of Philosophy: A 1912 Book by the Philosopher Bertrand Russell, in Which the Author Attempts to Create a Brief and Accessible Guide to . . . Focusing on Knowledge Rather Than Metaphysics*. Les Prairies Numeriques, 2020.

Sagan, Carl. *Pale Blue Dot: A Vision of the Human Future in Space*. Reprint edition. New York: Ballantine Books, 1997.

Seeliger, Wes. *Western Theology*. Atlanta: Forum House, 1973.

Sexton, Jared Yates. *American Rule: How a Nation Conquered the World but Failed Its People*. New York: Dutton, 2020.

Shorto, Russell. *Descartes' Bones: A Skeletal History of the Conflict Between Faith and Reason*. Reprint edition. Vintage, 2009.

Shroyer, Danielle. *Original Blessing: Putting Sin in Its Rightful Place*. Minneapolis: Fortress Press, 2016.

Smith, Walter C. "Immortal, Invisible, God Only wise," 1868.

Ståhl, Tomas. "The Amoral Atheist? A Cross-National Examination of Cultural, Motivational, and Cognitive Antecedents of Disbelief, and Their Implications for Morality." *PLOS ONE* 16, no. 2 (February 2021): e0246593. https://doi.org/10.1371/journal.pone.0246593.

TheBibleforNormalPeople. "A Technical Term That Will Change Your Life Forever," February 2019. https://vimeo.com/296014219?utm_campaign=5250933&utm.

The International Council on Biblical Inerrancy. "The Chicago Statement on Biblical Inerrancy." *Journal of the Evangelical Theological Society* 21, no. 4 (December 1978): 289–96.

Thielicke, Helmut. *Christ and the Meaning of Life*. Lutterworth Press, 1988.

Thomas, Anthony. "Questioning Darwin." HBO, August 2014.

Watson, Richard A. *The Breakdown of Cartesian Metaphysics*. Indianapolis: Hackett Publishing Company, Inc., 1998.

Wright, N. T. "How Can the Bible Be Authoritative? (The Laing Lecture for 1989." *Vox Evangelica* 21 (1991): 7–32.

Wright, N. T. *Surprised by Hope: Rethinking Heaven, the Resurrection, and the Mission of the Church*. Reprint edition. HarperOne, 2009.

Zahnd, Brian. *Sinners in the Hands of a Loving God: The Scandalous Truth of the Very Good News*. Colorado Springs, Colorado: WaterBrook, 2017.

Zuckerman, Phil. "Atheism, Morality, and Society." *Psychology Today*, August 2020. https://www.psychologytoday.com/us/blog/the-secular-life/202008/atheism-morality-and-society.

AUTHOR BIO

Alden Swan spends a lot of his time thinking and drinking coffee, not necessarily in that order. Growing up on a small farm in northern Minnesota, he had the luxury of having plenty of time to wonder about God and church and life. That sense of wonder has remained with him.

Raised Lutheran, he has spent much of his adult life in evangelical churches while never abandoning his more historic theological roots. He has devoted considerable time to Christian ministry, serving on church boards, teaching Bible studies, playing in worship bands, and always believing that God was bigger than the theological boxes that people constructed to house God. In the 1990s he started the Small Voices Journal, an early alternative online Christian magazine, exploring ideas about church and life. For many years he has blogged at aldenswan.com where he continues to express his thinking on a number of subjects. He co-authored *The Gospel Uncensored* with Ken Blue.

Alden currently resides in Oregon with Jo, his wife of 41 years. His favorite thing is to spend time with their three children and two grandchildren. He is very happily retired, which once again gives him ample time to think and write and drink too much coffee. On occasion he plays the banjo but will stop if you ask nicely.

Made in the USA
Columbia, SC
27 October 2024

44757440R00211